Planning for Cities
and Regions in Japan

Frontispiece: Principal cities and regions of Japan

Planning for Cities and Regions in Japan

edited by
PHILIP SHAPIRA, IAN MASSER and
DAVID W. EDGINGTON

LIVERPOOL UNIVERSITY PRESS

First published 1994 by
LIVERPOOL UNIVERSITY PRESS
PO Box 147
Liverpool
L69 3BX

British Library Cataloguing-in-Publication Data
A British Library CIP Record is available
ISBN 0 85323 248 2

Set in Linotron 202 Plantin by
Wilmaset Limited, Birkenhead, Wirral
Printed and bound in the European Union by
Redwood Books, Trowbridge, Wiltshire

Table of Contents

List of Figures   vi

List of Tables   vii

Abbreviations   viii

Contributors   x

1. Introduction
   Ian Masser, Philip Shapira and David W. Edgington   1
2. Some strengths and weaknesses of Japanese urban planning
   Jeremy D. Alden and Hirofumi Abe   12
3. Challenges for Japanese urban policy
   John Zetter   25
4. The impact of recent urbanisation on inner city development in Japan
   Jeremy D. Alden, Moriaki Hirohara and Hirofumi Abe   33
5. Land use planning and control in Japan
   David L. Callies   59
6. *Sen-biki* amidst *desakota*: urban sprawl and urban planning in Japan
   Michael Hebbert   70
7. Tokyo's land market and its impact on housing and urban life
   Michael Wegener   92
8. The institutional context of Japanese planning: professional associations
   and planning education
   Ian Masser and Takahiro Yorisaki   113
9. Planning for technology development and information systems in
   Japanese cities and regions
   David W. Edgington   126
10. Industrial restructuring and economic development strategies in a
    Japanese steel town: the case of Kitakyushu
    Philip Shapira   155

   Appendices
1. Chronology of major urban and regional planning legislation in Japan
   David W. Edgington   184
2. Selected literature on Japanese urban and regional planning
   Philip Shapira, Chet Askey and David W. Edgington   190

List of Figures

Frontispiece: Principal cities and regions of Japan

2.1   Trends in the net migration to metropolitan regions, 1955–1989   14

4.1   Regions and prefectures in Japan   36

4.2   Seven metropolitan areas designated by the Central Statistical Office of Japan   54

6.1   Unconsolidated growth of suburban Tokyo: Mitaka, Kokubunji and Minitama   75

6.2   Sample land prices in Chiba prefecture, 1989–1992   84

6.3   Agricultural belt around Kashiwa, Chiba prefecture, 1971   85

6.4   Development in the Kashiwa Urbanisation Control Area, 1970–1987   86

6.5   The Urbanisation Control Area today   87

7.1   Central Tokyo   94

7.2   Land prices in the Tokyo metropolitan area in 1969 and 1987, in ¥1000   97

7.3   Advertisement for the Kioicho Building, with location map enlarged   98

7.4   Urban structure and society in large cities in Japan   103

9.1   Tsukuba Science City and environs   129

9.2   Kansai Science City   130

9.3   Designated technopolis areas and the three largest metropolitan regions   135

9.4   Generalised model showing technopolis activities   137

9.5   Location of Tokyo Teleport   144

9.6   Plan of Yokohama's Minato Mirai 21   146

9.7   Plan of Technoport Osaka   148

10.1   Kitakyushu City   158

10.2   Yawata Steel Works, production and employment, 1955–1992   162

10.3   Steelworks restructuring at Nippon Steel   164

10.4   Nippon Steel, steelmaking employment and production, 1970–1992   166

List of Tables

2.1   International comparison of housing conditions   13
2.2   Concentration of economic activities in Tokyo: share of Tokyo
      metropolitan region in Japan, 1980s   15
2.3   The designated cities of Japan and their population as at 1991   16
2.4   Japan's economic vitality   18
2.5   Japan's quality of urban life: selected indicators   22
2.6   The sewerage diffusion rate in designated cities of Japan, 1990   23
4.1   Population growth in Tokyo and designated cities   37
4.2   Population trends and prospects by region, 1970–2025   38
4.3   Population trends and prospects of city region by the size of central
      city, 1970–2000   40
4.4   Employment by region and occupation in Japan, 1975 and 1985   43
4.5   Change in occupational share by region, 1975–1985   44
4.6   Change in regional share by occupation, 1975–1985   44
4.7   Growth rate of employment by region and occupation, 1975–1985   45
4.8   Employment by city and occupation in Japan, 1975 and 1985   46
4.9   Growth rate of employment by city and occupation   48
4.10 Change in occupational share by city   49
6.1   City planning area designation in Japan, 1991   74
6.2   Planning and development in the five case-study cities   78
7.1   Comparison of Tokyo, New York and Paris: area, population,
      employment and commuting   100
7.2   Impacts of policies on the land market and commuting in Tokyo   109
9.1   Kansai Science City: plan of development   132
9.2   National Japanese programmes for technology infrastructure   139
9.3   Conceptual model of programmes for high-technology development
      in Japanese cities   149
10.1 Kitakyushu City, manufacturing employment, 1965–1988   159
10.2 Employment change in Kitakyushu and Fukuoka districts and
      Fukuoka prefecture, 1974–1987   160
10.3 Kitakyushu City and Japan, employment change by sector, 1970–1990 172

Abbreviations

APAs	Agricultural Promotional Areas
BF	Blast furnace (steelmaking)
CATV	Community Access Television
CC	Central city
CCPC	Cooperative Credit Purchasing Company
CNDP	Comprehensive National Development Plan
CPIJ	City Planning Institute of Japan
CR	City region
CRDC	Chubu Regional Development Committee
CSA	Construction Standards Act
DIDs	Densely Inhabited Districts
EA	Environment Agency
FARs	Floor/area ratios
FY	Fiscal Year
GDP	Gross Domestic Product
GNP	Gross National Product
HDTV	High Definition Television
HUDC	Housing and Urban Development Corporation
KRDC	Kinki Regional Development Committee
IC	Integrated circuit
KPEC	Kitakyushu Prosperity Enrichment Council
KRI	Kansai Research Institute
KSC	Kansai Science City
LAN	Local Area Communications Network
LDP	Liberal Democratic Party
MAFF	Ministry of Agriculture, Forests and Fisheries
MITI	Ministry of International Trade and Industry
MOC	Ministry of Construction
MOE	Ministry of Education
MOF	Ministry of Finance
MOW	Ministry of Welfare
MM21	Minato Mirai 21
MPT	Ministry of Posts and Telecommunications
NCRDC	National Capital Regional
NKK	Nippon Kogaku KK (steel company)

NLA	National Land Agency
NLUP	National Land Use Planning Act, 1974
NMC	New Media Community
NTT	Nippon Telegraph and Telecommunications Limited
NUST	Nagaoko University of Science and Technology
OECD	Organisation for Economic Cooperation and Development
R and D	Research and Development
RTPI	Royal Town Planning Institute
SA	Surrounding area of major cities
SII	Structural Impediments Initiative
SMEs	Small and medium enterprises
TMG	Tokyo Metropolitan Government
UCAs	Urbanisation Control Areas
UPAs	Urbanisation Promotion Areas
WAN	Wide Area Network
¥	Yen

Contributors

HIROFUMI ABE is an Associate Professor in the Department of Civil Engineering at Okayama University, Japan.

CHET ASKEY, formerly a Graduate Research Assistant in the School of Public Policy at Georgia Institute of Technology, Atlanta, USA, now works as a policy analyst in Florida.

JEREMY D. ALDEN is head of the Department of City and Regional Planning of the University of Wales College of Cardiff, UK.

DAVID L. CALLIES is a Professor of Law at the William S. Richardson School of Law of the University of Hawaii at Manoa, Honolulu, USA.

DAVID W. EDGINGTON is Associate Professor in the Department of Geography, University of British Columbia, Vancouver, Canada.

MICHAEL HEBBERT is Professor in the Department of Planning and Landscape, University of Manchester, UK.

MORIAKI HIROHARA is President of the Kyoto Prefectural University, Japan, and was a Professor in the University's Department of Housing and Planning.

IAN MASSER is Professor in the Department of Town and Regional Planning at the University of Sheffield, UK.

PHILIP SHAPIRA is Associate Professor in the School of Public Policy at Georgia Institute of Technology, Atlanta, USA. In 1993 and 1994, he was a Visiting Fellow at the Japan Institute of Labour, Tokyo.

MICHAEL WEGENER is Deputy Director of the Institute of Spatial Planning at the University of Dortmund, Germany. In 1988 and 1989, he was a Professor of Infrastructure Planning at the University of Tokyo's Department of Civil Engineering, visiting Japan for further research in 1991.

TAKAHIRO YORISAKI works as a planner for Pacific Consultants in Tokyo.

JOHN ZETTER is Assistant Secretary in the Planning Services Directorate of the UK Department of the Environment, London. Until 1987, he was head of the Urban Affairs Division of the Organisation of Economic Development and Cooperation in Paris.

Chapter 1

Introduction

IAN MASSER, PHILIP SHAPIRA and DAVID W. EDGINGTON

Most visitors to Japan have been struck by the vitality of its economy and the extent to which the Japanese appear to have adapted imported ideas to their own requirements. The country presents an intriguing mix of internationally-oriented business institutions and technological products blended with seemingly traditional, even conservative, cultural and social norms. Equally puzzling for most Western planners is the extent to which Japanese cities have grown over the last forty years into some of the largest urban agglomerations in the world without apparently experiencing the economic and social problems that are so evident in cities elsewhere. At the same time, curiosity is provoked about how to reconcile these successes with the visual evidence of congestion, low personal and public space standards, and poor housing quality frequently evident in Japanese cities.

It is inevitable that impressions such as these should stimulate efforts to find out more about the nature of the Japanese experience. Indeed, 'learning from Japan' has become a minor growth industry in recent years. This is true especially in the fields of business management, manufacturing systems, and technology, where Japan's methods and results have attracted worldwide attention.[1] There are often motives other than simple curiosity for undertaking such projects. Some observers have been concerned with using Japanese experience to pinpoint perceived deficiencies at home.[2] Others have been interested more in the potential implications of Japanese expansion for their own national economic development. Nevertheless, despite these differences in approach, a considerable body of knowledge has been built up and made available to Western audiences on Japanese economic and industrial strategies and methods.

With some notable exceptions,[3] Japanese urban development has attracted much less attention from outside observers than Japanese business, industrial and technological development. This is certainly remarkable since the scale of the country's urban growth over the last forty years is in many ways on a par with that of its economic growth. During this period Japan's urban population has more than quadrupled from 20 million to over 90 million. Now, 45 per cent of Japan's population lives in one of the three massive urban concentrations associated with Tokyo, Nagoya and Osaka. This urban growth has taken place at a time when the overall rates of natural increase in population have been low, and is largely due to a massive inflow of population from rural areas.[4] In quantitative terms, it is arguable that Japan has gone through the same stages of urban growth during the last forty years that Britain went through in the hundred and fifty years between 1800 and 1950.

The extent of urban change and development in Japan over the last few decades has produced a complex and rich urban fabric. As in modern Western cities, specialised urban districts have emerged. Tokyo, in particular, has a profuse array of specialised quarters, ranging from head office finance and business functions in Marunouchi and Otemachi, and government in Kasumegaski, to high-class shopping in the Ginza and mass transportation nodes such as Shinjuku. The electronics shopping district of Akihabara has attained worldwide fame, but this is just one of numerous specialised shopping areas in Tokyo. Traditionally, these areas have been packed with small family-run shops, although there is now a noticeable emergence of chains and franchised stores. Gleaming modernist and post-modernist architectural edifices have been built, among the most recent of which is the towering Tokyo Metropolitan Government complex. Yet the city also manages to maintain a human scale, particularly in its residential neighbourhoods which sprawl out almost endlessly along a dense railway network.

These urban features are replicated, albeit at not so large a scale, in other Japanese cities. It is a pattern of development which reflects Japan's economic success but also poses a series of significant challenges for Japanese planners. In the large urban complexes of the Tokyo-Nagoya-Osaka core, these challenges include those of congestion, housing quality, public facilities, infrastructure provision, urban sprawl and fragmentation, commuting times, land values, neighbourhood stability, and accommodating the pace of economic and technological change. Cities in outlying regions have less intense growth pressures, and some face population and economic decline, but most also are confronted by issues associated with the quality of urban living.

This book brings together a series of contributions which examine the processes of contemporary city development and urban planning in Japan. A central theme of the book is to consider, from a range of perspectives and situations, the role, policies, methods, and effectiveness of planning in guiding city development in Japan and in addressing present and emerging urban issues. Areas of particular concern include inner city development, the urban periphery, the institutional and regulatory context of planning, and planning for urban and regional economic and technological change. In many instances, the book draws parallels between Japan's urban experience and planning approach with those of Europe and North America. Although earlier versions of all but two of the chapters were published in issues of the *Town Planning Review*, the book brings these contributions together in one volume, which has also allowed the authors to update their work and incorporate new developments. The editors have also added a chronology of Japanese planning legislation and an annotated guide to selected English-language literature on Japanese urban and regional planning.

The scene for understanding Japanese urban planning and policy is set by Jeremy Alden and Hirofumi Abe in their contribution to the book. They examine the nature and extent of urban problems in Japan and how the planning system has attempted to tackle them. Alden and Abe compare the history of Japanese planning since the turn of the century with that of Britain, and draw attention to the growth of gross national product over the last forty years in Japan. They note that Japan's economic success, in terms of economic growth and per capita income, has yet to be matched by the improvement of qualitative living standards as measured by indices such as civic amenities and public utility provision. The basic task for Japanese urban planners is to bring these qualitative indicators up to the level of the quantitative indicators of Japanese well-being. This will be difficult given the continued overcrowding of people and economic activities in the Tokyo metropolitan region. However, the authors suggest that the 1990s will see a marked increase in public investment which should lead to a significant upgrading of Japan's urban and social infrastructure.

One feature that emerges very clearly from studies of Japan is the extent to which the Japanese have systematically drawn upon Western experience and adapted it to suit their own needs in all fields. For instance, Japan's system of tiered general and local development plans has been influenced by European models, while its methods of land use zoning draw from American experience, as David Callies and Michael Wegener note in their contributions. What is less apparent, but nonetheless of considerable import-ance, is the extent to which the Japanese have sought help from outside observers in evaluating their own experiences. Hebbert, in the opening discussion to his chapter, notes how Japanese planners called upon the French regionalist, Jean Gottmann, to assess their plans for the huge Tokyo-Nagoya-Osaka 'megalopolis'. Another example of outside planning influence was the Urban Policy Review conducted in the mid-1980s by the Paris-based Organisation for Economic Cooperation and Development (OECD). This was the first urban review of its kind whereby the Japanese government invited the governments of the other OECD member countries to send officials and observers to examine recent Japanese urban experience, with a view to identifying matters which needed further attention. John Zetter, who was involved in the review, draws upon and updates this assessment in his contribution. He identifies a series of urban policy challenges for Japanese planners in the areas of housing policy, infrastructure provision, land prices, urban sprawl, urban decline, and public infrastructure investment. The Japanese government has initiated policies both to upgrade urban infrastructure and to promote the decentralisation of population and industry although, in Zetter's view, such policies have not yet had significant effects. High urban land prices, while encouraging some decentralisation, have also proven to be a brake on public infrastructure improvement. Zetter hints that a more potent force affecting urban development in future years might be the changing expectations of Japan's younger generation, whom he feels are now looking for a higher quality urban environment and greater leisure opportunities than provided to date in Japan's largest cities.

If there is a new generational search for a different kind of living environment in Japan, how will this affect Japan's inner city areas? In the advanced Western countries, there has been a shift of educated and middle- and higher-income households from the inner cities to the suburbs. Here, the long-term loss of well-paid industrial employment and the often poor wages in service jobs, when available, has compounded the difficulties faced in Western inner cities. The more recent drift back to selected renovated inner city neighbourhoods has barely begun to counter these problems. Japanese urban planners are aware of inner city issues in other countries, and are starting to debate whether Japan will experience a comparable phenomenon. This question forms a central theme of the chapter by Jeremy Alden, Moriaki Hirohara and Hirofumi Abe. They examine the impact of post-war urban trends on metropolitan and inner city development in Japan in terms of both population dispersal and employment growth. They look at the extent to which Japan may be described as having an inner city problem, and whether or not any such characteristics of cities in Japan may be compared or contrasted with those facing big European cities. Alden, Hirohara and Abe show that while the central cities of the three major metropolitan regions (Tokyo, Osaka and Nagoya) experienced some decline during the 1970s and exhibit certain inner city characteristics, the 1980–90 period led once again to a resurgence of growth in these areas. There appears to be no consensus of opinion regarding inner city problems in Japan, although this topic remains one of considerable current interest among planners there.

The legislative and administrative system used by Japanese planners in seeking to influence urban development and to control land use forms the subject of the chapter by David Callies. At the central level, plans emanating from several different agencies provide broad principles and objectives to guide development and investment in Japan. These national plans deal with economic issues and targets, land use, infrastructure investment, and, increasingly, social concerns and the quality of life. They generally embody a strong national growth orientation, together with redistributive elements for the less economically-favoured (but politically significant) cities and regions outside the Tokyo-Nagoya-Osaka-Kobe growth corridor. But, while such plans provide an overall framework, the real day-to-day work of planning and land use control in Japan is carried out at the local level, often with much discretion by local political leaders and ongoing negotiation and log-rolling with central government ministries. Callies details the basic legal and regulatory framework within which such localised urban planning and control occurs. Prefectural governors, in consultation with central government, can designate urban or near-urban land into one of two types of planning areas: urban promotion, where development is encouraged, and urban control, where in theory development is restricted but where in practice exemptions are frequently allowed. Planning and zoning schemes are developed for these areas, with special procedures for larger urban planning, development, and construction projects. The full implementation of this planning and land use system has only come about comparatively recently. For example, in the case of Hiroshima, a city which now houses more than one million people, Callies notes that a comprehensive approach to planning properly began only with the local implementation of Japan's city planning act of 1968. Since then, overall plans have been prepared for Hiroshima and neighbouring cities, along with detailed land use zones. In areas where city government is seeking to promote urban development, development permissions and even necessary re-zonings are readily granted by local officials, although developers may be asked to make public facility concessions. In Kyoto and Osaka—two other cities discussed by Callies—local planning procedures are essentially similar, with other special provisions and regulations applied to protect the historic areas of the former.

The planning and land use control framework which Callies describes has many elements which are comparable with, if not modelled upon, Western practice. How well does this framework function in the Japanese context, given not only the Japanese style of public administration, but also the particular economic, social, and political conditions found in post-war Japan? Both Michael Hebbert and Michael Wegener argue that, put to the test, the Japanese planning system has not done well in controlling and coordinating new development and in improving the quality of life for metropolitan residents. In his chapter, Hebbert points out that planners at all levels have failed to constrain successive waves of fragmented and sprawling development on the fringes of Japanese cities. Their failure is due to structural factors such as the segmentation of land ownership and the role played by small farmers in the land readjustment process in a situation where land prices are rising rapidly. Hebbert shows that planning powers have been used only to a limited extent in situations of this kind, and much development is exempted from planning conditions. Yet, he also suggests that the consequences of failure are apparently less serious in Japan than might have been expected on the basis of European or North American criteria. Hebbert maintains that the divide between urban and rural often demonstrated in Western approaches to land use planning is not so clearly replicated in Asia. Here, intense landscapes of mixed agricultural, industrial, service, and residential uses are commonly found between large urban cores. In Japan and elsewhere in Asia, such landscapes have high population densities—a factor which differentiates them from the low-density strip development seen at the edge of American and, now, some European cities. Significantly, Japanese planners, despite importing Western ideas of green belts and strict land use control, have been unable to limit the outward sprawl of their cities against an alliance of small landowners and property developers. Land use regulations, tax laws, subsidies, and rising land prices have further worked against the planners. Such forces and contradictions are, of course, well-known in the West. The fact that they are evident in Japan should remind us that this is not the centralised, bureaucratically-coordinated state that some popular accounts would have us believe, but a capitalist market economy, with powerful private political and financial lobbies and public policies which are often quite inconsistent. Japan's urban development can only be understood in this context.

Michael Wegener further develops the argument that analyses of the particular characteristics of Japanese urban form need to be situated in the broader fabric of Japanese society, economics and politics. In his view, the spatial organisation of large Japanese cities has been subordinated to Japan's overall orientation towards economic growth. Wegener's case in point is Tokyo, where 30 million people live in a huge, decentralised and sprawling metropolis. He argues that Tokyo's decentralisation is greater than in the large metropolitan areas of other advanced nations, forcing households to live increasingly further away and generating long commutes to still centralised workplaces.

In European and North American cities, households typically move outward to obtain more space, a more pleasant environment, lower housing costs, or better school systems. These factors do not apply to the same extent to Tokyo, where housing far from the centre remains hugely expensive and is still cramped, and where the quality of state schooling is rather uniform. There is also little in the way of the outer or edge city employment complexes which have developed most noticeably in the United States,[5] producing a considerable degree of (car) cross-commuting, as opposed to the radial (rail) journey routes from distant houses to central city offices which are typical in Tokyo. In the Tokyo case, high land prices, land hoarding and deficiencies in planning have underwritten a highly dispersed and, suggests Wegener, unsatisfactory settlement pattern. Wegener argues that this pattern combines with other features of Japanese society, including long working hours, restricted housing conditions, the organisation of family life, the situation of women, and the educational system, to oblige households to conform to business and economic objectives. While the collapse of Japan's 'bubble economy' of the mid-1980s to early 1990s has, temporarily at least, stemmed the implementation of new projects and caused the Japanese government to prop up failing banks and real estate firms, the core elements of Japan's development system for promoting speculative, uncoordinated, and decentralised development remains in place. It is a system in need of reform, and Wegener considers a number of policy alternatives which promise to lead to better results, drawing from both Japanese and European experience.

While numerous organisations in both the public and private sector and at national and local levels have joined in efforts to address Japan's urban challenges, how much leverage do Japanese planners have themselves, as a professional body, to push for urban policy improvement and reform? A reading of the chapter by Ian Masser and Takahiro Yorisaki on the institutional context of Japanese planning would suggest not so much. The status of planning as a profession in Japan is weak, certainly when compared with architecture (although this is true in other countries too). The regular rotation of jobs, which is a common practice in government as well as business in Japan, means that personnel engaged in urban and regional planning may do so only for a few years before being transferred to other administrative areas. This system builds loyalty to the employer, rather than to specific occupations. Furthermore, Japanese planning practice emphasises the physical and infrastructural aspects of planning, rather than the social and environmental concerns which are now important in Japanese cities. To a large extent, as Masser and Yorisaki note, this physical orientation reflects the ongoing city building process Japan has been engaged in since the late nineteenth century, and which has not slowed down even in recent years. This is a notable factor distinguishing Japanese planning from the situation in most other advanced countries (Masser and Yorisaki make the comparison here with Britain). However, one welcome development, described by the chapter authors, is the heterogeneous and increasingly inter-disciplinary nature of undergraduate and graduate planning education in Japan, which is taking its students beyond traditional physical considerations. Urban planning is not seen as exclusively a public function in Japan, and a significant proportion of students educated in planning take jobs in the private sector, with developers and real estate companies. This leads Masser and Yorisaki to raise a question about whether Japanese planners have the antagonism to private developers seen among some planners in Britain and America, although there has yet been little comparison of Japanese planners' attitudes with those in other countries to provide much in the way of an answer.

The extent to which Japan's planning system can rationally coordinate development, shift beyond a traditional physical infrastructural approach, and blend urban development with regional and economic concerns is further probed by David Edgington in his account of planning for technology development and information systems in Japanese cities and regions. Over the last few decades, as Japan has emerged as an industrial and technological force, issues of regional disparity have come to the fore. With Japan's technological modernisation, agriculture, mining and traditional heavy industries such as steel and shipbuilding have declined in outlying regions, accelerating the flow of people to the already congested urban complexes of the Tokyo-Osaka corridor where new growth industry, head office and technology-intensive jobs have concentrated. Japanese policy makers have tried to counter these trends, through regional planning and location incentives for new private investment in areas outside the central core. Most recently, planners have tried to use technology itself as a tool to stimulate outlying regions. Examples of these efforts, which Edgington analyses, include Tsukuba Science City and the Technopolis programme.

Although Tsukuba is beginning to attract private R and D firms, this project to establish a new technology-living complex outside Tokyo has depended heavily on massive central government investments in physical infrastructure and new national laboratories. Subsequent efforts, such as Kansai Science City, have sought a greater private industry and local government role. Industry and local government partnership has also been an organising theme of the Technopolis programme to develop greenfield regional high-tech centres, although the guiding hand of central government, through the Ministry of International Trade and Industry, is evidently present too. More than two dozen Technopolises have been designated, mostly outside the Tokyo-Osaka-Nagoya growth corridor. They have achieved only a mixed record of success, tending to attract more routine branch-plant production activities rather than indigenously innovative firms. In addition to these, Edgington examines a series of other programmes directed at upgrading the development of advanced technology industries and promoting more balanced development throughout Japan.

These programmes and projects illustrate the overall trend towards using technology as a method not only for stimulating economic growth but also for promoting a more efficient spatial organisation in Japan. While these efforts still rely on infrastructural investment, now in the form of technology parks and research buildings as well as roads and airports, they also embody important institutional efforts to forge new public-private partnerships (known in Japan as third-sector groups) and upgrade the capacity for technological innovation. Edgington points to the complicated pattern of seemingly uncoordinated programmes set up by national ministries and local governments. In part, this is due to inter-ministerial rivalry and inter-city competition. However, despite an apparent confusion in the roles and functions of the different programmes, Edgington discerns a structure which reflects both national and local policy goals. Thus, while Tokyo and Osaka are set to retain their pivotal functions as international gateways to Japan and centres of technology innovation, there is an important set of initiatives which are more local in their scale and impact, aimed at assisting a balanced regional development pattern.

The difficulties faced by local planners in adjusting to structural changes in Japan's economy are still daunting, however, notwithstanding the profusion of central government assistance mechanisms. This is shown by Philip Shapira who, in the book's last chapter, examines the processes and consequences of restructuring in Kitakyushu—one of Japan's major heavy industrial cities, located in northern Kyushu. Kitakyushu grew up around a government-established steelworks, now owned by Nippon Steel. Recently, the company has been rationalising production, causing a decline in steelmaking employment in Kitakyushu. Although, as Shapira shows, the sudden mass unemployment seen in declining European and North American industrial cities has been avoided, the city of Kitakyushu has been challenged to find new sources of employment and income. This, as in other Japanese 'industrial castle towns', has put local planners in a new role, since the city had grown accustomed to private industry and central government assuming responsibility for employment and other community facilities and services. New development initiatives have been put into place to promote high technology, small business and tourism; public-private partnerships have been formed between local government and the private sector; and visits have been made abroad to see how industrial restructuring has been dealt with elsewhere. Economic regeneration and development has become a key local planning priority, as in most Western industrial cities, and efforts are being made to redevelop unwanted industrial facilities into new uses. In Kitakyushu's case, part of the old steelworks is being turned into a space-age leisure centre; a former chemical factory housing area is now a hotel, shopping and sports complex; and a techno-centre for small firms has been built.

But, despite the construction of a handful of showplace projects, Shapira demonstrates how hard it is, even in Japan, for local planners to build a new economic and technological base in a traditional industrial city. Kitakyushu is relatively inexperienced in promoting economic development, pursuing new projects without full assessments of likely outcomes. Also evident is a tension between national and local policies for economic and regional development. While central planning agencies espouse policies to promote technological and economic decentralisation, in practice these are superseded by government support to expand Tokyo's international role in the global hierarchy of cities. Policies to promote regional greenfield technological centres may also conflict with efforts to regenerate older industrial cities such as Kitakyushu.

In a sense, the story of Kitakyushu, together with the other cases and issues discussed in this book, tell us that Japanese planners have to grapple not only with substantive problems such as economic restructuring, urban fragmentation and sprawl, and the quality of city life, but also with the procedural deficiencies of the planning system itself. While Japanese planning is good at producing strategic frameworks and visions, effective and rational implementation at the local level is often much more difficult to achieve. As the chapters of this book indicate, the problems of local implementation reflect the struggle of the planning system with the power of political, financial and land-owning interests, conflicting legal and regulatory codes, bureaucratic disorder, policy conflicts, weak professional organisation, and, of course, market forces (or, arguably in the case of high land prices, non-market social, political and institutional forces as well). Planners in Japan, as elsewhere, try to find ways to work within this multifarious environment. Compared with Western planners, they are handicapped in that individual initiatives to respond to complex local situations are usually not supported by the administrative culture and centralised supervising agencies. There is also considerable central control over local government finances and capital budgets. On the other hand, Japanese bureaucratic inertia seems to lead to planning policies and programmes which are maintained over a longer time horizon than is often seen in the West (which can, of course, have positive or negative impacts, depending on the situation).

The chapters in this book frequently make comparisons of Japan's approach to planning with those of Europe and the United States. But, given the parallels that exist between the processes of urbanisation that have occurred in Japan since the Second World War and those currently under way in many developing countries, it is not surprising to find that there has been a great deal of interest in Japanese experience from this quarter. Thus, while Japanese planners have not constrained urban sprawl, one aspect of Japanese planning that has received attention is the land readjustment technique that is used to organise new developments, especially on the urban fringe.[6] Although Hebbert's chapter shows that there are important differences in opinion about the overall utility of land readjustment techniques as planning tools, a number of planners from both Japan and outside have become interested in their possible application in developing countries experiencing rapid urbanisation. For example, in a study sponsored by the Japan-based United Nations Centre for Regional Development, Bijayanand Misra not only carried out an exhaustive evaluation of Japanese land readjustment experience, but also examined the potential use of these procedures for controlling the development of the unauthorised areas that surround Delhi.[7]

It should be noted, however, that other commentators have questioned the extent to which Japan's experience provides a model for other developing countries. These analysts argue that Japan's development is associated with a number of factors that are not likely to be found in most developing countries. Gedik, for example, points out that, despite two world wars and social change on a massive scale, there has been a basic stability in Japanese government which makes planning feasible.[8] This kind of basic stability is markedly absent in many developing countries. Japan has always had a highly educated population and well established bureaucratic institutions, which again represent elements not always found in other developing countries.

While the applicability of Japan's experience for cities in developing countries can be debated, the reality of Japan's economic success is proving to be a magnet attracting growing numbers of people from developing countries into its cities. Without wishing to understate the inequitable treatment of existing minorities in Japan, such as those of Korean origin, the country has been relatively homogeneous, with much less marked disparities between different groups within the population than would be the case in most other countries. There are small, but significant, signs that this is changing. Japan has sought severely to restrict immigration into the country, and make it difficult for foreigners to obtain permanent residency and citizenship. Nonetheless, driven by the needs of its economy, hundreds of thousands of people from developing countries have been drawn in, clustering in Tokyo and certain other cities. How to accommodate and treat these new workers and their families is emerging as one of the major critical issues Japanese cities and society as a whole will need to face in the coming decade.

The contributions in the book raise several important insights for Western planners. In a number of instances, it is shown that Japanese planning rests upon different assumptions from those commonly held in Europe and North America. The attitude towards development on the urban periphery is a case in point. Here, the Japanese approach can be regarded as a useful antidote to some of the preoccupations that underline planning thinking in the West. Furthermore, Japanese planning introduces a new dimension into the discussion of fundamental questions such as the economics of urban sprawl and the mechanisms of urban expansion. The contributions also indicate that there is still a great deal to be learnt from the evaluation of Japanese urban planning experience in its own right as the product of rapid economic development accompanied by unprecedented urbanisation. A particularly fruitful field for further investigation is likely to be the division of responsibilities between the public and private sectors. In this context, there may be much to learn from Japanese planning, where private-sector interests play a central role both in inner city renewal and urban fringe development.

Over the balance of this decade, it is likely that urban development policy and planning in Japan will experience considerable change. Demographic developments, coupled with shifts in the lifestyle and expectations of younger city dwellers, will comprise one set of driving factors. Another will be ongoing economic and technological developments, with their effects on employment and business location decisions. The rise of Morihiro Hosokawa's New Japan Party in 1993 and the subsequent realignment of Japanese politics seems to have ended the four-decade long monopoly of national political power by the Liberal Democratic Party, and promises to diminish the over-representation of rural and agricultural interests over urban ones (and also to remedy the political corruption often linked to land development and speculation). Sustained pressure from Japan's trading partners, particularly the United States, will also have urban impacts, for example through forcing open Japanese retail markets which may accelerate the demise of small neighbourhood shops, and compelling a shift in investment from production to social infrastructure. While the main aim of the book is to provide a detailed interpretation of current urban planning issues and policies in Japan, the chapters also provide a foundation for understanding how Japanese city planning may evolve in the future.

NOTES AND REFERENCES

1 See Vogel, E. F., *Japan as Number One: Lessons for America*, New York, Harper and Row, 1979; Pascale, R. T. and Athos, A. G., *The Art of Japanese Management*, New York, Simon and Schuster, 1981; Feigenbaum, E. A. and McCorduck, P., *The Fifth Generation: Artificial Intelligence and Japan's Computer Challenge to the World*, Reading, MA, Addison Wesley, 1983.

3 2 A good example is Ronald Dore's *Taking Japan Seriously: A Confucian Perspective on* *Leading Economic Issues*, which not only develops insights and lessons from Japan for Britain but also for the USA (in the American edition, published by Stanford University Press, Stanford, CA, 1987).

3 See Glickman, N., *The Growth and Management of the Japanese Urban Systems*, New York, Academic Press, 1978; and Gottmann, J. (ed.), 'Japan's Organisation of Space', *Ekistics*, 48, 1981, pp. 256–325.

4 Harris, C. D., 'The Urban and Indus-

trial Transformation of Japan', *Geographical Review*, 72, 1982, pp. 51–89.

5 Garreau, J., *Edge City: Life on the New Frontier*, New York, Doubleday, 1991.

6 For example, Doebele, W. A. (ed.), *Land Readjustment: A Different Approach to Financing Urbanisation*, Lexington, MA, Lexington Books, 1983; Masser, I., 'Learning from the Japanese', *Town and Country Planning*, 53, 1984, pp. 16–17; Minerbi, L. et al., *Land Readjustment: The Japanese System: A Reconnaissance and a Digest*, Honolulu, Department of Urban and Regional Planning, University of Hawaii, 1984.

7 Misra, B., 'Japanese Experience in Physical Development and Land Management' in Okita, S. (ed.), *Transferability of Development Experience: Case Studies on Japan* (special issue of *Regional Development Dialogue*), Nagoya, United Nations Centre for Regional Development, 1984.

8 Gedik, A., 'The Spatial Distribution of Population in Post War Japan: Implications for Developing Countries' in Friedrich, P. and Masser, I. (eds.), *International Perspectives on Regional Decentralisation*, Baden Baden, Nomos, 1986.

Chapter 2

Some Strengths and Weaknesses of Japanese Urban Planning

JEREMY D. ALDEN and HIROFUMI ABE

Urban planning in Japan has had to cope with the problems created by substantial post-war reconstruction which was largely unplanned, together with the very rapid rate of urbanisation in the 1950s and 1960s. Japan now has a population of 123 million (1990 figures) which has doubled in the past sixty years. However, many planners in the mid-1980s saw the slow-down in population growth nationally, together with the three metropolitan regions of Tokyo, Osaka and Nagoya expecting to grow through natural increase rather than net migration gains, as a hopeful sign that Japan would experience a period of greater stability in the latter 1980s and 1990s. This would provide an opportunity to tackle more effectively its existing urban problems, particularly the deficiencies in urban infrastructure, public amenities, and to make improvements in the quality of the urban environment. Unfortunately, recent events have shown that the Tokyo metropolitan region has been difficult to contain, and that once again the growth and dynamics of this city region are presenting new challenges.

Over the last decade, questions have been asked about the position of the Tokyo metropolitan area in the urban system of Japan, and about what were the right policies to adopt for the city. Although decentralisation policies have been actively pursued, should further decentralisation be encouraged? Is it time to relax such policies, especially when some central cities have begun to lose their residential populations as people have sought housing in local towns? For example, the central Tokyo ward of Chiyoda-ku has a day/night-time population ratio of more than 15:1). Will Japan in the future face the situation which has arisen already in other advanced economies where major cities require regeneration?

Japan is concerned for the future of its urban areas for a number of reasons. Firstly, it already exhibits a high level of urbanisation, with an urban population of some 85 million of its 123 million population. This urban concentration is very high in Japan at both national and metropolitan levels compared with other advanced industrial countries. Secondly, there is an urgent need to cope with urban redevelopment and urban growth. Thirdly, the nature of urban development policy has been changing, with less movement from rural to urban areas and more movement from inner cities to suburban areas. Fourthly, there has been a rapidly-expanding concern for the quality of the urban environment of Japanese towns and cities. Japan, having four cities with a population of over two million (i.e. Tokyo 8.0 million, Yokohama 3.2 million, Osaka 2.5

million and Nagoya 2.1 million) and 13 designated cities (including Tokyo's 23 wards) with a population close to or exceeding 1.0 million, can be expected to provide some of the most challenging examples of urban problems and policies of any of the advanced industrialised countries. This chapter seeks to assess the nature and extent of urban problems facing Japan, with particular reference to the continued success and economic vitality of the Tokyo metropolitan region. The development of urban planning policies is reviewed, and the response of the planning system in Japan to problems of urban development, infrastructure provision and its financing, is assessed.

Any assessment of urban problems requires a working definition of urban problems, whether they are associated with urban growth or decline. However, the classification of phenomena as 'strengths' or 'weaknesses' raises a number of issues, as illustrated by Alden.[1] Comments or views expressed about urban conditions or urban policies in Japan must be qualified to some extent by a recognition that what may be perceived as a problem to the Western analyst may not be seen as such by the Japanese, given their own distinctive cultural background. For example, some observers point to the fact that Japan continues to build high-rise, high-density and often cramped housing units, in sharp contrast to the more generous standards of Western societies. While this may have been the case in the past, it is certainly less so today. Indeed, in 1988 the total number of housing units in Japan reached 4.2 million, and the number of housing units per household was 1.11. These figures show that the housing stock has already met the demand in quantitative terms and is improving in quality. As shown in Table 2.1, the floor space per housing unit has been increasing in recent years, reaching 89.3 square metres in 1988, which exceeds the average floor space for France and West Germany. However, the floor space per person is still about 25 square metres, which is about 70 per cent of the figure for West Germany, France and the UK. The qualitative aspect of housing therefore remains to be addressed.

Post-war Migration Patterns in Japan

The post-war interregional pattern of migration in Japan can be broadly classified into three periods, as shown in Figure 2.1. The first period up to the early 1970s was

Table 2.1 *International comparison of housing conditions*

	Total (average)	Floor space per housing unit (m²) Owner occupants	Renters	Floor space per person	% of owner occupants (m²)
USA (1987)	153.6	160.3	115.9	61.8	64.0
UK (1988)	95.0	n.a.	n.a.	35.2	64.1
W. Germany (1987)	86.3	112.7	69.2	37.2	38.5
France (1984)	82.3	96.1	67.9	30.7	51.2
Japan (1988)	89.3	116.3	44.3	25.0	61.3

Source: Compiled from housing statistics, Ministry of Construction, Tokyo.

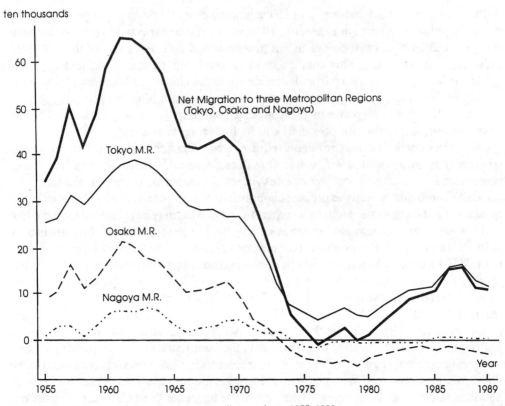

ten thousands

Net Migration to three Metropolitan Regions
(Tokyo, Osaka and Nagoya)

Tokyo M.R.

Osaka M.R.

Nagoya M.R.

Year

Fig. 2.1 Trends in the net migration to metropolitan regions, 1955–1989

characterised by large-scale migration of young people from local regions to metropolitan regions (i.e. Tokyo, Osaka and Nagoya regions) for new jobs.

During the second period from the first oil crisis of 1973 to the late 1980s, the return migration from metropolitan regions to local regions was dominant, and the concentration of migration to the three metropolitan regions had been reduced markedly. However, from the end of the 1980s and into the 1990s, net migration into the Tokyo metropolitan region increased, and the overcrowding of people and economic activities in the capital remains one of the most serious city regional problems in Japan. Table 2.2 illustrates the extent of this economic concentration within the Tokyo metropolitan region.

The Development of Urban Planning in Japan

Japan's planners have generally worked within a strong urban tradition which, when combined with centralised planning powers, has led to a fostering of their cities. Since the Meiji Restoration in 1868, when feudal Japan ended, Tokyo has been growing

Table 2.2 *Concentration of economic activities in Tokyo: share of Tokyo metropolitan region in Japan, 1980s*

Indicator	Percentage (year)	Percentage (year)
Foreign companies	82.2 (1974)	86.6 (1986)
Amount of bill clearing	69.6 (1981)	84.8 (1987)
Head offices of companies capitalised more than 10 billion yen	60.7 (1983)	62.2 (1988)
Bank loans	51.0 (1982)	55.4 (1988)
Companies listed on the Tokyo Stock Exchange	56.4 (1983)	54.6 (1988)
University students	45.0 (1980)	43.4 (1987)
Annual commercial sales	35.2 (1979)	38.6 (1985)
Bank deposits	32.7 (1982)	34.4 (1987)
Employment in finance and insurance companies	31.8 (1981)	33.0 (1986)
Employment in service industries	26.5 (1981)	27.8 (1986)
Office workers	26.1 (1981)	26.9 (1986)
Manufacturing output	26.6 (1980)	25.2 (1986)
Population	24.3 (1980)	25.2 (1988)
Offices	23.0 (1981)	23.3 (1986)
Area of Tokyo metropolitan region	3.6 (1980)	3.6 (1985)

Source: Compiled from Economic Planning Agency, *Tokyo no Sekaitoshika to Chiiki no Kasseika* [*Internationalisation of Tokyo and the Vitalisation of the Regional Economy*], Tokyo Printing Bureau, Ministry of Finance, Tokyo, 1988.

rapidly as the country's capital city. However, the growth of Tokyo brought about various city problems, most notably the lack of public facilities and environmental problems. This led to the establishment of comprehensive city planning, with the Tokyo Rebuilding Act (1888) and Land-use and Building Restriction Act for Tokyo Rebuilding (1889). They were the first city planning legislations in Japan, although the area was limited to Tokyo.

After the First World War, the other major cities, such as Osaka, Nagoya, Kobe, Yokohama and Kyoto, also grew rapidly as regional industrial centres in Japan, and urban problems became serious in these cities. At first, the Tokyo Rebuilding Act was applied to these cities. However, more comprehensive city planning legislation soon became necessary and, under these circumstances, the City Planning Act (1919) and the Urban Building Act (1919) were enacted. These acts were the first comprehensive city planning legislation to be applied to all Japanese cities. The timing of these acts may be compared with Britain's first Town Planning Acts passed in 1909 and 1919. It is generally recognised that the 1919 City Planning Act in Japan became the cornerstone of planning for the next fifty years.

However, the rapid urbanisation of Japan in the 1950s and 1960s brought with it new urban problems, particularly that of urban sprawl, and the City Planning Act of 1968 was passed to deal with these problems. Prior to 1968, there were no land use controls relating to the location and form of development, nor standards for urban infrastructure.

The 1968 City Planning Act introduced Urbanisation Promotion Areas and Urbanisation Control Areas to prevent urban sprawl, and a development permission system to provide a sufficient level of infrastructure in the development of serviced land (see also Chapter 5 of this book). The 1968 Act reduced central control of planning and delegated planning powers to prefectures (47) and municipalities (3255).

The local government system in Japan is a two-tier one, with *To-Do-Fu-Ken* (equivalent to prefectures) and *Shi-Cho-Son* (equivalent to municipalities). Municipalities which have the largest populations and in which most people live in urban areas, are designated *Shi* (city). Smaller municipalities which are urbanised are designated *Cho* (town); *Son* (villages) have small populations and are normally located in rural areas. The capital, Tokyo, has special administrative arangements and powers, containing 23 wards as well as many municipalities. Some cities with populations of more than 500 000 are known as 'designated cities', which take over important functions from prefectural governments. Under the Local Autonomy Law, the 'designated city' is defined as a major city in the region which has a population of more than half a million. However, the actual condition of designation is that the city has a population of more than one million or the population is expected to reach one million in the near future. Outside Tokyo, there are currently twelve such designated cities, namely Osaka, Nagoya, Yokohama, Kyoto, Kobe, Kitakyushu, Sapporo, Fukuoka, Kawasaki, Hiroshima, Sendai and Chiba. While Tokyo qualifies in terms of population size, the Tokyo 23 wards are not usually classified into the group of designated cities. The 'designated cities' and their population as at 1991 are shown in Table 2.3.

The 1968 City Planning Act also incorporates provisions for planning authorities to seek public participation in urban planning. The introduction of district plans from 1980 provides an opportunity to involve the public in plan-making, and the customary

Table 2.3 *The designated cities of Japan and their population as at 1991*

City	Prefecture	Designated year	Population in 1991
Tokyo 23 wards*	Tokyo	—	8 006 386
Sapporo	Hokkaido	1972	1 663 246
Sendai	Miyagi	1989	898 173
Yokohama	Kanagawa	1956	3 210 607
Kawasaki	Kanagawa	1972	1 152 639
Chiba	Chiba	1992	821 003
Nagoya	Aichi	1956	2 097 765
Kyoto	Kyoto	1956	1 401 171
Osaka	Osaka	1956	2 512 386
Kobe	Hyogo	1956	1 447 726
Hiroshima	Hiroshima	1980	1 061 864
Kitakyushu	Fukuoka	1963	1 019 501
Fukuoka	Fukuoka	1972	1 192 805

*Tokyo's 23 wards are usually not classified into the group of designated cities. Thus there are 12 designated cities in Japan.

Japanese approach of seeking consensus suggests that participation may develop more successfully in Japan than it has in Western countries. The Harajuku project in Tokyo provides an example of how local traders, residents and interest groups have joined together to revitalise and improve the physical and economic environment of their community. Although this successful project has been based on private finance, the extension of such schemes on a more comprehensive basis may require some public sector support.

Japan's interest in urban planning following its own period of rapid urbanisation, economic growth, and growing concern for the quality of life in its urban areas can be compared with the development of urban planning in Britain. The history of statutory town planning in Britain stemmed from a background of concern for the physical environment, social conditions, and quality of life. The concern for urban planning in Britain also arose from a period of rapid economic growth and urban population growth. However, it is important to emphasise that Japanese attitudes to the role of government and planning have been very different from those in Britain. While the Japanese system does have regulatory features, it also allows room for the operation of market mechanisms. This can be illustrated by the relatively small proportion of central government expenditure to Gross Domestic Product in Japan, at 16 per cent compared with 29 per cent in the UK and 23 per cent in the USA (see Table 2.4). However, while central government spending is relatively small in Japan in terms of GDP share, there are a variety of less visible but important government interventions in the private sector and in the operations of local government. These include administrative guidance, approval of local projects, financial control, and *amakudari* (placing retiring senior central bureaucrats in high-level positions in the private sector and local government). This pattern is reflected in Japanese urban and regional planning, where direct regulation can be minimal while the influence of these forms of indirect government intervention is often considerable.[2]

While urban planning at a micro level does tend towards minimalist regulations and intervention when compared with European countries, at a macro level the government establishes partnerships with the private sector in planning major projects for Japanese cities and regions (a similar feature to that found in European countries). These joint projects are called 'third sector' arrangements in Japan, and are illustrated by recent collaborative schemes to develop airports, transport links, science cities and other large projects. The term 'third sector' was first used by the government in 1973 in its Seventh National Economic Plan. In Japan, the third sector company usually means a corporate body which is established jointly by the public sector (first sector) and the private sector (second sector).[3] Public-private partnerships are therefore a feature of both Western and Japanese programmes for urban and regional development.

The provision of social overhead capital in Japan has been conducted primarily by the public sector. However, when the period of rapid economic growth ended in the 1970s, the shortage of public finance for the provision of social overhead capital soon became a serious problem for both national and local governments. These circumstances prompted the establishment of third sector companies in various fields of urban and regional planning.

Table 2.4 *Japan's economic vitality*

Indicator	Japan	UK	USA	France	Germany (West)
1. Population (1989, millions)	123.1	57.2	248.8	56.2	62.0
2. Unemployment rate (1990, per cent)	2.1	5.9	5.5	9.0	7.2
3. GDP average annual change (1985–90, 1985 price, per cent)	4.6 (1990)	3.2 (1989)	3.0 (1990)	2.9 (1990)	3.1 (1990)
4. Households' savings ratio as percentage of disposable income	14.2	2.4	7.1	12.0	13.3
5. Imports as percentage of GDP (1990)	8.0	23.0	9.6	19.8	23.7
6. Exports of goods as percentage of GDP (1990)	9.8	19.1	7.3	18.3	28.1
7. Consumer price index (1990, 1985=100)	106.9	133.4	121.4	116.4	107.0
8. Central government expenditure as percentage of GDP	15.6 (1990)	29.0 (1990)	23.2 (1990)	21.9 (1989)	13.0 (1989)
9. TV sets per 1000 pop. (1987)	587	434	811	333	385
10. Telephones per 1000 pop. (1987)	555 (1985)	524 (1984)	792 (1980)	608 (1985)	640 (1986)
11. GDP per capita (1990, US$)	23 810	16 893	21 446	21 015	23 698

Source: Compiled from Economic Planning Agency, *Economic Statistics Handbook*, 1992.

Furthermore, while Japanese governments have held a favourable view of the role of urban and regional development for purposes of economic development, a much lesser role has been given, hitherto, to the role of urban and regional development for amenity and environmental purposes (issues which have attracted considerable attention in Western countries).

The financing of urban development has also become a major issue in Japanese planning. How are local services to be provided and paid for? It seems inevitable, given the relatively low level of urban infrastructure provision in Japanese cities, and the sheer size of the task ahead, that urban planning will require a stronger public-sector commitment. At present, public expenditure restrictions pursued by central government have meant that city authorities have had to involve the private sector to an increasing extent. There seems to be a major problem here in respect of financing urban public expenditure, even given Japan's relatively high ratio of savings to Gross Domestic Product at over 14 per cent compared with only 2.4 per cent in the UK (Table 2.4). The options available include increased taxation, increased borrowing (already used to a considerable extent), increased economic growth to provide extra resources, or redistributing the budget to favour urban development. If the Japanese government wishes to seek greater involvement in urban development by the private sector in future, there are fears that this may lead to deregulation and relaxation of planning controls. The problems facing urban development in Japan, given the budget restrictions, are illustrated very well by the competing claims of urban renewal versus new urban development.

Watanabe has attempted to identify major periods of planning activity in Japan. He summarised the history of planning in Japan as being pro-economic and pro-urban, which together with its centralised planning powers has produced a strong interest and support for cities.[4] The Japanese concern for its cities represents a considerable strength for its urban planning system. There are many reasons for this concern: for example, the Tokyo metropolitan region dominates national space with its contribution of over 31 per cent of Japan's Gross Domestic Product.[5] Moreover, with the three metropolitan areas containing 45 per cent of the nation's population, there is a natural focus upon the performance of the largest cities such as Tokyo, Yokohama, Osaka and Nagoya.

The rather special nature of urban development in Japan is further illustrated by the many urban disaster prevention projects. The prevention of urban disasters is an important feature of urban planning, as earthquakes, wooden structures (which account for over 77 per cent of housing types, including fireproof and non-fireproof structures, according to the 1983 Housing Survey of Japan), floods and explosions present a continual threat of loss of life and property in Japan. The current urban renewal programme of the Tokyo Metropolitan Government stresses the importance of these issues. Although it is difficult to assess the priority given to disaster prevention in overall urban development, it does certainly occupy a special place in the urban life of Japan given the frequent occurrence of significant earth tremors throughout the country.

Rising Land Prices

The problems of rising land prices have been examined by the Japanese Economic Planning Agency. Over the last decade, land prices began to rise, starting with the commercial area of central Tokyo in 1983, and the rate of increase grew in 1986 and 1987. In the late 1980s, prices stabilised in central Tokyo, dropping somewhat with Japan's recession of the early 1990s. There are, however, some residential areas surrounding Tokyo where land prices continued to increase after 1988. The increase in land prices in the 1980s spread to Osaka and Nagoya, as well as to regional centres and cities elsewhere in Japan.

The current escalation in land prices is one of the largest-scale and most serious in Japan's post-war history. The increase in land prices (the average of all types of uses) for the greater Tokyo metropolitan area more than doubled between 1986 and 1988. A rise in land prices on a comparable scale also occurred in 1972 and 1973, but although prices came close to doubling within these two years, they dropped in 1974 in reaction to this increase. Since the early 1990s, there are now many residential and commercial districts in the Tokyo metropolitan area where land prices have fallen, and the downward trend is rippling outwards. Yet, while the recent slow-down in Japan's economic growth has softened Tokyo's land prices, by international standards they still remain extraordinarily high.

When examined by region, land prices rose first in the greater Tokyo region, later spreading to the greater Osaka and Nagoya regions. While the rate of increase was close to 80 per cent per year at the peak for the Tokyo region in the latter 1980s, it was only about half this in the greater Osaka region, and less than half in the greater Nagoya region and other areas. In contrast to this, the previous escalation in land prices in 1972–1973 occurred virtually simultaneously and on the same scale throughout the nation.[6]

Why did land prices rise so quickly in Tokyo in the 1980s? In recent years, along with the advance in internationalisation of the Japanese economy, economic functions have become progressively more concentrated in the greater Tokyo region. Tokyo, in particular, grew as an international financial centre, generating excess liquidity and causing the supply and demand for office space in the centre of the city to become tight. It is also believed that there have been increases in the productivity of land in Tokyo and its expected value. Conversely, in the early 1990s, Tokyo's land prices fell back somewhat as recessionary conditions hit the financial and development sectors.

Economic Success and Social Progress

The economic context for urban planning in the UK and many advanced industrial nations is one of little economic growth, little increase in population, and a marked decline in manufacturing industry and employment. The need for regional policy to combat regional income differentials has continued, while new social issues and ethnic minority concentrations have developed in the inner cities. In marked contrast, Japan's economic context has been one of economic success, particularly in the 1960s and early 1970s, with signs of a slowing down of the success rate in the latter 1970s and 1980s, although followed by another period of rapid economic growth in recent years up to 1991. In relative terms, of the advanced industrial nations, Japan continues to be economically successful, and in the 1980s Japan's Gross Domestic Product per capita passed that of the UK. A comparison of Japan's economic vitality with that of other major countries is shown in Table 2.4.

The buoyant economic context for urban planning in Japan can be seen from recent trends in economic growth rates and expected population growth. Between 1967 and 1973 the average annual growth rate of Japan's GDP was 9.5 per cent. Subsequently it faltered, averaging only 3.4 per cent between 1973 and 1978, and 4.1 per cent between 1978 and 1983. However, a rate of 5.0 per cent was achieved in 1984. Between 1985 and 1990, Japan's average annual change in GDP was again 5.0 per cent, compared with 3.0 per cent in the UK, USA, France and Germany (see Table 2.4 and OECD Main

Economic Indicators). The significance of these figures is that, with the high economic growth rates of the 1960s and 1970s, tax revenue increased rapidly, but tax revenue had in later years failed to keep pace with expenditure (with lower growth rates) and borrowing had increased. In addition to economic growth, the population of Japan is expected to grow by 14 million between 1980 and 2000. The Ministry of Health and Welfare's Institute of Population Problems has estimated Japan's population to increase from 117 million in 1980 to 131 million by the year 2000. This demonstrates the scale of new urban development required, in addition to which Japan is seeking to catch up with infrastructure provision for its existing 123 million people. Fortunately, four years of rapid growth since the latter 1980s have generated tax income for the government which can be used for increased public expenditure.

As well as experiencing both economic growth and population growth, Japan has been able to reduce regional income differentials to a point where they are now less than in the UK.[7] Japan's strong regional policy has been closely related to its policy towards its metropolitan areas. Japan has been able to maintain fairly full employment, with a national rate of less than three per cent unemployment throughout the 1980s and 1990s.[8] It has also been able to maintain its level of manufacturing jobs to a large extent.

Japan has a remarkably homogeneous social structure and its inner cities do not contain large proportions of disadvantaged groups, as seen in many cities in the USA and Europe. Additionally, while there are other ethnic or national groups living in Japan (most notably Koreans), outright racial or ethnic conflicts are less common than in the large cities of other industrialised countries. The Japanese government has imposed strong restrictions on immigration into Japan, although the number of foreign workers has increased in recent years.

However, although the specific context for cities differs in Japan compared with the West, a number of inner city problems do exist. For example, poor housing in the large cities has become an important issue in Japan. High land prices have encouraged people to live in local towns outside the large cities, and this has increased commuting for work in the central cities. Net migration to the three metropolitan areas in the 1980s has fallen to near zero. Industrial activity has tended to shrink or stagnate in inner city areas and some vacant land has appeared. However, the underlying economic strength of Japan has continued to exert a beneficial impact on urban growth. The Japanese are also facing a marked decline in their youthful population and a rapidly ageing society. This is having important implications for the provision of services and infrastructure in both the private and public sectors. Japanese-type inner city problems require greater consideration and analysis. At this stage, however, they are certainly not so severe in either nature or extent as those experienced in the USA and Europe.

While Japan has more houses than households (except in the largest cities), people are constantly demanding higher housing standards. For example, the high demand in the 1960s for wooden apartments, with their communal toilets and kitchens, had fallen away by the 1980s. Improvement of housing through urban renewal projects has become a major issue in the inner city areas of Japan. The quality of life in terms of infrastructure and amenity provision must also constitute part of the social problem facing Japan's cities.

There is no doubt, however, that the very rapid economic growth of Japan has brought very real benefits in terms of material living standards, as illustrated in Table 2.4. It also seems certain that the scale of urban development associated with continued population growth and the improvements required in infrastructure provision will dominate urban policy issues for many years to come in Japan. This raises the central question of how the required expenditure will be financed. Some observers point to increased public expenditure financed from increased taxation; some see funding through greater reliance on user charges; others see the private sector as providing goods and services which might otherwise be provided by the public sector; while others again point to borrowing as the inevitable method of filling revenue/expenditure gaps.

Japan now enjoys a high standard of living as measured by its per capita GDP. It has caught up and overtaken many other OECD countries. Kagami has provided evidence to show that the Japanese economy has reached the stage of maturity in its development.[9] However, qualitative living standards remain low compared with OECD standards, as shown by the indicators in Table 2.5. Indicators used to measure the quality of urban life in Japan have focused particularly upon the physical infrastructure provision of roads, sewerage, and city parks. There are, however, marked variations between cities in Japan regarding infrastructure provision, and urban Japan is certainly not homogeneous in this respect. This situation is illustrated in Table 2.6 in relation to the sewerage diffusion rate (i.e. percentage of population provided with sewerage services) for Japan's designated cities. A high level of sewerage diffusion provision has already been achieved in the major metropolitan regions, with rates between 85 and 100 per cent for Tokyo, Sapporo, Osaka, Nagoya, Yokohama, Kobe and Kitakyushu. The diffusion rate is, however, much lower for other cities, with rates of 54 per cent for Hiroshima, 61 per cent for Chiba and 66 per cent for Kawasaki. It should be noted that the average sewerage diffusion rate of Japan, as at 1990, still remains at 44 per cent (as

Table 2.5 *Japan's quality of urban life: selected indicators*

Indicator	Japan	UK	USA	France	West Germany
1. Percentage of total length paved	68 (1980)	100 (1988)	90 (1988)	92 (1988)	99 (1988)
2. Length of expressways (metres per 10 000 pop.)	88 (1990)	116 (1988)	455 (1988)	269 (1988)	281 (1988)
3. Sewerage diffusion rate (per cent)	44 (1990)	95 (1982)	73 (1986)	64 (1983)	91 (1983)
4. Per capita size of city parks in major cities (metres per person)	2.5 Tokyo (1988)	30.4 London (1976)	45.7 Washington DC (1976)	12.2 Paris (1984)	37.4 Bonn (1984)

Source: Compiled from Japan Regional Development Corporation's *Regional Statistics Handbook*, 1992, and OECD data.

Table 2.6 *The sewerage diffusion rate in designated cities of Japan, 1990*

City	Sewerage diffusion rate (%)
Tokyo (prefecture)	85.1
Sapporo	94.6
Sendai	75.3
Yokohama	85.2
Kawasaki	66.5
Chiba	61.3
Nagoya	89.4
Kyoto	84.0
Osaka	99.8
Kobe	95.5
Hiroshima	54.2
Kitakyushu	88.8
Fukuoka	83.6

Source: Compiled from *Summary of Sewerage Statistics 1990*, Japan Institute of Sewerage.

already shown in Table 2.5). In smaller towns and the rural areas, the level of sewerage provision is extremely low. Urban planning has the task of enabling Japan to match its qualitative living standard with its quantitative one.

Another of the problems facing urban planning in Japan which deserves some attention is its youthfulness compared with the long tradition of rural development and the importance attached to agriculture in the economy and the extent of food subsidies. The Ministry of Agriculture is actively involved in the development of rural areas, as is the Ministry of Construction in the development of urban areas. The 1969 Arrangement of Regional Agricultural Promotional Act designated Agricultural Promotional Areas (APAs). The Act provides a national system of zoning of agricultural land in use, together with potential agricultural land. If a developer wants to develop land which includes agricultural land, then because of the Land Law, Ministry of Agriculture permission is required. Moreover, if an Urbanisation Control Area (UCA)—a zone which in principle constrains urban development—overlaps with an APA, then the developer normally will have to omit from a project that part of the agricultural land lying in the UCA. However, a 1984 revision to the 1969 Act requires mayors of townships in APAs to have regard to employment generally and recreational needs as a whole when administering this restriction. An example of urban development that required using land in an APA, and which was re-zoned by the Ministry of Agriculture to facilitate the urban development, was Tskuschino New Town in Fukuoka prefecture, under construction in 1984. In a variety of ways, therefore, urban policy is closely linked to rural policy.

A considerable impetus to upgrading Japan's urban and social infrastructure has recently been given by the 'Basic Plan for Public Investments', published under the US-sponsored Structural Impediments Initiative (commonly referred to as the SII) in April 1990. The SII was approved by the Cabinet in June 1992, and the Plan provides the framework and basic direction of public investments during the fiscal years 1991–2000. The plan proposes the raising of public investment from an estimated demand of 263 trillion yen to 430 trillion yen (i.e. between $290 billion and $473 billion) during this 1991–2000 period. The plan emphasises the importance of public investments on residential environments and cultural facilities in order to achieve a better quality of life. Furthermore, specific goals are proposed for important facilities such as sewerage and city parks.

Conclusions

The response of the planning system in Japan to problems of urban development, infrastructure provision and its financing, in terms of scale and quantity, must impress any observer. Japanese urban planning may be criticised as being too project-orientated in the past, but this has to a large extent been the nature of the task.

In terms of economic development, Japan has caught up and overtaken most OECD countries. In terms of urban development, infrastructure provision and quality of life, Japan is attempting to catch up very quickly. While the financing of the scale of development and improvements required remains a central issue, the Japanese seem determined to improve the quality of their lives as they have done so successfully with their income levels.

NOTES AND REFERENCES

1 Alden, J., 'Metropolitan Planning in Japan', *Town Planning Review*, 55 (1) 1984, pp. 55–74.

2 Samuels, R. J., *The Politics of Regional Policy in Japan*, Princeton, NJ, Princeton University Press, 1983.

3 Ide, N., *Dai San Sekuta Bizinesu* [*The Third Business Sector*], Place?, Nikkan Nogyo Shimbun Co., 1990.

4 Watanabe, S., 'Garden City Japanese Style: The Case of Den-en Toshi Company Ltd.' in Cherry, G. E. (ed.), *Shaping an Urban World*, London, Mansell, 1988, pp. 129–44.

5 See 1992 *Annual Report on Prefectural Accounts* published by the Japanese Economic Planning Agency, Tokyo.

6 Japan Research Institute of Real Estate, *Tochi Mondai Jiten* [*The Encyclopaedia of Land Problems*], place? Toyo Keizai Shinpo,

7 Abe, H. and Alden, J., 'Regional Development Planning in Japan', *Regional Studies*, 22 (5) 1988, pp. 429–38; and unpublished update on regional income data for the UK and Japan undertaken by the authors.

8 See *International Labour Organisation Year Book of Labour Statistics*, Geneva, ILO, various years.

9 Kagami, N. A., 'Maturing of the Japanese Economy in the 1980's, *National Westminster Bank Review*, November 1983, pp. 18–28.

Chapter 3

Challenges for Japanese Urban Policy

JOHN ZETTER*

Japan has met its urban challenges more effectively than is often thought in other countries. It has certainly handled urbanisation more successfully than any of the countries which have experienced comparable rates of urban growth. This has been achieved through a range of initiatives taken by those who have participated in the urban development process. In general, government policies have taken the form of supporting framework legislation and direct intervention in the development process.

However, despite this success, urban Japan is in a transitional phase. In the coming decades, it will be confronted with considerable challenges of urban restructuring and the quality of urban community life. Some of these challenges may assume dramatic proportions unless great vigilance is shown. This will involve a major challenge for Japanese society, which cannot be met without the progressive definition of a consistent long-term urban policy. One of the major objectives should be to encourage systematically the development of local and private initiatives.

This chapter considers issues and challenges for urban policy in Japan. It draws upon the author's involvement in the Organisation for Economic Cooperation and Development review of urban policies in Japan in the mid-1980s,[1] as well as an updated analysis of recent developments.

The Main Urban Policy Challenges

HOUSING POLICY

There has been a marked improvement in the housing situation in Japan. Despite the exceptional urban population growth rate, the number of housing units per household rose from just under unity in 1958 to just over unity in 1968, and to 1.1 in 1988. However, the number of unoccupied housing units rose from two per cent of total units in 1958 to 10.9 per cent in 1988. More encouraging, the average size of existing housing units rose from 75.5 square metres in 1963 to 80.3 square metres in 1978, and then to 89.3 square metres in 1988.[2]

Nevertheless, significant problems remain. In 1980, in terms of housing unit size,

*The opinions expressed in this paper are those of the author and not necessarily those of the Organisation for Economic Cooperation and Development.

19 million households out of 33 million (57 per cent) were below the Average Housing Standards,[3] and 4.7 million, or 14.5 per cent of the total, were below the Minimum Housing Standards.[4] By 1988 there were still 3.6 million units (or 11 per cent) below the Minimum Housing Standards. The situation is particularly difficult in the major metropolitan regions. In the 1980s, about half of the households below the Average Housing Standards and just over half below the Minimum Housing Standards were in the two regions of Tokyo (Kanko-Rinkai) and Osaka (Kinki). Two-thirds of Tokyo families said their dwellings were too small, too old, under-equipped or did not get enough daylight. One-third of detached houses were under 29 square metres in size.

About sixty per cent of the existing housing stock is owner-occupied, with most of the balance rented. However, renting is higher in the major metropolitan regions. In 1988, 59 per cent of Tokyo's units were rented, as were 51 per cent of Osaka's units. About three-quarters of the Japanese dwellings below the Minimum Housing Standards are rented units. Further, the difference between owner-occupied housing and rented housing seems much greater than in other OECD countries. In 1988, the average size of the former was 112 square metres and of the latter 45 square metres. In the case of housing starts, the average size of new owner-occupied houses increased from 120 square metres to 136 square metres between 1980 and 1990, while the average size of new rental units fell from 57 square metres to 45 square metres over the same period. In 1980, almost two-thirds of new housing starts were for owner-occupied units, but by 1990, the situation was reversed, with rental units comprising 62 per cent of new starts.[5] The last decade—which has been one of rapidly rising urban land prices—has seen more Japanese households occupying smaller rental units. Relatively fewer households were able to owner-occupy new homes, but those who did enjoyed larger new houses—often in suburban locations where land was cheaper and more plentiful.

Lastly, it is to be noted that the share of residential construction in GDP is substantially higher in Japan than in other major developed countries (7.4 per cent against 6.4 per cent in France, 4.8 per cent in the USA and three per cent in the United Kingdom).[6] The total construction sector has 5.9 million jobs (9.5 per cent of total employment) and 508 000 enterprises, 99 per cent consisting of small to mid-size companies or one-person contractors.[7]

INFRASTRUCTURE PROVISION

The delay in providing public facilities in line with development is an extremely serious problem in Japan. It concerns not only total budget allocations for urban facilities, but also rapidly rising costs due to very high urban densities and the need to cater for major natural hazards. An opinion poll on the improvement of public facilities and infrastructure held in 1981 in towns with over 100 000 inhabitants showed that demand was mainly centred, in order of priority, on sanitation, areas for green space and sport and the road system. In the case of sanitation, the average rate for connection with the sewerage system is only 77 per cent in towns with over 100 000 inhabitants (73 per cent in Tokyo), and 50 per cent in towns with 50 000 to 100 000 inhabitants.

It has taken a major effort to raise the average amount of public green space per inhabitant in the major Japanese towns (three square metres in Tokyo). Even so, it is low in comparison with the figure of between 10 and 70 square metres in other similarly sized OECD cities. In addition, the natural environment is diminishing. In the Tokyo region, the area of farmland and forests declined from 44 per cent to 14 per cent of the total between 1945 and 1980.

Another illustration of the density and congestion of urban Japan is that the percentage of urban space used for the road system is considerably lower than in other major OECD cities. In 1988, it was about two times less than London and three times less than Bonn.[8]

NATURAL HAZARDS

The risks from natural hazards, which are exceptionally serious in Japan, are compounded by dense urban development. Minimising their effects involves heavy financial costs. Earthquakes are the hazard which have made the deepest impression on the Japanese. It is considered that over 100 000 people would be killed and injured in Tokyo in an earthquake of the same scale as that of 1923. The problems associated with landslides, floods, fires and typhoons are acute in very many towns.

LAND PRICES

The most intractable problem in Japanese towns is the price of land, which is astronomical compared with other OECD countries. The average price in residential areas exceeds $6600/square metre in Tokyo, and $3700/square metre in Osaka. What is probably an even more serious factor, due to its practical and psychological effects, is that land prices have continually risen much more rapidly than prices in general. Between 1980 and 1986, urban residential land prices in Japan's six largest cities rose by 47 per cent, compared with a 15 per cent increase in consumer prices. Since 1986, the increase in the price of urban land has been even more dramatic, rising by 145 per cent in the six largest cities between 1986 and 1991, as against a nine per cent growth in consumer prices.[9] The Long-Term Plan for Tokyo notes that the average price of building land in Tokyo has tripled in the past 10 years. Partly for this reason, small plots of under 100 square metres represent half of all building land.

Another point to be noted is that housing construction costs in Japan are high by Western standards. This is due not only to high land costs, but also to the patchwork structure of the building industry. New three-bedroom houses with a 40 minute commuting time to central Tokyo are advertised at approximately $625 000.[10] The average price of housing is between six and nine times the average annual salary, as against three to four times in the United States and the United Kingdom.[11]

The effects of the land reform instigated in the late 1940s have been extremely marked. At that time, large agricultural estates were parcelled out to approximately two million small-scale former tenant farmers. This resulted in the emergence of small farm units of approximately a hectare per household on average.

No close analysis of the current pattern of land ownership, nor of changes in it, is available. However, a very high degree of fragmentation appears to persist. It seems clear that, with present price levels, the land question involves numerous and powerful interests.

The agriculture sector in Japan, although decreasing in size, remains powerful and protected. In 1991, 2.3 million households were still considered as farming households, against 6.1 million in 1960. But only 16 per cent were working full-time in agriculture, and 70 per cent earned over half their incomes from non-farming activities. Farming in Japan does not pay. In 1991, 4.4 million persons, or seven per cent of the total working population, were engaged in primary activities (chiefly farming and fisheries), but these activities accounted for only 2.6 per cent of GDP.[12] Yet the average income of 'farming' households is considered to be 12.5 per cent higher than the average Japanese household income. The explanation of this seems to be the combination of farming with other sources of employment, government subsidies and lower tax rates.

On a more general basis, it is considered that the rise in land prices has been a key factor in recent economic development in Japan. Rising land prices provided the capital necessary to stimulate the growth of the Japanese economy and for this and other reasons political difficulties have arisen over controlling the rising price of land.

URBAN SPRAWL

Although it is difficult to come by precise figures, it seems that the combined effect of many factors has been to force a growing proportion of new urban development further and further out from existing urban areas. In summary these factors are:

  (a) the price of land;
  (b) the division of land into small plots;
  (c) infrequent use of expropriation powers;
  (d) the possibility of avoiding heavy development costs;
  (e) the remarkable efficiency of the Land Readjustment Projects; and
  (f) exemptions for small-scale building operations, of under 1000 square metres in Urbanisation Promotion Areas and under 3000 square metres in Urbanisation Control Areas.[13]

URBAN DECLINE

Conversely, declining population in a number of towns has become progressively more serious since 1970. It is affecting town or conurbation centres; towns where industries are in a critical situation or are being relocated; and towns with serious housing price density or environmental problems. The example of Osaka seems significant, although somewhat exceptional in certain respects: the city population decreased from 3.15 million in 1965 to 2.62 million in 1991.

However, trends similar to those in other OECD cities are occurring elsewhere in Japan. The move to the outskirts has been more pronounced in the case of middle-income families, with the proportion of low-income households rising in cities. The drop in population has been steeper in the inner city areas, especially for the 15–29 age group, while the number of elderly people (over 65) has risen in absolute terms. In urban Osaka, the increase was from 26 per cent of the population in 1965 to 65 per cent in the 1980s.

In response to this situation, the city has drawn up the Osaka Comprehensive Plan

1990. This sets the ambitious—but perhaps not realistic—objective of raising the population to three million by the year 2000 by creating employment, but also by developing a policy of various forms of aid for housing to young married couples and middle-income families.

HOUSING RENOVATION

An idea making increasing headway is that one of the main challenges, about which relatively little has been done so far, is the renovation of existing housing, an often difficult task considering the type of accommodation involved and its environment. The development and town planning scheme for Tokyo (1983) puts demand for housing in the period 1981–2000 at 2.7 million units, consisting of 800 000 new and 1.9 million renovated units. According to the scheme, an essential point is that the heaviest demand in the future will be for renovated housing and that the redevelopment of residential districts will become an important task.

As the urban population levels off (corresponding to the question raised from time to time of zero-sum urbanisation), the rivalry between towns and between town centres and the outskirts is becoming serious, as each endeavours to attract the maximum number of inhabitants. Apart from this question of rivalry, in view of the demand for a better kind of housing and environment, a key challenge in future Japanese urban policy is to restructure the cities and win back population and employment for existing urban areas.

PUBLIC PARTICIPATION

Although the price of land and fragmentation are major challenges affecting Japanese towns, as elsewhere in the OECD another trend has shown an increase in recent years. This concerns the obstacles and delays to development, especially to urban renovation or restructuring operations, arising from the direct or indirect resistance of the population in question. This shows the increasing importance attached to consultation and securing cooperation.

PUBLIC INFRASTRUCTURE INVESTMENT

In the 1970s, government spending on public works and facilities grew at an annual rate of 13 per cent in real terms. Between 1980 and 1985, there was an unprecedented cut in public investment, and it fell at an average annual rate of nearly six per cent over this period. However, between 1985 and 1991, public works and facilities investment picked up again, growing at an annual real rate of about eight per cent a year.[14] Most recently, in Japan's 'post-bubble' recession, public investment has again been constrained.

In the early 1980s, financial transfers from central to local government and the latter's borrowing capacity were strictly limited. This helped to focus attention on private funding for urban development and infrastructure, though how this approach could be implemented to good effect is not yet clearly perceived. In the land price boom after 1986, many 'third sector' public-private projects were established, particularly to develop recreational and leisure projects. But a number of these projects have run into difficulty in the post-1991 recession.

DEVELOPMENTS IN THE LATE 1980s AND EARLY 1990s

Since the OECD Review of Urban Policies was completed in the mid-1980s, Japan has continued to participate in the work of the Urban Affairs Group at the OECD. In particular, recent projects on housing policies and social integration, social demographic change, urban travel and transport, the urban environment, urban infrastructure and urban land markets have included Japanese contributions.[15] The picture presented has been one of the incremental, steadily-paced introduction of new policy measures.

The 1989 Basic Land Law has set out to tackle a number of the main issues identified in the OECD Review. In particular, the exclusion of agricultural land from urban zoning and its favourable tax treatment have been reviewed. New stricter measures took effect in 1992. The Land Tax Committee, said to be meeting weekly, is at the centre of this process.

Under the Land Price Publication Act 1969, the threshold has been progressively lowered on the area of land for which sale notifications have to be given. Evidently, there is only one recorded case of a vendor going against advice to reduce a land price. An amendment to the National Land Use Planning Act 1990 introduced punitive taxation rates on the resale of land within three months of acquisition. Pressure to bring land forward for development has been increased by the designations of specific districts for 'Promoting the Utilisation and Conversion of Idle Land'.

Land prices continued to boom in the late 1980s. In 1986, a 70 per cent increase was recorded in the average price of land in the 23 wards of Tokyo. By 1987, land prices in central Tokyo were three or four times those of the London equivalent. However, the more general effect has been to widen the geographical spread of higher prices rather than to lead to rises in the top prices. No doubt the very recent bust in the office price boom in Tokyo may be leading to a considerable rethink on the land price issue. The continuing reluctance to take strict measures partially relates to the benefits which accrue to central and local governments through land taxation.

In the face of the relentless increases in land prices, the sixth Housing Construction Five Year Plan, starting in 1991, gives additional emphasis to public housing provision and to the private rented sector. The 1995 target for floor space in the average dwelling has been raised to 95 square metres. The Tokyo Development Plan was also reviewed in 1991. In central Tokyo, decentralisation of office, shopping and other commercial activity continues to take place away from the traditional focus of Marunouchi/Tokyo Station towards the newer subcentres on the Yamanote railway loop line. Shinjuku is already well established and Ueno is also developing quickly.

More speculatively, the well-known Japanese architect Kisho Kurokawa has proposed a major man-made island in Tokyo Bay for two million extra people. One of several proposals made for the Bay area, it is based on two massive circular canals with high rise buildings on the perimeter and lower rise buildings in the centre of the circular development. Also, a proposal has been made for the State to acquire land to a depth of 40 metres below the surface in urban areas. This would be used for the provision of service networks, with sunlight provided via fibre optics.

Looking more broadly, the Fourth Comprehensive National Development Plan is based on a 'multi-polar' approach. Only one new technopolis has been identified recently (see Chapter 9), but two new pieces of legislation back up the multi-polar approach. First, a Key Facilities Siting Law has been introduced to secure the decentralisation of high-tech industries. Second, 18 plans have been agreed under a new multi-polar law to assist decentralised development. The general assessment is that these laws are too indirect to influence trends, which have seen Kanto (Tokyo region) and Tokai (Nagoya region) as the only regions experiencing population growth in Japan. It is likely that labour market shortages in the long run will have a greater decentralisation effect. However, there have been innovations in regional policy, including the recent use of proceeds from the privatisation sale of the telephone company NTT to provide low interest loans for social infrastructure.

The general decentralisation within the Tokyo region is having its impact on transport conditions. The average rail passenger density index, which in the mid-1980s had a value of 200 ('. . . bodies in contact and a sense of pressure . . .'), is being replaced by one of 250 ('. . . you cannot even move your arms . . .').

The Advisory Group on Economic Structural Adjustment[16] (following up the Maekawa Report of the mid-1980s) has commented that high land prices are depriving the Japanese people from enjoying the full benefits of recent economic growth. This ensures the continued attention to this area of policy as a high priority, given the wealth tied up in land; the potentially divisive social effects of different wealth levels between property owners and non-property owners; and the increasing cost of the land element in infrastructure provision (98 per cent of a recent *cause célèbre* for providing road access to a vacant railway site).

The Future

Reference should be made in closing to some questions of major importance for the future of Japanese cities. First, the ageing of the population. Japan is still young, with nine per cent of the population over 65 against 11 per cent in the USA, 14 per cent in France and 15 per cent in Germany. But the country is now ageing at a speed unparalleled in the OECD. The proportion of over-65s rose from five to 12 per cent in the 40 years from 1950 to 1990, whereas the same rise took 175 years in France and 80 years in Germany. At 15.6 per cent in the year 2000, the proportion of over-65s will have either reached or exceeded that of other OECD countries.

In Japan, questions are being asked about the possible changes in the attitude of young people to work, society, leisure and the environment. Osaka has been affected sooner than other towns by an outflow of economic activity and of young and middle-class families. The question has been raised of whether the young generation, brought up during the recent period of rapid urbanisation, may have different attitudes to urban living from those who moved to the cities from rural areas. Greater importance now seems to be attached to urban aesthetic standards and to the quality of architecture and the environment.

Even if it is still far behind OECD standards in this area, Japan is on an irreversible trend towards more recreational time and activities. Free time has risen by 28 per cent since 1960. Thirty per cent of employees were on a five-day working week in 1980 as against 26 per cent in 1975 and only 8.4 per cent in 1970. The proportion of Japanese playing sport of some kind rose from 45 per cent in 1965 to 68 per cent in 1979. The younger generation are mainly behind the rapid development of the leisure and travel industry, and this will have many consequences on the demand for a more pleasant environment in and around towns.

NOTES AND REFERENCES

1 Organisation for Economic Cooperation and Development, *Urban Policies in Japan*, OECD, 1986.

2 *Japan Statistical Yearbook*, Tokyo Management and Coordination Agency, 1992.

3 50 square metres for two persons, 86 square metres for four.

4 29 square metres for two persons, 50 square metres for four.

5 *Japan Statistical Yearbook*, op. cit.

6 OECD, *Economic Surveys: Japan 1983*, Paris, Organisation for Economic Cooperation and Development, 1983.

7 Ministry of Construction, 1990 data, in *Japan Almanac 1993*, Tokyo, Asahi Shimbun Publishing Company, 1992, p. 142.

8 Ibid., p. 188. Chapter 3

9 *Japan Statistical Yearbook*, op. cit.

10 Japan Real Estate Institute data, *Japan Almanac 1993*, op. cit., p. 184.

11 *Nikkei Shimbum*, 18 February 1993.

12 Ministry of Labour, Tokyo, 1990 data, in *Japan Almanac 1993*, op. cit., p. 188.

13 See the chapter in this book by David Callies for an additional discussion of Urbanisation Promotion and Control Areas.

14 Ministry of Construction data, adjusted by GDP deflator, in *Japan Almanac 1993*, op. cit., p. 142.

15 See the following publications by the Organisation for Economic Cooperation and Development: *Environment Policies in Cities in the 1990s*, Paris, OECD, 1990; *Urban Infrastructure: Finance and Management*, Paris, OECD, 1991; and *Urban Land Markets*, Paris, OECD, 1992.

16 *On the Progress of Economic Structural Adjustment: Follow-up Measures Presented in the Maekawa Report*, Tokyo, The Advisory Group on Economic Structural Adjustment for International Harmony, July 1991.

Chapter 4

The Impact of Recent Urbanisation on Inner City Development in Japan

JEREMY D. ALDEN, MORIAKI HIROHARA and HIROFUMI ABE

The incidence of inner city problems in the central cities of metropolitan regions in advanced Western countries has been recognised as an important planning issue for many years. In terms of economic development, Japan has caught up and overtaken many OECD countries. In terms of urban development, infrastructure provision and quality of life, Japan is attempting to catch up very quickly. This situation has been well documented by the OECD.[1] However, there is a growing concern in Japan that the inner city problems which have become such a feature of urban planning in many advanced Western nations may soon spread to become a feature of urban planning in Japan.

The main purpose of this chapter is to examine the impact of recent urbanisation on inner city development in Japan, the extent to which Japan may be described as having an inner city problem, and whether or not this can be compared with the problems facing European cities. After a brief review of trends in the urbanisation of post-war Japan, the chapter focuses upon the main issues of concern that emerged in the face of new trends in Japanese metropolises and metropolitan regions from the second half of the 1970s. There is an examination of population and employment trends for both central cities and surrounding city regions for Japan's major cities in the 1970s and 1980s. The chapter concludes with some comments on likely future problems and prospects facing Japan's metropolitan regions and metropolises in terms of inner city problems.

Urbanisation, Urban Policies and the City Planning System in Post-War Japan

The Japanese mainland, particularly its cities, was devastated by the Second World War. While 115 cities suffered large-scale war damage, it was concentrated in the five largest cities, i.e. Tokyo, Osaka, Nagoya, Yokohama and Kobe. Tokyo suffered a quarter of the nation's war damage. Faced with this situation, the post-war government gave priority to the increased production of foodstuffs, the reconstruction of basic industries, and construction of new dwellings to replace the 2.65 million homes which had been destroyed (the absolute housing shortage was some 4.2 million units).

Consequently, the birth of a new city planning system had to wait until the enactment in 1968 of the new City Planning Law.

Japan's post-war policy of rapid economic growth, which attracted a great deal of international attention, developed quickly as national economic plans such as the 'Economic Self-Sufficiency Plan' (December 1955) and the 'New Long-Term Economic Plan' (December 1957) were repeatedly revised. With the 'National Income-Doubling Plan' (December 1960), this policy was linked to regional development plans for the first time. The 'National Income-Doubling Plan' (1961–70) was a plan for highly intensive income growth, i.e. 8.8 per cent growth of GNP (actual growth: 11.6 per cent). Regional development measures to implement this policy were made public in the 'Pacific Belt Concept' (August 1961) by the Industrial Location Subcommittee of the Economic Council, the advisory body concerned with this plan. This concept was a major plan to develop the Pacific coastal belt, joining four major industrial areas (Tokyo, Nagoya, Osaka and Kitakyushu) into a key industrial zone. For an idea of the scale of the plan, the goal was to concentrate (a) 85 per cent of the 128 000 newly-built factories, (b) 88 per cent of the 61 380 hectares of new factory sites, and (c) 70 per cent of all public investments in the belt, and to generate 87 per cent of all industrial production in that region.[2]

The 'Pacific Belt Concept' was a nationally directed, regional development plan, the industrial location policy of which was based on a respect for economic principles under a free market economic system. It perceived the development of industrial infrastructure through public investment as the major means of inducing enterprises to locate in a given area, and it was aimed at concentrating public investment in a limited region in order to put it to most effective use. However, there were strong protests from less developed regions that were not included in this development concept. Figure 4.1 shows the regional divisions of Japan, together with prefectural boundaries. Consequently, a political compromise resulted in the establishment of the 'First Comprehensive National Development Plan' (October 1962), which took as its approach the fostering of regional development nuclei and the decentralisation of industry in order to prevent the over-expansion of cities and reduce regional differences. As a result, the 'Pacific Belt Concept' and the 'First Comprehensive National Development Plan', though each represents a regional development version of the 'National Income-Doubling Plan', offer sharp contrasts in their content: industrial centralisation versus decentralisation, development weighted in favour of certain areas versus balanced development, and the efficient distribution of public investment versus balanced distribution. However, the Comprehensive National Development Plan was actually a plan of guidance and inducement and had no legal binding power; thus, in reality the tendency was to place the emphasis on *laissez-faire* economic principles.[3]

The policy of intensive economic growth initiated in the 1950s led to a concentration of population in metropolitan regions that was unprecedented in Japanese history. The numbers of people who moved from provincial areas to the three metropolitan areas of Tokyo (Tokyo and Kanagawa, Saitama, and Chiba prefectures), Osaka (Osaka, Kyoto, and Hyogo prefectures) and Nagoya (Aichi and Mie prefectures) during five-year periods between 1950 and 1975 were 2 172 000, 2 491 000, 3 030 000, 2 031 000 and

1 010 000, or a total of 10 734 000 (of whom 5 684 000 moved to the Tokyo region). When the growth through natural increase is added, the percentage of the national population accounted for by the three metropolitan regions is seen to have grown rapidly from 32 per cent (or 26 624 000 persons) in 1950 to 44.9 per cent (or 50 610 000 persons) by 1975 and to 45.4 per cent (or 55 007 000 persons) in 1985. In particular, the concentration of population in the Tokyo region was remarkable. The percentage of the national population in the Tokyo region grew from 15.5 per cent (or 12.9 million persons) in 1950 to 24.2 per cent (or 27.1 million persons) by 1975.[4]

Another characteristic of migration during the period of intensive economic growth was a substantial movement of population from farming areas to cities within provincial regions simultaneous with the movement from provincial regions to the three largest metropolitan regions. This concentrated movement of population, from the farming villages to provincial cities, and from provincial cities to metropolises (called the 'billiards phenomenon') led to new patterns of city and regional population growth.

Regions of widespread and serious depopulation were the other side of the coin of capital and population concentration in the three metropolitan regions.[5] The depopulation problem had calmed down in the 1970s when the Japanese economy went into a period of low economic growth after the first oil crisis. Thus the 1980 population census showed population growth for all local prefectures during 1975–80. However, the population census for 1990 revealed population losses in 18 prefectures (one prefecture in three metropolitan regions and 17 prefectures in local regions) during 1985–90. Depopulation of local regions has therefore become a serious regional problem again.

Land prices also rose sharply, reflecting the rapid and large-scale concentration of capital and population in cities. Land prices in Japanese cities increased rapidly because effective measures to control them, such as the creation of taxes on increases in land prices and development profits, were not taken over the long term, and because land speculation fuelled by excessively liquid capital was repeated continuously over the short term.

Sharp increases in land prices occurred three times in post-war Japan. If one looks at the rate of change over the previous year in land price indices for the urbanised areas of the six largest metropolises, then 1961, 1973 and 1988 represent the peak years for land price increases. The average land prices in residential areas rose by 61.9 per cent in 1961, by 42.5 per cent in 1973 and by 30.7 per cent in 1988. As a result, although the post-war consumer price index (base year 1955 = 100) rose to 108 in 1960, 188 in 1970, 445 in 1980 and 529 in 1989, land prices as calculated according to the average urban area price index for all zones of use rose to 294 in 1960, 1692 in 1970, 4094 in 1980, and 12 848 in 1989, in the six largest metropolises (i.e. Tokyo, Yokohama, Osaka, Nagoya, Kyoto and Kobe), or approximately 24 times the consumer price index during the period 1955–89.[6] Rising land prices have been one of the most serious urban problems in post-war Japan and have devastated the major cities, although increases have now stabilised in most cities. The Japanese government enacted the Basic Law on Land in 1989 to cope with these problems.

The new City Planning Law was enacted in the latter half of the 1960s, when various urban problems of this nature caused by the policy of intensive economic growth

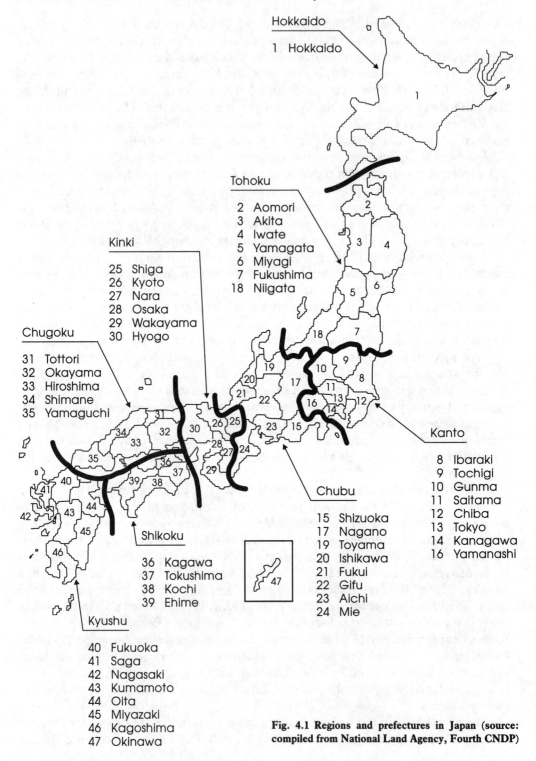

Hokkaido

1 Hokkaido

Tohoku

2 Aomori
3 Akita
4 Iwate
5 Yamagata
6 Miyagi
7 Fukushima
18 Niigata

Kinki

25 Shiga
26 Kyoto
27 Nara
28 Osaka
29 Wakayama
30 Hyogo

Chugoku

31 Tottori
32 Okayama
33 Hiroshima
34 Shimane
35 Yamaguchi

Kanto

8 Ibaraki
9 Tochigi
10 Gunma
11 Saitama
12 Chiba
13 Tokyo
14 Kanagawa
16 Yamanashi

Chubu

15 Shizuoka
17 Nagano
19 Toyama
20 Ishikawa
21 Fukui
22 Gifu
23 Aichi
24 Mie

Shikoku

36 Kagawa
37 Tokushima
38 Kochi
39 Ehime

Kyushu

40 Fukuoka
41 Saga
42 Nagasaki
43 Kumamoto
44 Oita
45 Miyazaki
46 Kagoshima
47 Okinawa

Fig. 4.1 Regions and prefectures in Japan (source: compiled from National Land Agency, Fourth CNDP)

gradually became more severe. Although the 1968 City Planning Law has not been very successful in coping with urban problems which occurred during the period of rapid economic growth (such as urban sprawl, soaring land prices, etc.), it produced an extensive land use zoning system and is an important landmark in post-war urban planning in Japan.

To summarise, when one reviews the history of urban policy and the urban planning system in post-war Japan, it can be seen that regional development and urban policies have been consistently adapted to the aim of achieving rapid economic growth, and that the city planning system has been designed to support those policies. In contrast with the growing concern with de-urbanisation problems in the UK and USA in the 1960s and early 1970s, one of the greatest concerns of city planning in Japan up to the mid-1970s was not about urban decline, but the exact opposite, i.e. the depopulation of rural communities. However, as a result of rapidly-rising land prices which occurred in Tokyo and major Japanese cities in the mid to late 1980s, the provision of housing and infrastructure became extremely difficult in major cities. This problem led to the devastation of their communities as well as the urban environment. It is likely to have an effect on inner city communities in future years.

Metropolitan and Inner City Development Problems in Japan

Population growth in the major cities of Japan slowed down in the 1970s. Table 4.1 shows the population of these cities as at 1975, 1980, 1985 and 1990, and the changes for each five-year period between 1970 and 1990. Population growth was generally

Table 4.1 *Population growth in Tokyo and designated cities* (1000s and per cent)*

	1975	1980	1985	1990	1970/75	1975/80	1980/85	1985/90
Tokyo 23 wards	8647	8349	8355	8164	−2.2	−3.4	−0.0	−2.3
Yokohama	2622	2755	2993	3220	17.1	5.8	7.9	7.6
Osaka	2779	2648	2636	2624	−6.8	−4.7	−0.5	−0.5
Nagoya	2080	2083	2116	2155	2.1	0.4	1.6	1.8
Sapporo	1241	1402	1543	1672	22.8	13.0	10.1	8.3
Kobe	1361	1367	1411	1477	5.6	0.5	3.2	4.7
Kyoto	1461	1473	1479	1461	3.0	0.8	0.4	−1.2
Fukuoka	1002	1089	1160	1237	15.0	8.6	6.5	6.6
Kawasaki	1015	1041	1089	1174	4.3	2.5	4.6	7.8
Hiroshima	853	899	044	1085	14.2	5.5	16.1	4.0
Kitakyushu	1058	1065	1056	1026	1.5	0.6	−0.1	−2.8
TOTAL	24 119	24 190	24 882	25 295	2.8	0.3	2.9	1.7

*Rank order by 1990 population; excludes Sendai and Chiba.
Source: Statistics Bureau, Population Census of Japan 1970–1990.

considerably slower in the latter periods, although there are some exceptions in the 1985–90 period. The table also shows that the two most important cities of Japan, Tokyo and Osaka, lost population throughout the 1970s and 1980s. This situation must not be confused with the position where in the mid-1980s the three metropolitan regions as a whole had a larger share of the nation's population than they had in the mid-1970s. The population declines recorded for these 'central' cities (as defined in Japan, and shown in Fig. 4.1.) may be contrasted with continuing population growth over the same period in the larger Tokyo and Osaka metropolitan regions (boundaries shown in Fig. 4.1.). This indicates that the lion's share of urban population growth during the 1970s and 1980s, whether by in-migration or natural growth, occurred in the suburban towns and communities lying in the 'surrounding areas' shown in Figure 4.1.

The emphasis of Japanese regional development and urban policies remains largely unchanged in terms of their underlying strategies. The National Land Agency, which published the Fourth Comprehensive National Development Plan in 1987, foresees, with regard to the future distribution of population, the growth of the three largest metropolitan regions, particularly the Tokyo metropolitan region, and the growth of central provincial cities in provincial regions.

As shown in Table 4.2, compared with 1990, the distribution of population in 2025 is

Table 4.2 *Population trends and prospects by region, 1970–2025 (1000 persons)*

	1970	1990	2025	1990/1970 (%)	2025/1990 (%)
Japan	104 665	123 611	133 180	18.1	7.7
	(100.0)	(100.0)	(100.0)		
Hokkaido	5184	5644	5830	8.9	3.3
	(5.0)	(4.6)	(4.4)		
Tohhoku	11 392	12 213	11 450	7.2	−6.2
	(10.9)	(9.9)	(8.6)		
Kanto	30 258	39 396	45 960	27.4	16.7
	(28.9)	(31.9)	(34.5)		
Chubu	16 511	19 486	21 030	23.2	7.9
	(15.8)	(15.8)	(15.8)		
Kinki	17 401	20 414	22 500	17.3	10.2
	(16.6)	(16.5)	(16.9)		
Chugoku/Shikoku	10 901	11 940	11 430	9.5	−4.3
	(10.4)	(9.7)	(8.6)		
Kyushu	13 017	14 518	14 980	11.5	3.2
	(12.4)	(11.7)	(11.2)		

Source: National Land Agency, *Kokudo Shingikai Shiryo: Jinko, Toshi King Kara Mita Kokudo Kozo no Tenbo* [*National Land Council Source Material: Prospects for the National Land Structure from the Viewpoint of Population and Urban Function*], 1985, and Statistics Bureau, Management and Coordination Agency, *Final Report of the 1985 Population Census*, Printing Bureau, Ministry of Finance, 1990 (in Japanese).

expected to show: (a) the population of the Hokkaido, Tohoku, Chugoku, Shikoku and Kyushu regions has decreased relatively speaking from 44 315 000 persons (or 35.9 per cent) to 43 690 000 persons (or 32.8 per cent); (b) the population of the Kinki region, including the Osaka metropolitan region, and the population of the Chubu region, including the Nagoya metropolitan region, has levelled off, from 20 414 000 persons (or 16.5 per cent) to 22 500 000 persons (or 16.9 per cent), and from 19 486 000 persons (or 15.8 per cent) to 21 030 000 persons (or 15.8 per cent) respectively; and (c), in contrast, the population of the Kanto region, including the Tokyo metropolitan population of the Kanto region, including the Tokyo metropolitan region, will have increased significantly from 39 396 000 persons (or 31.9 per cent) to 45 960 000 (or 34.8 per cent). Table 4.3 displays a government forecast of population for different city regions and for different classes of cities by population size. The table also separates the population figures and future estimates by 'central city' and 'surrounding area' (boundaries shown in Fig. 4.2). Table 4.3 indicates that average growth of national population up to the year 2000 is expected to be 5.9 per cent. However, as shown in Table 4.3, whereas the sum of all city regions (i.e. City region, CR) is expected to grow in population from 74 512 000 to 98 843 000 or the population share in Japan from 71.2 per cent to 77.8 per cent during the period 1970–2000, the outside city region in Japan (i.e. 'The rest' region) is expected to experience population decline from 30 153 000 to 29 273 000 or the population share from 28.8 per cent to 22.2 per cent during the same period, resulting in the division of the country into 'growing urban regions' and 'declining non-urban regions'. For the urban regions, it is expected that the Chyuko metropolitan region, centred around the cities of Nagoya, Toyota, Gifu and Yokkaichi, and provincial urban regions with central cities of over 500 000 population, will experience a high 12 to 16 per cent rate of growth. For the Tokyo metropolitan region, centred around the 23 wards of Tokyo, and the Kyoto/Osaka/Kobe metropolitan region, centred around the cities of Osaka, Kyoto, Kobe and Wakayama, it is expected that both will maintain a growth rate of slightly less than nine per cent, but it should be noted that, of the central cities of these two metropolitan regions, Tokyo, at −13.9 per cent, and Kyoto/Osaka/Kobe, at −6.6 per cent, are expected to show population decreases. Consequently, what is depicted here of the country and the city goes one step beyond the old idea of the 'three main metropolitan regions plus the Pacific Belt', and is instead a regional and urban development plan involving 'the capital region plus the provincial metropolitan regions plus a national network' and is a plan for reorganising regions and cities accordingly (see Tables 4.2 and 4.3).[7]

The view of the future held by the government, that urbanisation will progress further in Japan and that metropolitan regions, particularly the capital region, will experience further growth and expansion, leads the government to hold a positive view regarding the problem of the decline of metropolitan regions. Neither the central government nor metropolitan governments have in the past publicly used the phrase 'inner city problems'. Consequently, among the various ministries and agencies of the central government, or between the central government and local governments, or among the different local governments, opinions differ regarding the question of where the inner city problems of Japan lie.

Table 4.3 Population trends and prospects of city region by the size of central city, 1970–2000 (1000 persons)

		1970	1980	1985	2000	1985/1970 (%)	2000/1985 (%)
Japan	CR	104 665 (100.00)	117 060	120 924	128 116 (100.0)	15.5	5.9
Keithin	CR	21 688 (20.7)	25 848	27 268	29 685 (23.4)	25.8	8.9
(Tokyo)	CC	8841	8352	8273	7123	-6.4	-13.9
	SA	12 828	17 496	18 995	22 562	48.1	18.8
Keihanshin	CR	13 911 (13.3)	15 819	16 328	17 748 (14.0)	17.4	8.7
(Osaka, Kyoto Kobe)	CC	6045	5889	5784	5401	-4.5	-6.6
	SA	7857	9930	10 544	12 347	34.2	17.1
Chukyo (Nagoya)	CR	5886 (5.6)	6797	7049	7913 (6.2)	19.8	12.3
	CC	3272	3505	3544	3707	8.3	4.5
	SA	2614	3292	3505	4210	34.1	20.1
1 000 000 plus city	CR	7419 (7.1)	8932	9414	10 908 (8.6)	26.9	15.9
	CC	5204	6202	6496	7421	24.8	14.2
	SA	2215	2703	2918	3487	31.7	19.5
500 000 to 1 000 000 city	CR	3720 (3.6)	4377	4583	5151 (4.1)	23.2	12.4
	CC	2529	2916	3037	3354	20.1	10.4
	SA	1191	1461	1546	1797	29.8	16.2
300 000 to 500 000 city	CR	8699 (8.3)	9924	10 326	11 174 (8.8)	18.7	8.2
	CC	5205	6046	6304	6884	21.1	9.2
	SA	3494	3878	4022	4290	15.1	6.7
300 000 & less city	CR	13 209 (12.6)	14 859	15 360	16 264 (12.8)	16.3	5.9
	CC	8307	9415	9717	10 296	17.0	6.0
	SA	4902	5444	5643	5968	15.1	5.8
Total City regions	CR	74 512 (71.2)	86 556	90 327	98 843 (77.8)	21.2	9.4
	CC	39 412	42 325	43 155	44 182	9.5	2.4
	SA	35 100	44 231	47 173	54 661	34.4	15.9
'The rest' region		30 153 (28.8)	30 504	30 597	29 273 (22.2)	1.5	-4.3

CR = City region   CC = Central city   SA = Surrounding area. Source: National Land Agency, *Nihon: Nijuisseiki e no Tenbo* [*Japan: Prospects for the 21st Century*], 1984; National Land Agency, *Kokudo Shingikai Shiryo: Jinko, Toshi King Kara Mita Kokudo Kozo no Tenbo* [*National Land Council Source Material: Prospects for the National Land Structure from the Viewpoint of Population and Urban Function*], 1985. Note: The results of the population census for 1990 are not available by metropolitan region/city size.

However, the increasing concern expressed in Japan over the future economic vitality of its cities can be seen from statements made by various ministries of central government in the mid-1980s on the subject of inner city problems. For example, the Ministry of Construction has noted that:

> The central cities of the three largest metropolitan regions are being emptied of their population and are experiencing the loss or stagnation of their settled population. However, this does not necessarily mean the decrease of their day-time, active population, for that is continuing to increase. Nevertheless, the day-time population has been decreasing since 1970 in Osaka, indicating a weakening of Osaka's fundamental strength. The emptying of the urban area caused by a decrease in the night-time population and the growth in the ratio of the day-time population to the night-time population may lead to problems such as the inefficient use of social overhead capital and an undermining of the basis for a comfortable life.[8]

The National Land Agency has voiced its concern over emerging inner city problems in Japan, although it has recognised that these have not yet reached the scale being faced in European cities:

> The problem of the decline of metropolises was pointed out quite early in Western countries, and the problem is quite serious. At present, although a decline in vitality in the cores and surrounding areas is evident in Japanese metropolises, conditions have not become as serious as in Western countries. Nevertheless, the decline of regional vitality in areas other than inner cities due to new factors such as the possible exodus of structurally depressed types of industries from coastal regions or the possible degeneration into slums of old residential areas that become out-dated as living standards rise is a matter of concern.[9]

The link between the economy of inner city areas and the vitality of cities as a whole has been emphasised by the Ministry of Home Affairs:

> In recent years, there have been places in the cores and areas surrounding the cores of metropolises where factors such as a decrease in population and the exodus of factories have begun to create a vacuum. Such a phenomenon has major economic and social implications such as the under-utilisation of public facilities, commercial stagnation, and the transformation of the community, and is perceived as an important problem related to the overall function of the metropolis. In particular, there exist extensive districts within inner-ring areas that have been late in adapting to structural changes in the metropolis and are consequently weakened. If nothing is done about their decline, there is the danger that it might lead to a lowering of vitality of the city as a whole.[10]

The work of both Sassen[11] and Nakabayashi[12] has illustrated the impact of continuing inner city population decline facing Japanese cities in the 1980s, the explosion of land values and property speculation which have devastated traditional communities, substantial inner city redevelopment schemes, and the increasing social problems due to a changing social mix which is a result of large numbers of illegal workers from Asia living in the inner districts of Tokyo, as well as Osaka and Nagoya. Sassen has suggested that perhaps the most important process of change in the social geography of Tokyo is the emergence of an inner city problem. The decline in the employment base and in the physical conditions of older areas in central Tokyo has been the most visible sign of emerging inner city-type problems.

The most detailed empirical study of the social geography of Tokyo has been that undertaken by Nakabayashi, who analysed government data on thirty-two variables for each of Tokyo's twenty-three wards in 1986. The data included demographic and employment variables, land prices, environmental conditions, and the presence of minority populations. The incidence of these variables and their geographic concentration allowed the author to establish the extent to which there are in Tokyo social, economic and physical conditions which replicate the inner city problems in Western cities such as London and New York. Taking Nakabayashi's four broad indices of neighbourhood social decline, local economic decline, physical decline and presence of disadvantaged minorities, the areas with the overall highest incidence of these conditions were the Arakawa, Taito and Sumida wards of Tokyo, all immediately adjacent to the central business districts. Sassen concurs with Nakabayashi that the key factor in the social, economic and physical decline of inner city areas in Tokyo has been the decline of traditional manufacturing and trading, which in turn has affected the viability of a whole range of secondary local activities.

Recent Trends in Employment in Japanese Regions

While the preceding analysis has focused largely upon issues of population change and dispersal, some assessment must also be made of recent trends in employment for both regions and central cities in Japan, particularly in relation to occupational structure. Table 4.4 identifies the employment structure of Japan as at 1975 and 1985 by both occupation and region. The occupational classification used for the purposes of the 1985 population census is based upon the International Labour Office classification. Occupational classifications are summarised into four main groups, namely (1) Agriculture, forestry and fishing, (2) production and transport, (3) sales and service, (4) clerical, technical and managerial. These latter three groups are often referred to as 'blue', 'yellow' and 'white' class occupational groups respectively.

The data presented in Table 4.4 show that the share of the agricultural sector in Japan fell from 13.8 per cent of total employment in 1975 to 9.2 per cent in 1985, and that of the 'blue' sector from 36.4 per cent to 35.6 per cent. However, the 'yellow' and 'white' sectors in Japan increased their share by 1.6 per cent and 3.8 per cent respectively. There was a clear shift to the 'white' sector in Japan during this period.

Table 4.5 illustrates that these employment trends in Japan as a whole were experienced in each region between 1975 and 1985. Kanto and Kinki regions, which

Table 4.4 *Employment by region and occupation in Japan, 1975 and 1985*

Region	1975					1985				
	Total	Agri	Product (Blue)	Sales (Yellow)	Clerical (White)	Total	Agri	Product (Blue)	Sales (Yellow)	Clerical (White)
Japan	52.955	7.290	19.280	11.241	15.144	58.193	5.360	20.719	13.288	18.826
(Occupational share %)	100.0	13.8	36.4	21.2	28.6	100.0	9.2	35.6	22.8	32.4
(Regional share %)	—	100.0	100.0	100.0	100.0	—	100.0	100.0	100.0	100.0
Hokkaido	2.456	379	818	567	692	2.622	317	805	661	839
(Occupational share %)	100.0	15.4	33.3	23.1	28.2	100.0	12.1	30.7	25.2	32.0
(Regional share %)	—	5.2	4.2	5.0	4.6	—	5.9	3.9	5.0	4.5
Tohuku	5.776	1.628	1.840	1.024	1.284	6.058	1.135	2.139	1.193	1.591
(Occupational share %)	100.0	28.2	31.9	17.7	22.2	100.0	18.7	35.3	19.7	26.3
(Regional share %)	—	22.3	9.5	9.1	8.5	—	21.2	10.3	9.0	8.5
Kantoh	15.727	1.323	5.573	3.566	5.264	18.307	967	6.189	4.361	6.790
(Occupational share %)	100.0	8.4	35.4	22.7	33.5	100.0	5.3	33.8	23.8	37.1
(Regional share %)	—	18.2	28.9	31.7	24.8	—	18.0	29.9	32.8	36.1
Chubu	8.808	1.136	3.693	1.734	2.245	9.688	809	4.066	2.009	2.804
(Occupational share %)	100.0	12.9	41.9	19.7	25.5	100.0	8.4	42.0	20.7	28.9
(Regional share %)	—	15.6	19.2	15.4	14.8	—	15.1	19.6	15.1	14.9
Kinki	8.528	513	3.342	1.988	2.684	9.198	359	3.362	2.320	3.157
(Occupational share %)	100.0	6.0	39.2	23.3	31.5	100.0	3.9	36.5	25.2	34.3
(Regional share %)	—	7.0	17.3	17.7	17.7	—	6.7	16.2	17.5	16.8
Chugoku/Shikoku	5.634	1.049	2.083	1.066	1.436	5.820	795	2.014	1.209	1.712
(Occupational share %)	100.0	18.6	37.0	18.9	25.5	100.0	13.7	36.2	20.8	29.4
(Regional share %)	—	14.4	10.8	9.5	9.5	—	14.8	10.2	9.1	9.1
Kyushu	6.027	1.261	1.931	1.296	1.539	6.499	978	2.053	1.534	1.934
(Occupational share %)	100.0	20.9	32.0	21.5	25.5	100.0	15.0	31.6	23.6	29.8
(Regional share %)	—	17.3	10.0	11.5	10.2	—	18.2	9.9	11.5	10.3

Source: Compiled from population censuses of Japan in 1975 and 1985. Agri = agriculture, foresty and fishing.

Table 4.5 *Change in occupational share by region, 1975–1985*

| Region | Total | Change in 1975–1985 | | | |
		Agri	Product (blue)	Sales (yellow)	Clerical (white)
Japan	—	−4.6	−0.8	1.6	3.8
Hokkaido	—	−3.3	−2.6	2.1	3.8
Tohoku	—	−9.5	3.5	2.0	4.0
Kanto	—	−3.1	−1.6	1.1	3.6
Chubu	—	−4.5	0.0	1.1	3.5
Kinki	—	−2.1	−2.6	1.9	2.8
Chugoku/Shikoku	—	−5.0	−0.8	1.8	3.9
Kyushu	—	−5.9	−0.4	2.1	4.2

Source: Compiled from population censuses of Japan in 1975 and 1985.

Table 4.6 *Change in regional share by occupation, 1975–1985*

| Region | Total | Change in 1975–1985 | | | |
		Agri	Product (blue)	Sales (yellow)	Clerical (white)
Japan	—	–	—	—	—
Hokkaido	—	0.72	−0.36	−0.07	−0.11
Tohoku	—	−1.17	0.78	−0.13	−0.02
Kanto	—	−0.12	0.97	1.10	1.31
Chubu	—	−0.49	0.47	−0.31	0.07
Kinki	—	−0.33	−1.11	−0.23	−0.96
Chugoku/Shikoku	—	0.44	−0.65	−0.39	−0.39
Kyushu	—	0.94	−0.10	0.02	0.11

Source: Compiled from population censuses of Japan in 1975 and 1985.

include Tokyo and Osaka respectively, have a larger share in the 'white' sector. Table 4.6 shows regional patterns of change in occupational structure during this 1975–85 period. These regional changes have been fairly similar and not very large.

Table 4.7 shows the growth rate by region and occupation for the period 1975–85. The 'white' sector shows the largest growth rate in each region, which means a large shift in occupational structure towards the 'white' sector. While the differences in growth rates between regions are small in the 'yellow' and 'white' sectors, the growth rate of the 'blue' sector shows a marked difference between regions. While the Tohoku, Kanto and Chubu regions show substantial growth in the 'blue' sector, the Hokkaido, Kinki and Chugoku/Shikoku regions show very little growth, or even job losses. These regions have been dependent on the heavy and petro-chemical industries, and suffered from the restructuring of manufacturing industries in recent years.

Table 4.7 *Growth rate of employment by region and occupation, 1975–1985*

| Region | Total | Change in 1975–1985 | | | |
		Agri	Product (blue)	Sales (yellow)	Clerical (white)
Japan	9.9	−26.5	7.5	18.2	24.3
Hokkaido	6.8	−16.2	−1.6	16.6	21.2
Tohoku	4.9	−30.3	16.3	16.5	24.0
Kanto	16.4	−26.9	11.1	22.3	29.0
Chubu	10.0	−28.8	10.1	15.9	24.9
Kinki	7.9	−30.0	0.6	16.7	17.6
Chugoku/Shikoku	3.3	−24.2	1.0	13.4	19.2
Kyushu	7.8	−22.5	6.3	18.4	25.7

Source: Compiled from population censuses of Japan in 1975 and 1985.

Recent Trends in Occupational Structure in Major Japanese Cities

As shown in Table 4.8, the share of the 'agri' sector was less than three per cent in the central city (CC) of each city region. However, the shares of 'agri' in the surrounding area (SA) of major cities in local regions (i.e. Sendai, Hiroshima, Kitakyushu/Fukuoka) exceeded 10 per cent in 1985, although the shares were decreasing rapidly in 1975 to 1985.

The Chukyo metropolitan region, which includes Nagoya city, shows the largest share of the 'product' (blue) sector among major cities in both 1975 and 1985. However, the occupational structure is generally similar among major Japanese cities. Tables 4.9 and 4.10 illustrate the growth rate and changes in the share by city and sector. The growth rate of the 'product' (blue) sector differs among cities. While Hiroshima and Kitakyushu/Fukuoka cities lost employment in the 'product' (blue) sector in 1975 and 1985, Sapporo and Sendai cities showed large increases in this sector. Hiroshima and Kitakyushu/Fukuoka have been dependent on the heavy and petro-chemical industries, and have suffered since the oil crises. In contrast with these cities, the 'product' (blue) sector of Sendai city has been growing rapidly under the expansion of high-tech industries from Tokyo metropolitan region to Tohoku region.

The 'sales' (yellow) and 'clerical' (white) sectors showed large growth rates in all city regions in 1975 to 1985. This has led to these major cities growing as regional centres of business and commerce in each region. The surrounding areas (SA) of three large metropolitan regions (i.e. Keihin, Chukyo and Keihanshin), which include Tokyo, Nagoya and Osaka respectively, showed a larger growth rate in the 'sales' (yellow) and 'clerical' (white) sectors than the central cities (CC). There is a clear locational shift of business and commercial activities from central cities to suburban areas under the expansion of the city region, especially in large metropolitan regions.

Table 4.8 Employment (thousands and percentages) by city and occupation in Japan, 1975 and 1985

City		1975					1985				
		Total	Agri	Product (blue)	Sales (yellow)	Clerical (white)	Total	Agri	Product (blue)	Sales (yellow)	Clerical (white)
Japan		53 015	7290	19 014	11 507	15 144	58 357	5360	20 719	13 288	18 826
	%	100.0	13.8	35.9	21.7	28.6	100.0	9.2	35.5	22.8	32.3
Sapporo	CR	794	34	242	237	280	971	31	278	292	367
	%	100.0	4.3	30.5	29.8	35.3	100.0	3.2	28.6	30.1	37.8
	CC	559	7	173	165	213	695	6	195	214	278
	%	100.0	1.3	31.0	29.5	38.1	100.0	0.8	28.0	30.8	40.1
	SA	235	27	69	72	67	276	25	83	78	89
	%	100.0	11.4	29.2	30.7	28.6	100.0	9.1	30.2	28.4	32.1
Keihin (Tokyo)	CR	12 391	495	4287	3039	4544	14 767	390	4775	3681	5448
	%	100.0	4.0	34.6	24.5	36.7	100.0	2.6	32.3	24.9	39.6
	CC	5954	32	2020	1568	2317	6349	28	1891	1727	2662
	%	100.0	0.5	33.9	26.3	38.9	100.0	0.4	29.8	27.2	41.9
	SA	6437	463	2267	1471	2227	8418	362	2884	1954	3186
	%	100.0	7.2	35.2	22.8	34.6	100.0	4.3	34.3	23.2	37.9
Chukyo (Nagoya)	CR	3562	226	1584	764	984	4004	158	1734	878	1229
	%	100.0	6.3	44.5	21.4	27.6	100.0	3.9	43.3	21.9	30.7
	CC	1002	8	380	272	342	1054	6	369	299	378
	%	100.0	0.7	37.9	27.1	34.2	100.0	0.6	35.0	28.4	35.9
	SA	2560	218	1204	492	642	2950	152	1365	579	851
	%	100.0	8.5	47.1	19.2	25.1	100.0	5.2	46.3	19.6	28.8
Keihannshin (Osaka, Kyoto, Kobe)	CR	7338	267	2818	1818	2422	8057	183	2882	2092	2851
	%	100.0	3.6	38.4	24.8	33.0	100.0	2.3	35.8	26.0	35.4
	CC	2635	24	1030	737	839	2630	18	917	776	903
	%	100.0	0.9	39.1	28.0	31.8	100.0	0.7	34.9	29.5	34.3
	SA	4703	243	1788	1081	1583	5427	165	1965	1316	1948
	%	100.0	5.2	38.0	23.0	33.7	100.0	3.0	36.2	24.3	35.9

Table 4.8 *continued*

City		1975					1985				
		Total	Agri	Product (blue)	Sales (yellow)	Clerical (white)	Total	Agri	Product (blue)	Sales (yellow)	Clerical (white)
Hiroshima	CR	859	70	321	198	270	912	53	316	221	321
	%	100.0	8.1	37.4	23.1	31.4	100.0	5.8	34.6	24.2	35.2
	CC	407	13	144	103	146	495	13	155	133	193
	%	100.0	3.3	35.4	25.3	35.9	100.0	2.6	31.3	26.8	39.1
	SA	452	57	177	95	124	417	40	161	88	128
	%	100.0	12.5	39.2	21.0	27.4	100.0	9.6	38.6	21.2	30.6
Kitakyushu/ Fukuoka	CR	2069	200	733	508	625	2191	138	719	586	741
	%	100.0	9.7	35.4	24.6	30.2	100.0	6.3	32.8	26.7	33.8
	CC	899	22	318	246	312	973	16	296	297	360
	%	100.0	2.4	35.3	27.4	34.7	100.0	1.6	30.4	30.6	37.0
	SA	1170	178	415	262	313	1218	122	423	289	381
	%	100.0	15.2	35.5	22.4	26.8	100.0	10.1	34.7	23.7	31.3
Sendai	CR	737	130	218	167	222	876	100	279	213	282
	%	100.0	17.6	29.6	22.7	30.1	100.0	11.4	31.8	24.3	32.2
	CC	275	9	70	79	117	317	6	79	99	133
	%	100.0	3.2	25.3	28.7	42.7	100.0	2.0	24.8	31.2	41.9
	SA	462	121	148	88	105	559	94	200	114	149
	%	100.0	26.2	32.1	19.1	22.6	100.0	16.7	35.8	20.4	26.7

Source: Compiled from population censuses of Japan in 1975 and 1985.
CR = city region; CC = central city; SA = surrounding area.

Table 4.9 *Growth rate of employment by city and occupation*

| City | CR | Growth rate of employment 1975–85 (%) | | | | |
		Total	Agri	Product (blue)	Sales (yellow)	Clerical (white)
Japan		10.1	−26.5	9.0	15.5	24.3
Sapporo	CR	22.3	−8.8	14.9	23.2	31.1
	CC	24.4	−17.7	12.3	29.7	31.0
	SA	17.3	−6.5	21.3	8.4	31.3
Keihin	CR	19.2	−21.2	11.4	21.1	28.7
	CC	6.6	−12.8	−6.4	10.1	14.9
	SA	30.8	−21.8	27.2	32.9	43.1
Chukyo	CR	12.4	−30.1	9.5	14.9	24.9
	CC	5.1	−19.9	−2.9	10.1	10.4
	SA	15.3	−30.4	13.4	17.6	32.6
Keihannshin	CR	9.8	−31.5	2.3	15.1	17.7
	CC	−0.2	−23.2	−11.0	5.3	7.6
	SA	15.4	−32.3	9.9	21.7	23.1
Hiroshima	CR	6.2	−24.3	−1.6	11.6	18.9
	CC	21.5	−3.7	7.5	28.6	32.2
	SA	−7.7	−29.1	−8.9	−6.8	3.2
Kitakyushu/Fukuoka	CR	5.9	−31.0	−1.9	15.4	18.6
	CC	8.3	−28.1	−6.8	20.9	15.5
	SA	4.1	−31.4	1.8	10.1	21.6
Sendai	CR	18.9	−23.1	28.0	27.5	27.0
	CC	15.3	−27.9	12.9	25.5	13.2
	SA	21.0	−22.7	35.1	29.4	42.6

Source: Compiled from population censuses of Japan in 1975 and 1985.

Comparison of Inner City Problems in Japan and European Countries

This increasing concern of central government ministries in Japan over recent urbanisation trends and their impact on inner city development can be compared with that expressed by Western countries in the 1970s. During the 1950s and 1960s, most OECD countries enjoyed a high rate of economic growth based on rapid industrial development and expansion of the service sector. Business activities tended to concentrate in the larger urban areas, and people followed in search of job opportunities, higher incomes and social amenities. Urban population increase far outstripped overall population growth. The OECD has documented the substantial change which took place in the 1970s for many member countries in terms of urbanisation and urban growth trends.[13]

In Britain, the 1977 White Paper *Policy for the Inner Cities* identified the nature of the

Table 4.10 *Change in occupational share by city*

| City | CR | Change in occupational share by city | | | | |
		Total	Agri	Product (blue)	Sales (yellow)	Clerical (white)
Japan		0.0	−4.6	−0.4	1.1	3.7
Sapporo	CR	0.0	−1.1	−1.8	0.2	2.5
	CC	0.0	−0.4	−3.0	1.3	2.0
	SA	0.0	−2.3	1.0	−2.3	3.4
Keihin	CR	0.0	−1.4	−2.3	0.4	2.9
	CC	0.0	−0.1	−4.1	0.9	3.0
	SA	0.0	−2.9	−1.0	0.4	3.3
Chukyo	CR	0.0	−2.4	−1.2	0.5	3.1
	CC	0.0	−0.2	−2.9	1.3	1.7
	SA	0.0	−3.4	−0.8	0.4	3.8
Keihannshin	CR	0.0	−1.4	−2.6	1.2	2.4
	CC	0.0	−0.2	−4.2	1.5	2.5
	SA	0.0	−2.1	−1.8	1.3	2.2
Hiroshima	CR	0.0	−2.3	−2.7	1.2	3.8
	CC	0.0	−0.7	−4.1	1.5	3.2
	SA	0.0	−2.9	−0.5	0.2	3.2
Kitakyushu/Fukuoka	CR	0.0	−3.4	−2.6	2.2	3.6
	CC	0.0	−0.8	−4.9	3.2	2.3
	SA	0.0	−5.2	−0.8	1.3	4.5
Sendai	CR	0.0	−6.2	2.3	1.7	2.1
	CC	0.0	−1.2	−0.5	2.5	−0.8
	SA	0.0	−9.5	3.7	1.3	4.0

Source: Compiled from population censuses of Japan in 1975 and 1985.

inner city problem.[14] The Inner Area Studies of parts of Liverpool, Birmingham and Lambeth, and the West Central Scotland Study in relation to Glasgow, had underlined the erosion of the inner area economy and shortage of private investment which might assist the processes of regeneration. The 1977 White Paper identified in detail a number of features of inner city decline, focused upon economic decline, physical decay, social disadvantage, and the problems facing ethnic minorities.

The Economic and Social Research Council (ESRC) in the UK began to develop a programme of research on the inner city in the late 1970s. The ESRC looked at the process of urban economic adjustment across a range of types of cities. It was clear from the ESRC research that the problems faced by inner cities formed a trilogy of environmental dereliction, social malaise and economic distress.[15]

The very real problems identified as comprising the inner city problem in Britain have been examined in relation to Japanese cities by both practitioners and academics alike. For example, the Tokyo Metropolitan Government has looked closely at the extent to which it may face an inner city problem. It is generally recognised that inner city problems in England were the result of post-war urban policies that were intended to ease the overcrowding of cities. The objective of these policies was achieved in many cities and led to the dispersal of employment and population from cities. In contrast, Tokyo's problem is that enterprises are concentrated in the three central wards of the city (Chiyoda, Chuo and Minato), leading to problems in surrounding wards. If England's inner city problems are the result of the success of regional policies, then Tokyo's problems are the result of the failure of regional policies. If 'inner city problems' is interpreted as a geographical term, then Tokyo certainly has inner city problems, since in its inner city areas residential districts are being transformed into business districts, overcrowding is increasing as management functions continue to concentrate in Tokyo, and communities are being destroyed by the decrease in the settled population. However, if an economic decline and a consequent outflow of population are meant by that expression, then Tokyo does not have an inner city problem.[16]

While Osaka has often been quoted in Japan as exhibiting some of the symptoms of Western inner city areas, the Osaka Metropolitan Government has emphasised its continued current economic vitality, although recognising that the city is facing certain environmental problems.[17] Other city governments in Japan are certainly aware of the need to monitor closely the economic, social and environmental health of their cities.

While there is not as large a disparity among researchers in Japan as there is among government agencies, a difference can be observed in levels of perception. In particular, researchers in Osaka and the Kansai region in general have a strong sense of crisis. For example, Taguchi has shown that:

> (a) The main metropolitan regions in Japan are divided into two groups: the three major metropolitan regions where suburbanisation (the phenomenon in which population and employment growths are experienced not in the central city but in peripheral areas) is under way in earnest, and other urban regions where that process is only in its initial stages; (b) among the three major metropolitan regions, the difference between the Tokyo metropolitan region on the one hand and the Nagoya and Osaka metropolitan regions on the other is widening, in terms of the capacity for growth of employment in the central city and the capacity for growth of population and employment in peripheral areas; (c) in particular, the rate of suburbanisation of the Osaka metropolitan region is very high because it is a very mature metropolitan region, despite the fact that the potential for growth of the metropolitan region is weakening overall, and as a result the growth of the metropolitan region is being restricted to the peripheral areas and the central city is experiencing negative growth in population and employment; (d) this decrease in employment in the central city of the Osaka metropolitan region is very much like the average situation of SMSAs in the United States in that its effect has extended to white collar workers; (e) at the same time, the stagnation of the Osaka metropolitan region has taken place amidst the reorganisation of urban functions in Japan whereby, on the one hand, functions concentrate in the Tokyo metropolitan region out of the three major

metropolitan regions, and, on the other, other urban regions take over metropolitan functions; if the capacity for growth of urban regions is weakened in the future, then what has happened to Osaka may happen to any other urban region.[18]

These points made by Taguchi have been supported by Sakiyama:

(i) Although Japanese metropolitan regions grew rapidly during the process of intensive economic growth, an exodus of the settled population from the cores and areas surrounding the cores of central cities began from around 1960, and this creation of a vacuum has advanced and not halted to this day; (ii) since the 1970s, when the growth of population in metropolitan regions slowed down, population has come to level off or decrease in not only metropolises but adjacent satellite cities as well; (iii) with respect to employment, the absolute number of the working population, particularly in manufacturing, has decreased since the 1970s, and in Osaka city those employed in manufacturing decreased by 20 per cent in six years, from 721 000 (1972) to 580 000 (1978); (iv) the population had decreased uniformly within the central city, but a change was observed in the latter half of the 1970s. For example, within Osaka city there were three types of wards: those that continued to decrease in population, those in which the population decrease slowed, and those in which the population increased; and the decrease in population in inner-ring areas is notable; (v) strictly from the above population and employment trends in metropolises, it might be said that Japanese metropolises were continuing to follow the path of metropolises in advanced countries; (vi) however, the rate of economic growth in Japan is high compared with the rates in other countries, despite the many references about this being the era of low growth, and this growth rate is exerting a beneficial influence on urban growth; (vii) moreover, the young workers who left the farms in great numbers in the period of intensive economic growth uniformly possessed a high level of education and did not collect in ghettos or slums in cities; instead they adapted to modern industries and urban ways of life and continue to do so; (viii) this accounts for the fact that social and spatial discrimination stemming from minority problems and problems of foreign workers has not become as serious in Japan as in the West; (ix) however, the farming population, which has decreased drastically from 17 770 000 (or 48.8 per cent of the total working population in 1950) to 6 090 000 (or 11.8 per cent of the total working population in 1970), contributing 11 680 000 persons to the non-agricultural labour force, can no longer serve as a source of additional labour. If the need for additional labour leads to foreign workers settling in Japan in the future, inner city problems as serious as those in the West will arise.[19]

A comparison of inner city problems in Japanese and European cities has been undertaken by Kurasama. He has noted the following similarities:

(a) Japan is at a major turning point as far as its thirty-year, post-war population pattern of rapidly-growing metropolises and declining provincial regions is concerned, as suggested by the 1980 census which showed that the rate of increase over the previous period registered by metropolitan populations had dropped to nearly the same level as the rates of provincial regions, and the population growth of metropolises is beginning to halt or to be reversed; (b) the inner city population is decreasing drastically, as for example in the six central wards of Tokyo (Chiyoda, Chuo, Minato, Taito, Bunkyo and Shinjuku), which have experienced a 30 per cent decrease in population over twenty years, from 1 540 000 (1960) to 1 070 000 (1980); (c) industrial activity, particularly in manufacturing, has tended to shrink or stagnate in the inner city areas of Tokyo; and (d) with respect to the population structure, there has been a drastic decrease in the youthful population and a rapid ageing of society.

However, Kurasama has also noted that there exist the following major differences between inner city problems facing Japanese and European cities.

Firstly, from the standpoint of population structure, problems of race of minorities have little meaning (although the Koreans and Burakumin represent under-privileged groups). Secondly, from the standpoint of employment structure, secondary industries still claim a large share, and the employment problem is not yet serious. Thirdly, there is not a serious personal security problem. Fourthly, there is no region that has markedly declined, and, fifthly, Japanese inner city areas still retain residential districts for the upper and upper-middle classes, in part because Japanese cities do not have a strongly segregated structure determined according to social and economic classes. At present, these differences are saving Tokyo's inner city areas, relatively speaking, from devastation.[20]

The concern in Japan over inner city-type problems is illustrated by the numerous meetings held between 1988 and 1990 to discuss various city problems and future perspectives of major cities in the Kansai region (i.e. Osaka, Kyoto and Kobe). The inner city problem in the Kansai region was a major concern of these meetings.[21]

As indicated by the above views, there is by no means a consensus of opinion regarding the present situation as far as Japan's inner city problems are concerned among persons of different positions and areas of expertise. However, there appears to be agreement on the following points. Firstly, inner city problems of the English type, characterised by the regional concentration in the central city of a metropolitan region of economic decline, social disadvantage, environmental devastation and racial problems, do not exist in Japanese metropolises. Secondly, some of the reasons for this are that relative economic growth has been sustained, employment is stable, the Japanese are strongly drawn to metropolises, Japan is freer of racial and immigration problems, and, as far as local urban structure is concerned, social classes are not differentiated (compared with, say, London or New York) and a mixed residential style of life prevails. However, as noted by Sassen, there has been a rapid increase over recent years in the number of foreigners who are working illegally in Japan, mostly in the Tokyo metropolitan area, Nagoya and Osaka. Almost all of these workers, estimated at some 200 000, were from Asia, with the largest groups from Taiwan, South Korea,

Bangladesh, the Philippines and Pakistan. The current immigration of Asian workers is geared to low-wage and physically-demanding manual jobs. Thirdly, however, the creation of a vacuum in terms of the night-time population and employment, primarily in manufacturing industries, in the central cities of metropolitan regions is steadily progressing, and inner-ring areas where small factories of depressed industries and dilapidated houses are crowded together and the population is ageing require particular attention. The term 'Japanese-type inner city problems' might be applied to the various economic, social and environmental problems that are already arising in these districts, although the problems may differ in their degrees of seriousness. In that case, the main research areas of study in this field may be: (a) an analysis of the qualitative and quantitative ways in which the English type and the Japanese type of inner city problems differ; and (b) an assessment of the homogeneity and heterogeneity of inner city problems from the standpoint of the stages of economic and urban development of the two countries.

Likely Future Trends of Urbanisation in Japan and Japanese-type Inner City Areas

The main thrust of the chapter so far has been to illustrate that the central cities of the three metropolitan regions of Japan experienced some decline during the 1970s, and have exhibited certain Western-style inner city characteristics. However, there is some evidence from the results of the 1985 census to suggest that these areas have once again experienced a resurgence of growth concerning the trend of urbanisation between 1980 and 1985. Firstly, if one looks at the resident populations and their rates of change for municipalities of different sizes of population, cities of different size having populations under one million have had uniformly sluggish rates of population increase, whereas cities of over one million have grown from 0.1 per cent (1975–80) to 2.5 per cent. Secondly, the population growth of the three major metropolitan regions which had declined sharply in the 1970s, grew again, with the Tokyo metropolitan region in particular showing a 5.5 per cent growth rate (versus a 3.4 per cent national average) and expanding to a population of 30 272 000 (or a 25.0 per cent share of the national population). Thirdly, whereas the Nagoya metropolitan region exhibited a 3.7 per cent growth, which was slightly above the national average, the Osaka metropolitan region grew by only 2.4 per cent and claimed a smaller share of the national population. It has been the four metropolitan regions in Eastern Japan which have enjoyed the highest population growth rates between 1980 and 1985, i.e. Sapporo, Sendai, Keihin and Chukyo. The three metropolitan regions in Western Japan, i.e. Kyoto/Osaka/Kobe, Hiroshima, and Kitakyushu/Fukuoka, have had low growth rates.[22] These seven metropolitan regions of Japan, as defined by the census, are shown in Figure 4.1.

Furthermore, if one looks at the population trends for 1980–85, distinguishing between the core, the inner ring, and the outer ring of the central city, with regard to the Tokyo ward area, Yokohama, Nagoya and Osaka, the following trends emerge. Firstly,

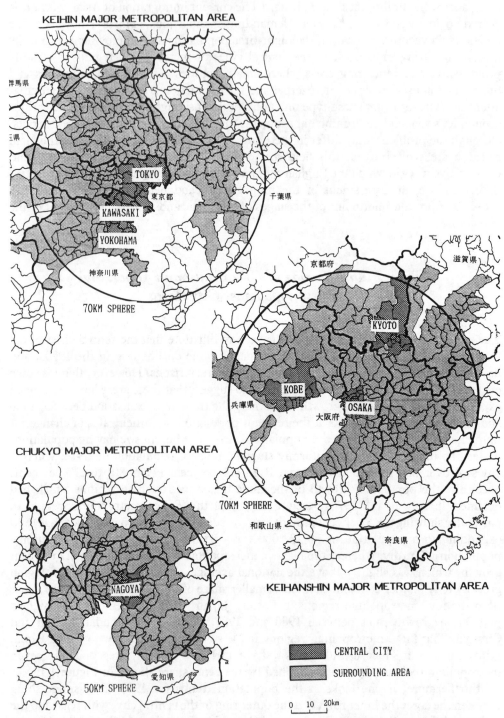

Fig. 4.2 (above and facing) Seven metropolitan areas designated by the Central Statistical Office of Japan

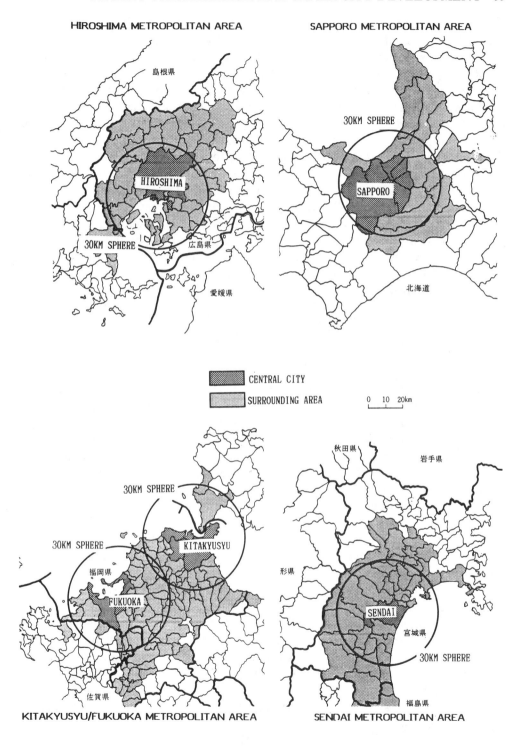

the cores and inner rings of all four metropolises and the outer rings of the Tokyo ward area and Osaka show trends of relative population growth compared with 1975–80. Secondly, the core populations of the Tokyo ward area (from −6.5 to −3.8 per cent), Yokohama (from −8.4 per cent to −2.3 per cent) and Nagoya (from −8.1 to −2.7 per cent), although still decreasing, are doing so at a slower rate. That of Osaka (from −2.3 to +2.4 per cent) is now increasing. Thirdly, the inner-ring populations of the Tokyo ward area (from −6.5 to −1.1 per cent), Nagoya (from −3.9 to −1.1 per cent), and Osaka (from −3.0 to −2.1 per cent) are still decreasing, but again at a slower rate than before, and that of Yokohama (from −2.8 to +1.6 per cent) is now growing. Fourthly, the outer-ring populations of the Tokyo ward area (from −2.4 to +0.9 per cent) and Osaka (from −2.8 to +1.3 per cent) are now increasing, and those of Yokohama (from 13.8 to 13.1 per cent) and Nagoya (from 20.5 to 10.4 per cent) are continuing to grow strongly.

These trends in the resident populations of metropolitan regions between 1980 and 1985 may be summarised as follows. Firstly, the trend of urbanisation in Japan remains strong. Secondly, the pressure of urbanisation is extending the regions of depopulation in provincial areas but is bringing about the growth of central cities in the provinces and provincial metropolitan regions. Thirdly, the rapid decrease in population that was observed in the central cities of the three major metropolitan regions in the 1970s has moderated, and while the metropolitan regions of Nagoya and Osaka maintain their shares of the national population, the share of the Tokyo metropolitan region is growing. Fourthly, with regard to that process, it should be noted that the rate of population decrease of the core and inner ring of the central city in the Osaka metropolitan region is beginning to decline, and that this is also happening in the Kyoto/Osaka/Kobe metropolitan region, which had had the most sluggish growth of any metropolitan region.

It is very interesting to compare these recent trends in Japanese cities with the experience of British cities. For example, while Greater London continued to lose population through the 1960s, 1970s and early 1980s (a loss of 1.2 million people between 1961 and 1984), it recorded a gain of population by the mid-1980s. Other cities in Britain have not been able to stem their population losses, with Merseyside, Greater Manchester and the Central Clydeside Conurbation all experiencing continued losses in recent years.[23] While Japanese cities like Tokyo (23 wards) and Osaka may have lost population in the past, these losses were experienced only in the 1970s.[24] There is now some evidence to suggest that even these losses are being reversed. In Britain, where the major cities have been losing population for more than three decades, there are at least some signs that Greater London itself has begun to hold and even increase its population since the mid-1980s.

It is not yet certain whether this phenomenon, i.e. the slackening off in the population decrease in the central cities of the three major metropolitan regions in Japan, represents the stage of re-urbanisation common to metropolitan regions in advanced industrial countries. Any assessment of inner city problems in Japan must recognise the continuing strong trends of urbanisation and of economic growth, albeit at lesser rates than in the past. How these trends will affect the future development of Japanese-type inner city problems remains to be seen.

NOTES AND REFERENCES

1 Organisation for Economic Cooperation and Development, *Urban Policies in Japan*, Paris, OECD, 1986. This review was the first of its kind by the OECD. It examined recent new approaches to policy making in Japan, where urban renewal schemes are becoming increasingly important after four decades of uninterrupted growth.

2 Economic Planning Agency, *Keizai Kikakucho Sanjunenshi* [*A Thirty-Year History of the Economic Planning Agency*], 1976; Sogo Seisaku Kenkyukai [Comprehensive Planning Research Association], *Nihon no Chiiki Kaihatsu* [*Japan's Regional Development*], 1963.

3 National Land Planning Association, *Nihon no Kokudo Sogo Kaihatsu Keikaku* [*Comprehensive National Development Plan in Japan*], 1963.

4 Ministry of Construction, *Nihon no Toshi* [*Japanese Cities*], 1983; National Land Agency, *Kokudo Shingikai Shiryo: Jinko, Toshi King Kara Mita Kokudo Kozo no Tenbo* [*National Land Council Source Material: Prospects for the National Land Structure from the Viewpoint of Population and Urban Function*], 1985; Management and Coordination Agency, *1985 nen kokusei chosa* [*1985 Census Survey*], 1985.

5 National Land Agency, *Kaso Taisaku no Quekyo* [*Present Situation with Regard to Measures to Deal with Depopulation*], 1986.

6 Kokusheisha, *Nihon Kokuseizue, Choki Tokeiban* [*Collected Charts of the Japanese Census: Long-Term Statistics*], 1981; Nihon Fudosan Kenkyujo [Japan Real Estate Research Centre), *Shigaichi Kakaku Shisu* [*Urban Land Price Index*], 1985. See also the 1990 and 1991 White Papers on Land published by the National Land Agency.

7 National Land Agency, *Nihon: Nijuisseiki e no Tenbo* [*Japan: Prospects for the 21st Century*], 1984; *Kokudo shingikai shiryo*, op. cit.

8 Ministry of Construction, *Nihon no toshi* [*Japanese Cities*], 1985.

9 National Land Agency [Zaidan Hojin], Shakai Kaihatsu Sogo Kenkyujo [Comprehensive Social Development Research Centre], *Daitoshi Chiiki ni Okeru Katsuryoku no Iji Hosaku ni Kansuru Chosa Hokokusho* [*Survey Report Concerning Measures to Maintain the Vitality of Metropolitan Regions*], 1984.

10 Ministry of Home Affairs [Zaidan Hojin], Jichi Sogo Centre [Comprehensive Self-Government Centre], *Daitoshi no Toshin Shuhenbu Deno Katsuryoku Kasseika no Tameno Shisaku no Arikata* [*Measures to Revitalize Inner-Ring Areas in Metropolises*], 1984.

11 Sassen, S., *The Global City: New York, London, Tokyo*, Princeton, NJ, Princeton University Press, 1991. Part 3 of this book focuses in particular on the nature and extent of inner city-type problems in Tokyo compared with those in London and New York.

12 Nakabayashi, I., 'Socio-Economic and Living Conditions of Tokyo's Inner City', reprinted from *Geographical Reports of Tokyo Metropolitan University*, 22, 1991, pp. 111–28.

13 Organisation for Economic Cooperation and Development, *Managing Urban Change, Volume 1. Policies and Finance*, Paris, OECD, 1983.

14 *Policy for the Inner Cities*, Cmnd 6845, London, HMSO, June 1977. For a comprehensive assessment of post-war urban planning policies in Britain, see also Department of the Environment, *Urban Renaissance: A Better Life in Towns*, London, HMSO, 1980.

15 Economic and Social Research Council, *Changing Cities*, London, Economic and Social Research Council, 1985.

16 S., Ikeda, 'Tokyo no Innaa Shitii Mondai' ['Tokyo's Inner City Problems'], *Jutaku*, July 1980.

17 'It is generally said that inner city areas are beset by an accumulation of negative economic, social and space-related structural phenomena such as the devastation and decline of local society that accompany the outflow of population and enterprises, but if one looks at the inner city of Osaka, it is by no means devastated or declining in terms of its economic

or social environment, although that description may apply to certain aspects of its physical environment' (Keijiro Iwama, Planning Department, Comprehensive Planning Bureau, Osaka Metropolitan Government, Metropolitan Planning Management Conference, 'Shimpozium, Daitoshi no Inaa Shitii' ['Symposium on Inner City Areas of Metropolises'], 1982).

18 Y., Taguchi, 'Wagakuni Toshiken no Kozo Henka to Seikaku no Bunka Gensho' ['Structural Changes and Differentiation in Character in Japanese Urban Regions'], *Daitoshi no Suitai to Saisei* [*The Decline and Regeneration of Metropolises*], University of Tokyo Publishing Centre, 1981.

19 K., Sakiyama, 'Toshika to Daitoshi Mondai' ['Urbanisation and Metropolitan Problems'], *Daitosi no Suitai to Seisei* [*Decline and Regeneration of Metropolitan Regions*], University of Tokyo Publishing Centre, 1981.

20 S., Kurasawa, 'Daitoshni: no Okeru Chiiki Shakai no Benbo' ['Transformation of Local Society in Metropolises'], *Toshi Heikaku* [*City Planning*], Tokyo, February 1983.

21 Nippon Toshi Mondai Kaigi, Kansai kaigi [Japan Conference on City Problems, Kansai Branch Conference] 1991. *Toshi no Mirai, Kyoto, Osaka, Kobe Karano Apurochi* [*Future of Cities, Approaches from Kyoto, Osaka and Kobe*], Toshi Bunka Sha Publishing (in Japanese).

22 Prime Minister's Office, *Daitoshiken* [*Metropolitan Regions*], Tokyo, 1973; *Daitoshiken no Jinko* [*Population of Metropolitan Regions*], Tokyo, 1983; *Kokusei Chosa, Zenkoku Todofuken Shikuchoson Betsu Jinko* [*1985 Census, Population by Municipality and Prefecture*], Japan Statistical Office, 1986.

23 For population trends 1961–1985 for the British conurbations, see *Regional Trends*, 22, 1987, p. 49.

24 References for both population and employment data include: Statistics Bureau, Prime Minister's Office, *Summary of the Results of the 1975 Population Census of Japan*, Printing Bureau, Ministry of Finance, 1975 (in Japanese); Statistics Bureau, Prime Minister's Office, *1980 Population of Japan*, The Series of Abridged Reports of the 1980 Population Census, No. 1, Printing Bureau, Ministry of Finance, 1982 (in Japanese); Statistics Bureau, Management and Coordination Agency, *Final Report of the 1985 Population Census*, Printing Bureau, Ministry of Finance, 1990 (in Japanese).

Chapter 5

Land Use Planning and Control in Japan

DAVID L. CALLIES

Land use controls, in order to have direction, are usually designed in accordance with a scheme of comprehensive planning. So it is in Japan. There are several salient components of Japanese planning. Principal among these is the general top-down method of planning, governed generally by economic goals rather than land use planning goals. At the top of the 'pyramid' is the series of national economic plans which have set out goals over the past 30 years. While these have recently included social goals, it is probably true to say that they continue to favour economic development. Other influential national plans include the Comprehensive National Development Plans, growth-oriented by means of favouring development. Regional plans—usually at the prefectural level—are responsible for some implementation of these important national economic and development plans. However, the principal implementation occurs at the local level by means of local plans, and finally through land use zoning at the bottom of the pyramid.[1]

This 'top down' system is in sharp contrast to land use controls in the United States where, until quite recently, local land use controls through zoning and subdivision ordinances regulated the use of land without guidance from even so much as a local comprehensive plan, much less a regional or national one. There is still no national plan of any sort in the United States, whether economic, developmental or land use, and only a handful of states carry out statewide (or regional) planning, often accompanied by partial land use controls (such as California and Oregon) or comprehensive land use control at that level (such as Hawaii). Instead, most states have zoning enabling statutes which set out the basic administrative and substantive requirements for local government zoning ordinances, should a local government choose to regulate the use of land (most urban local governments have so chosen). While these often recite the need for zoning to be in accordance with a comprehensive plan, it is common for American local governments to ignore them. More common since the 1970s, at least, are local comprehensive plans, often with a strong land use component, but conformance to such plans in the United States is irregular and unpredictable.[2]

In the UK, of course, there has for decades been a tradition of broad structure plans to which local plans must conform. Land use controls are loosely associated with such plans by forbidding any material development of land without planning permission (translate: development permission) from local government planning authorities.[3] Therefore, while there is a more top-down approach in the UK than in the United

States, this is still fairly broad-brush, and economic development is far less a goal in town planning and control as compared with Japan.

What follows is a selective introduction to how the use of land is regulated in Japan (see also the chronology of Japanese land use and planning legislation in Appendix 1). First, there is a brief summary of applicable planning legislation since, as noted above, Japan follows the model wherein land use regulations are based upon, though hardly strictly tied to, plans with a strong, but not overwhelming, land use component. There follows a more detailed summary of the Urban Planning Act and the Construction Standards Act, to which most local land use regulatory schemes appear to conform. Certainly this is true with respect to the number and kinds of zoning districts found in the principal examples of Hiroshima, Kyoto and Osaka. The examples taken together with the national laws and plans lead to the conclusion that whereas the general thrust of planning and regulation of land is indeed 'top-down', implementation is (at least in major urban areas) where it should be—at the local government level.

Basic Elements of Land Use Planning Control in Japan

There are a variety of laws that ultimately affect the use of land in Japan, including such statutes as the Agricultural Promotion Act and the Nature Conservation Act. However, as this chapter is restricted primarily to the subject of urban land development controls at the local level, what follows is a basic framework/summary of the principal statutes which are more or less enforced through the Japanese equivalent of zoning.

Broad land use policy for Japan is established primarily through the National Land Use Planning Act of 1974, or NLUPA. Administered principally by the Ministry of Construction and the National Land Authority, NLUPA was designed to help regulate land values. However, it also requires the preparation of a national land use plan providing for the placing of land in urban, agricultural, forest, natural parks and nature conservation areas. These are designated in regional or prefectural plans and local land use plans. The latter are more specifically provided for in the City (or Urban) Planning Act of 1968.[4]

City planning areas are those areas designated by the prefectural governor after consultation with the Ministry of Construction, and normally constitute already built-up regions or soon-to-be-developed areas. Altogether they are reported to cover about a quarter of Japan's land.[5] These city planning areas are further divided into urbanisation promotion areas (UPAs) and urbanisation control areas (UCAs). Designed to be built up within ten years, the UPAs are regulated by zoning, as described below. They are divided into eight primary use zones, the regulations for which control the use and volume of buildings constructed therein: exclusive residential categories I and II, residential, neighbourhood commercial, commercial, quasi-industrial, industrial, and exclusive industrial.[6] By the same token, development in the UCAs is in theory strictly controlled, though there is apparently evidence that such controls are frequently relaxed.[7]

Enforcement of Planning Policy:
The Urban Planning Act and the Construction Standards Act

There are a number of national laws that affect how land is regulated in Japan. Principal among them are the Urban Planning Act of 1968 (referred to also as the City Planning Act) and the Construction Standards Act of 1950. Both are principally administered by the Ministry of Construction.[8] What follows is a selective discussion of those parts of these Acts that most relate to the regulation of land.

THE URBAN PLANNING ACT

The Urban Planning Act, as noted above, is but one of the national laws which regulate the use of land in Japanese cities.[9] Basically, the Act permits a prefectural governor to designate cities or city centres (or village or town centres, for that matter) as urban planning zones (Article 15). Once this is done, an urban plan is adopted for the area, taking into consideration such factors as environmental and social conditions, public facilities and infrastructure, and so forth (Art. 15). The most critical basic decision in the plan is to decide what areas within the plan's jurisdiction will be designated as an 'urbanising zone' in which development is to be encouraged (though not without restrictions) and as a 'non-urbanising zone' in which development is discouraged.[10] While the plans are drawn up initially by the cities or prefectural governments, it is the Ministry of Construction that finally approves how the urban plan makes these decisions (see Art. 24).

A variety of zones, facilities and projects may or can be provided for in the urbanising zone, as follows:[11]

A. Under the Urban Planning Act,[12] the following zones may be used:
  (1) use area;
  (2) special use area:
     (a) special industrial zone;
     (b) educational zone;
     (c) other zones established by government order, e.g. retail store zone, office zone, welfare zone, recreational zone, sightseeing zone, special business zone;
  (3) highly developed area;
  (4) particularised district;
  (5) fire-resistant area;
  (6) beauty zone;
  (7) scenic zone;
  (8) parking place arranging zones;
  (9) portside zones;
  (10) zones where historical properties are specially preserved;
  (11) neighbouring zones where green zones are specially preserved;
  (12) wholesale area complex zones.

B. Under the Urban Planning Act, the following facilities may be designated:[13]
   (1) traffic facilities;
   (2) official open space;
   (3) supply facilities or disposition facilities;
   (4) waterways;
   (5) educational-cultural facilities;
   (6) health facilities or welfare facilities;
   (7) market, butchery, or crematory facilities;
   (8) public housing facilities (apartment complexes);
   (9) government and municipal office complexes;
   (10) wholesaling area complexes;
   (11) other facilities set up by government order.

C. Under the Urban Planning Act, the following projects may be designated:[14]
   (1) land readjustment projects under the Land Readjustment Act;
   (2) projects for developing new housing areas under the New Housing Development Act;
   (3) projects for improving industrial towns under the Act Concerning Arrangement of Neighbouring Regions and Urban Development Zones in the Metropolitan Area, or the Act Concerning Arrangement and Development of Neighbouring Zones and Urban Development Zones in the Kinki Area;
   (4) projects for redeveloping towns under the Urban Redevelopment Act;
   (5) new projects for maintenance of urban areas under the New Urban Maintenance Readjustment Act.

The enforcement of the contents of these zones proceeds along three possible routes, in part depending upon the zone in which the property is located.[15] These are: development licensing (Art. 29 et seq.), restrictions on areas and zones (Art. 53 et seq.), and restrictions on scenic zones (Art. 58 et seq.).

A development licence from the prefectural governor is generally necessary for most developments, and particularly housing developments which are large-scale in nature (usually over 1000 square metres—see Urban Planning Reg. Art. 19). This is not likely to be forthcoming unless the developer has already filed or prepared a development plan first. There is some evidence that public facilities for the proposed project must also meet a certain minimum standard.

There are exceptions to the requirement for such a licence for railroad and health facilities and others which serve the public interest, and developments serving agriculture, forestry and fishery in non-urbanising zones. Government projects and emergency projects are also excepted. It is apparently also possible to obtain a licence for development in a non-urbanising area, but in theory at least this can only occur rarely and with great difficulty (see Section 3, Art. 7). Basically, the development licence is granted only for developments classified or zoned for urban development in the urban plan for the specific city or town. If this is so, and the public facilities are adequate, then a developer is in theory entitled to his development licence. There is some indication that to deny a licence because a different sort of development is contemplated by the governor gives the developer the right to have his land acquired by the government (Art. 52.4). Further restrictions on areas and zones are applied under the Building Standards Act, Parking Place Act, and Act for Preserving Ancient Cities, but these are in addition to and beyond the standards contained in a development licence under the Urban Planning Act.[16]

For larger 'urban planning projects' which are usually local-government sponsored, it may be necessary to obtain a licence from the Minister of Construction (Art. 22).

THE CONSTRUCTION STANDARDS ACT OF 1950

The Construction Standards Act applies to all of Japan, whether or not in urban zones under the Urban Planning Act. It is, however, more than a building code, though it has aspects of this as well. It has specific provisions 'concerning overall regulations' or 'overall provisions' which are designed to deal with the use of land with respect to specific projects in urban zones.[17] For this purpose, the Construction Standards Act contains a use zone system (Art. 48), one of the purposes of which is to separate conflicting uses of land (e.g. heavy industry and residences) and to encourage concentration of buildings of similar uses in the same location. The Act provides for eight classifications:

1. Residential zones, which also permit limited shops and offices unless harmful to residential peace.
2. First-class, exclusive residential zones, in which low-rise dwellings are the rule and other facilities are heavily restricted.
3. Second-class, exclusive residential zones, in which middle- to high-rise dwellings are permitted.
4. Neighbourhood commercial zones, in which certain businesses are permitted to serve the residential neighbourhood.
5. Commercial zones, in which highly-centralised commercial enterprises are encouraged.
6. Quasi-industrial zones, in which home and light-industries are permitted.
7. Industrial zones, in which there are few if any restrictions on industrial use.
8. Exclusive industrial zones, in which residences and other non-industrial buildings are prohibited.

The Act further permits local government to designate yet another use zone for special uses. The Construction Standards Act also has provisions restricting building heights in the first-class exclusive residential zone and in other zones depending upon the width of the road upon which it fronts, aside from further height restrictions which depend upon the materials used in its construction. There is some indication that an urban plan may contain more stringent height restrictions.[18]

Urban Planning Implementation and Zoning in Hiroshima

To illustrate how land use controls work at the local level in Japan, the following section summarises the relationship between local urban plans and urban zoning, which is the principal mechanism for regulating the use of urban land. As appears below, the zoning itself is often divorced from the actual development process. This is in some contrast to zoning, say, in the United States, where much change in zones or granting of special permissions therein is directly tied to the land development process, even though theoretically development codes govern actual development.

TOWN PLANNING AND ZONING IN BRIEF

Hiroshima is located in the south of Japan's largest island, Honshu, about 550 kilometres west of Tokyo, and is the economic hub of its region. It is a major governmental and industrial centre, with a high concentration of companies engaged in the manufacturing of automotive parts and equipment. The city faces an inland sea to the south, and a mountain range to the north. The lowland region of principal development is a delta at the mouth of the Ota River. Much of the remaining area consists of steep-sided hills and mountains covered with forest.[19]

Originally 'municipalised' in 1889, Hiroshima has grown from approximately 27 square kilometres with 83 000 people to 740 square kilometres with a population of about 1.1 million in 1990. This is the more remarkable since the detonation of an atom bomb over the city by American forces in 1945 during the Second World War reduced the population from over 400 000 to something over 100 000. Hiroshima was designated as a city eligible to receive aid under a 1946 Special Town Planning Law, under the auspices of the War Damage Reconstruction Institute established in 1945. In 1952, the Hiroshima Peace Memorial City Construction Plan was promulgated under the auspices of the 1949 Hiroshima Peace Memorial City Construction Law. Military installations near the epicentre of the blast were replaced by park-like open spaces of nearly 100 hectares, together with buildings and monuments to peace. A new road network was also planned and implemented. An additional 1000 hectares were designated, replanned and rebuilt under the direction of the mayor of Hiroshima and the prefectural governor, who split their territorial responsibilities over the east and west parts of the city damaged by the blast, respectively. An example of the redevelopment is the 33.3 hectare Motomachi District Redevelopment Project which replaced destroyed (and temporarily rebuilt) wooden dwellings with blocks of apartments numbering 4570 units housing an estimated 12 000 people.[20] Today, the city is governed by a 64-member town council elected from eight wards.[21]

While town planning arguably dates back to 1589 with the construction of Hiroshima Castle, and some town planning was applied through national legislation in 1923, modern town planning in Hiroshima did not really commence until the local implementation of the City Planning Act in 1968, subsequent to the expansion of industry and associated uses. It is the City Plan and its enforcement, largely through zoning and other controls, that governs the use of land in Hiroshima today.[22]

In common with other major cities in Japan, large parts of Hiroshima are regulated by planning districts promulgated under the auspices of the national town planning laws. A Hiroshima Region Town Planning Jurisdiction was designated in January 1971, and covers both parts of Hiroshima and eight other nearby local governments. Within Hiroshima, the area covered is approximately 320 square kilometres or 31 912 hectares, out of a total city land area of 740 square kilometres or 74 037 hectares.[23] These are the more urbanised areas of the city, particularly around its extensive waterfront.

As already described, the City Planning Act requires the division of Hiroshima's town planning area into Urban Promotion Areas (14 045 hectares or 19 per cent of the area of the city) and Urban Control Areas (17 867 hectares or 24 per cent of the urban area of the city). According to maps which accompany Hiroshima's town planning literature, the remainder consists of rural and ocean areas. The town planning law provides for the further subdivision of these two basic classifications into zoning districts with the usual restrictions on the use of land as well as external features such as floor/area ratios (FARs).[24]

Of the 16 categories of zones provided for in the Town Planning Law, the city has 'provided for' or used seven, together with 'zones for certain uses'. There are eight categories of such 'zones for certain uses' which the city has divided into a total of 15, the first eight of which are the most important for developmental purposes. The tabulation below lists these zones, together with the area of the city devoted to them (in hectares) and the percentage this represents of the total land area of the city:[25]

1. Exclusively residential zone, class 1 (2963/4 per cent)
2. Exclusively residential zone, class 2 (1986/2.7 per cent)
3. Residential zone (5656/7.6 per cent)
4. Neighbourhood commercial zone (756/1 per cent)
5. Commercial zone (591/0.8 per cent)
6. Semi-industrial zone (1238/1.7 per cent)
7. Industrial zone (557/0.8 per cent)
8. Exclusively industrial zone (296/0.4 per cent).

IMPLEMENTATION

Obtaining permission to commence development, provided the proposal is a permitted use in the zone in which a parcel falls, is a comparatively straightforward process. However, deviations from the requirements of the district are not easily permitted, whether large or small. Indeed, it may well be easier to obtain a 'rezoning' by the town planning department, as appears below. In either event, contributions to public facilities are increasingly likely to be required as a prerequisite.

According to officials in the Hiroshima Planning Department,[26] the city divides applications for development into two categories: small-scale developments of between five and 25 hectares, and large-scale developments of more than 20 hectares. While up to thirty agencies and divisions of city government may be involved in reviewing projects in the larger development categories, two areas are critical in both categories: traffic (including parking) and housing. Most development proposals currently involve housing. As expected, little or no development is permitted in Urban Control Areas, but only in Urban Promotion Areas.

The subject of rezoning is one that apparently arises mainly at planning stages unrelated to pending developments. The architectural control division's architectural control council is principally responsible for giving and coordinating permission to develop. Always provided the property is in an urban promotion area, the council will approve a development if it is in an area undergoing change, and if it is clear that there will be a contribution by the development to needed city facilities (see discussion below on this subject). The same architectural control council has authority to approve variations in standards (height, etc.) proposed by a private landowner/developer. For major development variations, a change of zone is possible from the city planning division. It is notable that these and other permissions may be given directly by the officials concerned. There appears to be no concept of either rezoning or the granting of substantial variations from standards as legislative acts needing the approval of the equivalent of a city council. This appears to reflect the tendency in Japan for the plans, which govern the land use through zoning, to be 'top-down' through the chain of executive officers involved at the various levels of government.

There is very little land development which is permitted without some sort of permission. Thus, even the construction of a single-family house in an area properly zoned needs the approval of the architectural control division (though this is quickly and easily granted, often within three weeks or so) to make sure that all the district standards are met. These do not usually extend to design features unless the house is located within the precincts, say, of the famous Hiroshima Peace Park.

EXACTIONS

The practice of exacting public facility concessions for development permissions appears to be well developed, although at times ad hoc. Thus, for example, it appears to be quite common to require street and road dedications and school sites, and there appear to be standards in place for these requirements. The provision of open space, on the other hand, appears to proceed on a project-by-project basis. Developers may also be asked to share the cost of certain facilities as diverse as nature reserves and trails, and sanitary sewer systems. All of these are part of the urban plans applicable to Hiroshima, which target the provision of such facilities and many others by the government.

There is not a developed concept of nexus between facilities and the development, rational or otherwise, as there is in much of the United States. Thus, for example, officials relate that it would not be unusual to request, say, a golf course developer to provide an (unrelated) playground or a community centre. Other developers may be required to widen a road, provide sidewalks, or traffic signalisation, even if their development would not warrant such improvements. Finally, in large-scale residential construction, there does not seem to be any requirement for providing low-income housing as a condition for development approvals or permissions, as sometimes occurs in other countries.

Urban Planning and Implementation in Osaka and Kyoto

An examination of the zoning implementation of town plans in Kyoto and Osaka discloses essentially the same kind of enforcement mechanisms. The cities are divided into the same two broad classifications, and further subdivided by zoning in urban zoning plans. Of particular interest, however, is the special care taken by Kyoto to preserve its natural and built environment—to be expected, of course, in one of Japan's premier centres of culture, largely untouched physically by the ravages of allied bombing raids in the Second World War.

KYOTO

Established as the capital of the Heian emperors in 794, Kyoto remained the imperial capital of Japan even after real power shifted to the shoguns at Kamakura, near Edo (Tokyo), and then Tokyo itself, in the fifteenth century. Tokyo became the official imperial capital as well, with the restoration of the emperor to the head of state (Meiji restoration) in 1869. Town planning of a modern nature commenced in the 1970s for all practical purposes. Kyoto has a population in the range of 1.4 million in an area of about 130 square kilometres.[27]

As in Hiroshima, the key is the division of Kyoto into Urbanisation Promotion Areas and Urbanisation Control Areas, though there are separate restrictions on building heights and public facilities plans. The Promotion Area is divided into nine use districts: exclusive residential category 1, exclusive residential category 2, residential, neighbourhood commercial, commercial, quasi-industrial, industrial, exclusive industrial, and special industrial.[28]

Of special interest are the overlay zones for preservation of historical, cultural and natural resources. Presently, a quarter of the land area of Kyoto is designated in scenic area or suburban green area overlay zones, which overlap both Urban Promotion and Urban Control areas particularly in the northern parts of the city. The idea is to protect natural landscapes. No development is permitted in these areas without the permission of the mayor's office for the regulation of development and architectural activities.[29]

Moreover, under a Special Law for the Preservation of Historical Landscapes passed in 1966, about 15 additional square kilometres of the city are designated Special Areas for the Preservation of Historical Landscapes, or Aesthetic Areas. Additional areas are in areas or zones Restricted Against Enormous Constructions. Other select areas are designated as Preservation Areas of Historic Atmosphere, Preservation Districts for Groups of Historic Buildings, and Special Preservation Areas of Traditional Buildings. In all these areas, it is necessary to obtain permission from the mayor's office for development activity, which is 'severely restricted'.[30]

OSAKA

Osaka's importance as a commercial centre goes back at least to the fourth century. At that time, and for centuries thereafter, it flourished primarily as a port city. Early town plans date at least back to 1655. Indeed, after the restoration of the emperor Meiji in

1868, Osaka became the birthplace of Japan's industrial revolution and maintained its preeminence as a commercial and industrial centre in Japan until the 1950s, despite heavy American bombing during the Second World War.[31] It has a population of 2.64 million (to which another million is added during the workday) in a metropolitan area of nearly 17 million people.[32]

As in Hiroshima and Kyoto, Osaka uses the concept of urban zoning to enforce its comprehensive plan. While the divisions technically follow those in the other cities, based upon the national planning laws discussed above, Osaka's urban zoning plan groups land uses in the city in the following zones: residential areas, business areas, residential/business composite areas, residential/manufacturing composite areas, waterfront composite areas, Technoport Osaka site, and large parks/green belts.[33]

Conclusions

As noted in the introduction, the Japanese system of land use controls through zoning bears much resemblance to the American technique of local zoning. The groupings are familiar: residential, commercial and industrial (several zones in each category), with an occasional special development zone reflecting the need to deal with a particular large project in a separate and different fashion. The plans, however, are up to a point pure European (or at least pure British), at least with respect to the broad land use planning and similar geographic and use goals. The planning is clearly top-down and based on economic considerations, though there is some evidence that this is changing to reflect increasing concern about the environment, both natural and built. These concerns are often reflected in scenic, natural area and preservation zones, as, for example, in Kyoto.

In a manner similar to that experienced in the United Kingdom and the United States,[34] Japan is beginning to struggle with the relationship between infrastructure/ public facilities and development permissions. As the experience in Hiroshima indicates, issues of planning gain and nexus do not yet appear to be well-developed. The problems associated with such issues in the United States may never arise, given the lack of a counterpart to the Fifth Amendment to the US Constitution which has been interpreted to forbid taking of property through regulation without compensation.[35] For example, it would be possible for Japanese cities to require low-income housing as a condition for development permission, since they already require a variety of other 'contributions' unrelated to a particular project as development conditions, at least in Hiroshima.

It does not appear that Japan's relatively uniform system of plan-based urban land use controls has changed much in the past decade or so. However, it may not need to do so. The system is general enough to accommodate a range of conditions, both social and economic. It has clearly responded to (or at least not impeded) a redevelopment process that, in the instance of Hiroshima, was total in both economic and physical terms. Thus it might be fair to conclude that it would serve as well during an economic downturn as during a period of sustained economic growth. As some of the Hiroshima experience indicates, the Japanese tend to target particular areas for attention, when they need it, by means of special laws based upon or following upon special plans. Perhaps a more meaningful issue is the extent to which Japanese planning still responds adequately to changes in Japan today, but that is not the subject of this chapter.

NOTES AND REFERENCES

1 Barrett, B. F. D. and Therivel, R., *Environment Policy and Impact Assessment in Japan*, London and New York, Routledge, 1991, pp. 56–60.

2 For a summary of such US methodology and history, see Mandelker, D., *Land Use Law*, Charlottesville, The Michie Company, 1988, Chapter 3; Callies, D. L. and Garner, J., 'Planning Law in England and Wales and in the United States', *Anglo-American Law Review*, 1 (3) 1972, pp. 310–11.

3 Heap, D., *An Outline of Planning Law*, London, Sweet & Maxwell, 1987, Chapter 10; Cullingworth, B., *Town and Country Planning in Britain*, London, Unwin Hyman, 1988, Chapter 4; Grant, M., *Urban Planning Law*, London, Sweet & Maxwell, 1982, Chapter 5; Moore, V., *A Practical Approach to Planning Law*, London, Blackstone, 1990, Chapter 5.

4 Barrett and Therivel, op. cit., pp. 61–63.

5 Ibid., p. 63.

6 Ibid., note 43 to chapter 4.

7 Ibid., p. 63.

8 Ibid.

9 Arai, Hachitaro, 'Land Use and Zoning' in Kitagawa, Z., *Doing Business in Japan*, New York, Matthew Bender, 1990, Vol. 6, Chapter 7.

10 UPA Articles 5 and 7, as described in Arai, op. cit., p. 21.

11 Arai, op. cit., pp. 22–24.

12 Articles 14 and 9.

13 Article 11.

14 Article 12.

15 Arai, op. cit., p. 25.

16 Ibid., pp. 26–27.

17 Ibid., pp. 32–33.

18 CSA articles 48–58, as described in Arai, op. cit., pp. 40–43.

19 City of Hiroshima, *Town Planning in Hiroshima* (undated), p. 5.

20 Ibid., pp. 11–21.

21 Ibid., p. 7.

22 Ibid., pp. 9–23.

23 Ibid., pp. 7 and 25.

24 Ibid., p. 27.

25 Ibid.

26 Interview in Hiroshima, Department of Planning, Mr Yamamoto and staff, 29 May 1992.

27 Kyoto City, Planning Bureau, *Kyoto City Planning* (undated), p. 5.

28 Ibid., p. 11.

29 Ibid., p. 13.

30 Ibid., pp. 13–16.

31 City of Osaka, *Osaka City Comprehensive Plan for the 21st Century* (undated), pp. 4–5.

32 Ibid., pp. 14–15.

33 Ibid., pp. 16–17.

34 Callies, D. L. and Grant, M., 'Impact Fees, Development Agreements and Planning Gain: An Anglo-American Comparison', *The Urban Lawyer*, 22 (4) 1991.

35 See, for example, Lucas v. South Carolina Coastal Council, 112 S. Ct. 2886 (1992). For a thorough review of the issues raised and decided in that case and its implications for US town planning law, see Callies, D. L. (ed.), *After Lucas: Land Use Regulation and the Taking of Property Without Compensation*, Chicago, ABA, 1993.

Chapter 6

Sen-biki amidst Desakota: Urban Sprawl and Urban Planning in Japan

MICHAEL HEBBERT

Megalopolis was the name given by Jean Gottmann to the urbanised north-eastern seaboard of the United States. His book of 1961 offered an affectionate portrait of the great urban nebula that stretches from Washington to Boston. Rejecting the Malthusian image of an uncontrolled, destructive metropolitan sprawl, Gottmann argued that the 37 million residents of Megalopolis lived better and enjoyed a wider range of choice since their cities burst across the landscape.

The portrait had a deliberate ambiguity. On the one hand, as a French regional geographer, Gottmann stressed the uniqueness of the place and people he described. Their decentralised, car-based pattern of living was distinctively American, and among American regions Megalopolis had an unrivalled position as 'Main Street and Crossroads of the Nation', the hub of decision making, power and innovation. Megalopolis was unique, but it was also a prototype. 'So great are the consequences of the general evolution heralded by this present rise and complexity of Megalopolis that an analysis of this region's problems often gives one the feeling of looking at the dawn of a new stage in human civilization. The author has visited and studied various other regions of the world but has not experienced such a feeling anywhere else. Indeed', wrote Gottmann, 'the area may be considered the cradle of a new order in the organisation of inhabited space'.[1]

Whatever the author's original intentions, the word megalopolis was soon being applied around the world as a generic term for the overlapping of metropolitan systems into super-settlements of more than 20 million population. Peter Hall identified five such complexes in 1973. Four of these were the original Megalopolis, with 34 million population, the coffin-shaped area up the M1 and M6 motorways in England (32 millions), the Rhine-Ruhr megalopolis (29 millions), and the cities around the Great Lakes (20 millions).[2]

Largest of all was the Japanese megalopolis, the 600-kilometre-long urban belt joining the vast metropolitan areas of Tokyo-Yokohama, Nagoya and Osaka-Kyoto-Kobe. Not only did it have the greatest population (40 million in 1960), but it was also sustaining the fastest rate of expansion, under the stimulus of the building of the Shinkansen, the Tokyo-Nagoya-Kobe Highway, the Pacific Belt port-industrial complexes, and kindred projects under the National Income Doubling Plan of 1958. The unfamiliar geographical phenomena studied by Gottmannn on the US north-eastern seaboard were even more strikingly evident in the Tokaido (Tokyo to Kyoto) region. There was the same overlapping of functional urban regions, detected from census analysis of travel to work patterns, the same interpenetration of urban and rural living and nebulous intermingling of traditionally separate land uses. But there was also an absolute density of rural population and near-continuous building which made the interstices of Maryland, Pennsylvania and Massachusetts look sparsely populated by comparison. It was not surprising that Gottmannn's book made an immediate impact after its Japanese publication in 1964, or that it spawned an entire research literature on the Tokaido Megalopolis, or *kyotai-toshi*.[3] Gottmannn himself became one of the distinguished foreign experts regularly invited by the Government of Japan to sanction successive strategic plans for the long-term management of the megalopolis as it grew to its current size of seventy millions.[4]

The concept of *desakota*, recently coined by the Canadian geographer Terence McGee from the Indonesian *kota* (town), *desa* (village), has many echoes of Gottmannn's original portrayal of the north-eastern Megalopolis. Like Gottmannn, McGee uses a neologism to challenge standard assumptions about the urban-rural divide. He draws on land use and employment data to portray new landscapes where agricultural, industrial and service economies melt together, and entire metropolitan regions fuse into one. *Desakota* zones are defined as 'regions of an intense mixture of agricultural and nonagricultural activities that often stretch along corridors between large city cores'.[5] But his concept is not for general application to the Great Lakes, Rhine-Ruhr, Los Angeles and São Paolo. *Desakota*, as a geographical phenomenon, is distinctive to the Far East:

> In many parts of Asia, the spatial juxtaposition of many of the larger city cores within heavily populated regions of intensive, mostly wet-rice agriculture based on a mixture of 'skill oriented' and 'mechanical' technological inputs has created densities of population that are frequently much higher than in the suburban areas of the West. This juxtaposition permits demographic densities similar to urban areas over extended zones of intensely cultivated rural areas located adjacent to urban cores.[6]

Megalopolis was built on the outward movement into thinly populated hinterlands of suburban householders driving automobiles. *Desakota* is based on the incorporation into the urban economy of densely settled peasant householders riding two-stroke motor-bikes. Extended metropolitan regions with *desakota* characteristics occur throughout Asia. Their character varies according to the national level of economic growth and degree of urbanisation. The Jog-Jakarta region in Java, and Kerala in South India, are examples of 'Type 3' *desakota*, with a stagnant economy and high labour surplus. Nanjing-Shanghai-Hangzhou, and the Calcutta region, are 'Type 2' regions, exhibiting rapid growth. In the Three Tigers of Taiwan, South Korea and Japan we find 'Type 1' *desakota*, that is to say, nominally rural zones where most economically active work is non-agricultural. McGee offers as an alternative label to Type 1 the Japanese term *konjuka* which could be translated in Prince Kropotkin's words as 'fields, factories and workshops'. The emergence of this landscape in all three countries can be traced historically to the transfer of farms to peasant smallholders under post-war land reform, complemented by protective agricultural policies to maintain farm structure over the post-war period of rapid industrialisation. During its period of rapid economic growth, each tapped the labour reserve of farm households around the main urban-industrial centres by a combination of infrastructure improvements and rural mechanisation. The process has gone furthest in Japan, where it can also be mapped most precisely, thanks to the unrivalled quality of data available on the income composition of part-time farming households, a key indicator of Type 1 *desakota*.[7]

While *desakota*'s decentralised, open texture can make a fertile medium for economic growth, it poses problems for 'the conventional city planning mind-set'.[8] Planners have traditionally emphasised the separateness of town and country and the undesirability of the in-between environment, known pejoratively as 'urban sprawl', or as Raymond Unwin put it, in *Town Planning in Practice*, 'that irregular fringe of half-developed suburb and half-spoiled country which forms such a hideous and depressing girdle around modern growing towns'.[9] Town planning as we know it today has developed largely as a regulatory response to the destructive effects of modern transport and communication, and free land and property markets, on the quality of urban life. The unfettered exercise of property rights and consumer choice is opposed because they leave older districts devalued—or worse, abandoned—while newer urbanisation 'spreads outward in a haphazard pattern, consuming more land than is necessary, and creating excessive costs for municipal facilities and services. Instead of creating a series of well organised communities with well-defined centres of high activity, sprawl spreads housing thinly and intermittently across the landscape with higher intensity uses . . . scattered separately and unevenly on sites that are left over. This, in turn, frustrates a rational transportation system'.[10] Sprawl, from a conventional planning perspective, is environmentally harmful, fiscally inefficient—because of the higher unit costs of servicing scattered buildings—and destructive of civic culture. But as part of the American way of life, it has had many articulate defenders before and since Jean Gottmann.[11] The spirited debate over compactness or diffusion has recently been given a new twist by the discovery of global warming and the chemical erosion of the ozone layer.[12] McGee and Ginsberg's *desakota* concept takes the debate in a new direction. Their suggestion is that received planning ideas about urban sprawl and disorderly development reflect a distinctively Western obsession with the need to control cities and are alien to the dynamic economies of the Asia Pacific Rim.[13] In the remainder of this chapter, we shall explore the role of urban planning in Japan's *desakota* regions, asking where it operates, and how, and why.

Earlier chapters have discussed the close attention paid by Japanese town planning reformers to the Western example. Sir Raymond Unwin's concept of a permanent green belt of agricultural land around major cities was known, as was Sir Patrick Abercrombie's famous elaboration of it in the *Greater London Plan* of 1944, which became the basis for the post-war planning of the capital region. The success of English policies for planned decentralisation prompted the Japanese government in April 1956 to launch a similar 'mother city/green belt/satellite town' scheme for the containment of Tokyo. In the First Capital Region Improvement Plan, a green belt (*Kin Kochitai*) was declared around the built-up area (*Kisea-Shigaichi*) of Tokyo. It was perhaps the most famous instance of an inappropriate transplant of Western planning thought to Japan. The specific cause of failure of the Tokyo green belt was the formation of a political league between sixteen municipalities and several hundred farmers to frustrate the plan. In Koganei City, farmers prematurely subdivided and sold plots to prevent designation. The small landowners had a powerful ally in the form of the Japan Housing Corporation, owner and intending developer of large tracts of land in the heart of the proposed belt. The enshrinement of private property rights in the Japanese Constitution made implementation legally doubtful, and the green belt provisions were dropped in 1965.[14]

Quite apart from the specific property interests opposed to control of Tokyo's growth, the policy switch reflected a cultural incongruity in the very idea of a sacrosanct green belt of countryside around the built-up area. Green belts are based on a distinctively European dichotomy between town and countryside, *urbs* and *rus*. The physical contrast between built environment and natural environment, which mattered so much to Unwin and still forms the basis of British planning today, has no foothold in Japanese culture and language. Henry Smith observes that the relationship between town and country is one of opposition (either/or) in the West, but is seen in Japan in terms of complementarity (both/and) and interpenetration.[15] The French geographer Augustin Berqué links these different attitudes to underlying contrasts between occidental agriculture, based on animal husbandry and arable farming, and oriental rice-culture. In a rice-based civilisation, the dykes and paddies of the agricultural landscape are as artificial as the towns they support. The realm of nature begins not at the urban edge but with the wilderness (*yama*) of mountain and forest.[16] It is no task of city planning to stop development 'spoiling' countryside, to use that expressive English phrase.[17] These considerations perhaps help to explain the very different path taken by Japanese city planning after the failure of the Tokyo green belt.

When the modern land use planning system was introduced at the height of the rapid growth period, it had a more specific and modest rationale: not to restrain urban growth, but to phase it, improve the level of public service infrastructure, and dampen private land speculation. Earlier chapters have described the battery of law and policy that was wheeled into place, involving 27 major acts and a host of subsidiary legislation.[18] As noted in the previous chapter by David Callies, the key legal instrument for regulating urban growth was the City Planning Act (1968). This Act provided for the demarcation of Urbanisation Promotion Areas (UPAs)—areas already built up, or expected to become so within a decade—from Urbanisation Control Areas (UCAs) where, in the words of the Act, 'no development is allowed on principle, so as to control the disorderly expansion of the urban area'. City planning was to shape *desakota* by drawing the line— literally, *sen-biki*—between UPA and UCA, *shigaika-kuiki* and *shigaika-chosei-kuiki*. The formal distinction between promotion and control was not all it seemed. Significant concessions were won by the property lobby both in the passage of the 1968 Act, and in its implementation. As initially drafted, the bill made provision for a landscape protection zone, with the certainty and permanency of a green belt. But the government legislation bureau directed that outright prohibition in development would be unconsti-tutional, unless accompanied by compensation at market value. The control area, as

Table 6.1 *City planning area designation in Japan, 1991*

	Numbers	Area (km²)
Unzoned CPAs	920	42 945
Zoned CPAs	331	50 979
UCA		37 242
UPA		13 737
TOTAL	1 251	93 924

Source: Ministry of Construction.

enacted, allowed numerous categories of exempted development (see below) and the prospect of upgrading to UPA was held open through periodic revision. More seriously, the demarcation of control and promotion areas was not made mandatory. A quarter of a century after the Act was passed, almost half the total city planning area of Japan remains unzoned (see Table 6.1), implying a presumption in favour of promotion rather than control. And finally, in the areas that have been zoned, the planning authorities have made lavish provision for urban expansion. The promotion area is very widely drawn, embracing 13 700 square kilometres in all, of which perhaps half corresponds to the census definition of Densely Inhabited Districts (DIDs) with gross population densities in excess of 40 inhabitants per hectare. The city planning system operates—to use an industrial analogy—with generous buffer stocks of development land: whereas Japanese factories have perfected the technique of 'just in time' stock control, bringing in production factors to match demand, Japanese cities sit surrounded by swathes of UPA, designated on a 'just in case' basis.[19]

It is unsurprising, then, that a quarter of a century's city planning has left no imprint to compare with the green belts around London, or indeed neighbouring Seoul.[20] What remains striking about the Japanese pattern of land use is the interpenetration of farming, housing, industry and urban services, not just within a limited peripheral zone of transition, but far into the inner post-war suburbs, and out into the outer reaches of the functional urban region. Figure 6.1 illustrates how *desakota* land use patterns extend even into districts of suburban Tokyo. Equally noteworthy are the high proportion of undeveloped plots in Mitaka or Kokubunji, nineteen and thirty kilometres respectively from the city centre, and the sporadic scattering of development around Nishitama 40 kilometres away. While the outward sprawl of the Tokyo metropolis continues year by year, perhaps half the land within 40 kilometres of the central railway station remains undeveloped.[21] There are reported to be 36 000 hectares of agricultural land in Greater Tokyo, and agricultural remnants extend deep into the 23 ward core of the city. Despite an average population density of 14 000 people per square kilometre, the core has 1800 hectares of farm land (and an agricultural workforce of 12 500).[22]

It is hard to detect the city planner's hand in the loose-knit texture of *desakota*. For many kilometres around any sizeable population centre, the landscape is scattered with small housing developments, isolated villas, roadside factories and urban utilities.

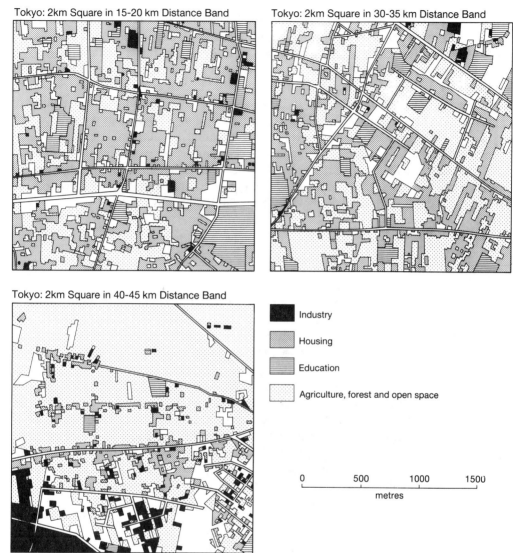

Tokyo: 2km Square in 15-20 km Distance Band

Tokyo: 2km Square in 30-35 km Distance Band

Tokyo: 2km Square in 40-45 km Distance Band

Industry

Housing

Education

Agriculture, forest and open space

0   500   1000   1500
metres

Fig. 6.1 Unconsolidated growth of suburban Tokyo: Mitaka, Kokubunji and Minitama (source: Tokyo Metropolitan Government Land Use Maps)

Although as we move towards the town we encounter large-scale residential estates, laid out in blocks of flats built either by local government (the prefectures or larger municipalities) or by the Japan Housing and Urban Development Corporation, most private sector building activity can be seen to proceed gradually on a plot-by-plot basis. Estates (*danchi*) are laid out by land developers who sell off building plots to individual buyers, producing a characteristically dense, variegated residential environment.[23] Three sites have been sold off here for small detached dwellings. A fourth, separately, is developed in small, dense, two-storey terraces of private rental housing. The land between continues under cultivation. Moving further in, the rate of building coverage increases, but a significant quantity of land lies undeveloped, some of it planted with trees, some cultivated for vegetables or as a rice paddy, and a small residue left idle. The undeveloped land within the urbanised area matches the scatter of new building activity at the outer periphery. Tsukio Yoshio puts it well: 'The cities and the country are not separated but joined together as if they were one unit. At one point, fields are encompassed by a colony of buildings: at another, a colony of buildings is encompassed by a field.'[24] As he goes on to observe, Jean Gottmannn's concept of megalopolis—'an irregularly colloidal mixture of rural and suburban landscapes'—applies all the more to the *desakota* along the route of the Tokaido Shinkansen line than to the open landscapes visible from the railway line between Washington DC and New York. Where, on the ground, are the boundaries laid down by any planning system?

Urban Growth on Tokyo's Edge

To explore this question about the boundaries of the planning system, Norihiro Nakai and the present author examined an area of fast urban growth on the edge of metropolitan Tokyo, in Chiba prefecture. Over the past two decades, the adjacent prefectures of Chiba, Saitama and Kanagawa have sustained the highest net in-migration and fastest population growth in Japan. Like the Tama area, to which they are in urban terms the annexe, their growth has been based on the household rather than the firm sector; for decades Chiba and Saitama prefectures have played a dormitory role. Their ratio of day-time to night-time population has always been the lowest of any prefecture in Japan—and the trend is still downwards, in contrast to the strongly developing local labour markets within the fifty-kilometre radius of London.[25] The majority of commuters—around two-thirds in the prefectures of Chiba, Saitama and Kanagawa—face journeys to work of more than an hour-and-a-half each way.[26] It used to be the case that these long-distance commuters were trading off the inconvenience and wasted hours of their journey to work for higher living standards. In Allinson's classic study of Tokyo suburbanisation, better housing was the lure that drew most people outwards—it was a 'pull' migration, not, as in the USA, a 'pushed' flight to the suburbs[27]—but the relative standard of new housing in the commuter belt has not kept pace with rising national expectations.[28]

For our study of *sen-biki* amidst *desakota* we selected five dormitory municipalities that lie in the north-east corner of the great Tokyo agglomeration, in Chiba prefecture: Abiko, Kamagaya, Kashiwa, Matsudo and Nagareyama. Most of these cities doubled their population in 1955–65 and again in 1965–75. Though the rate of expansion is slowing down, their population growth rates in 1980–90 were still running at between 14 per cent (Matsudo) and 31 per cent (Nagareyama). We began by looking at the process of preparing the city plan on which the urbanisation promotion and control areas are designated: *sen-biki*—the process of drawing the line. Leaving aside the detail of what proved to be an extremely intricate decision process, we can distinguish two basic positions. The property industry, represented by the Real Estates Association, the Urban Development Association and the National Federation of Land and Building Agents, lobbies energetically at local and central levels to get as much land as possible designated for building, and for more laxity (or flexibility) in the enforcement of controls. Further, the development lobby has pressed in recent years for the whole mechanism of promotion and control areas to be swept away. Two other powerful interests put their weight behind a maximalist position. First, the prefectural authorities, reflecting central Ministry of Construction policy, are keen to sustain a strong rate of growth in the outer suburban belt in order to relieve the inflationary pressure of housing demand upon land prices. Secondly, landowners—which is to say, in general terms, the farmers and their representative organisations—have a clear preference to see their holdings zoned as potential building land.

On the other side, local government tends to argue a minimalist case. It does so on strictly economic grounds. Japanese municipal authorities, unlike academic contributors to the 'costs of sprawl' debate,[29] are in no doubt that scatteration costs more than compact development. The additional tax revenue brought by residential expansion is not sufficient to cover its expenditure requirements. All the municipalities have severe infrastructure backlogs (see Table 6.2). They have been conspicuous victims of a postwar economic growth strategy which has favoured private over public investment and (for political reasons) favoured rural over urban areas in the allocation of the small budget share for housing and urban infrastructure.[30] The preference of City Treasurers is for a compact, efficient pattern of urban development, serviceable by water and sewerage networks, schools and clinics. A diffuse sprawl of development implies higher unit costs. The Japanese city planners' motivation to minimise the building area is quite distinct from that of their British counterparts. It owes nothing to *a priori* objection against building on farmland. Thus, there is no objection in principle to development projects in the control area (land readjustments for example) which undertake to provide their own infrastructure—land in such a case will automatically be rescheduled. But 'scatteration' they oppose.

It will come as no surprise that the outcome of the *sen-biki* struggle has tended to favour the maximalists. We have already seen the excessively liberal designation of UPAs in Japan as a whole—enough for a doubling in size of existing built-up areas. Our five cities show the physical effect of this loose-fit land supply system. The boundaries of the promotion areas have been liberally drawn, and with only one exception have been rolled forwards at each of the regular reviews, in 1970, 1973, 1978 and 1985. In Kashiwa, a city of 7300 hectares, the promotion area covered 3926 hectares in 1970, and 4250 hectares in 1990. The built-up part of the city—as measured by Densely Inhabited Districts—covers only 2200 hectares. Even at the height of the bubble economy, urbanisation no more than nibbled at the commodious supply of adjacent building land. Indeed the city of Matsudo set a precedent by applying to the Ministry of Construction to be allowed to declassify some of the huge 4600 hectare stock of building land which it had designated in 1970. After much negotiation (and against considerable resistance from the Ministry), it was allowed to lop off 208 hectares, though with no prejudice to the development rights of the local landowners.[31]

Table 6.2 *Planning and development in the five case-study cities*

	Matsudo	Kashiwa	Nagereyama	Abiko	Kamagaya
Planning (1987) UPA area (ha)	4443	4205	1488	1598	1007
UCA area (ha)	1677	3051	2042	2809	1046
Development (1985)					
in UPA (no.)	36	51	17	—	18
area (m^2)	80 809	162 703	53 958	—	34 142
average size	2246	3190	3174	—	1897
in UCA (no.)	23	23	23	—	15
area (m^2)	20 803	44 885	17 227	—	—
average size	904	1952	749	—	—
Land readjustment project (as of March 1985)					
completed (no.)	44	7	10	4	0
area (ha)	1457	243	139	170	0
under way (no.)	11	4	2	6	0
area (ha)	281	234	171	167	0
Urban infrastructure completion rate of City Planning Roads (%) 1986	45.7	28.7	33.3	49.7	9.7
Park area per head of population (m^2) 1985	3.71	1.63	3.83	6.44	1.53
Sewerage diffusion rate (%) 1986	41	33	2	33	10
Local finance (1985) Public borrowings as a percentage of the total budget	10.9	12.2	8.8	12.0	10.2

Source: compiled from official statistics of the five cities.

All these suburban municipalities display a common pattern. While the built-up area is expanding rapidly into the neighbouring farmland, their internal structure remains loose-knit, with large stocks of undeveloped land. A point sampling analysis of building coverage in the case of Kamagaya City estimated that the building cover was no more than 56 per cent of the level provided in the city plan.[32] The open texture is not the planners' doing. Thanks to the active opposition of property owners through their neighbourhood associations, very limited use is made of the open space designations available under planning law. In general, controls are applied only to river flood plains, waterfronts, and steep wooded slopes—in other words, to areas where hard engineering considerations preclude building. In the entire Tokyo metropolitan area, only 82 hectares are designated as Green Space Conservation Zone. Other zonings that can be used to restrict building activity in areas of special landscape quality, or traditional building types, are applied very sparingly, mostly to major tourist attractions. On closer inspection we find two kinds of unbuilt land within *desakota* cities: agricultural plots (sometimes classified as 'forest') and vacant building plots. Agricultural and forest land account for between a quarter and a third of the Urbanisation Promotion Areas in Kamagaya, Abiko and Matsudo—some 1840 hectares in all. Vacant building sites take up at least a further 10 per cent, and up to half of all residential land development in the case of Matsudo.

Far from encouraging consolidation of the built-up area, planning designation seems to have the opposite effect. Landowners in a Promotion Area are following a rational strategy of portfolio management when they bring just a small portion of their plot on to the market but leave the rest undeveloped for as long as possible. Consider, for example, a 270 hectare rectangle of rice paddy sandwiched between the River Edo and Matsudo's industrial belt, all of it designated UPA in 1974. The area is divided by a main irrigation channel, which imposes some obstacle to lateral movement. It is regularly laid out in a grid-pattern of holdings and access roads, thanks to an agricultural improvement scheme carried out during the late 1950s, but has no sewers. The effect of the agricultural improvements was to encourage local farmers to engage in speculative development, mostly of *minikaihatsu* or 'pocket-handkerchief' houses, packed on to narrow alleys laid at right angles to the streets. At the time of UPA designation, building was well advanced in the sector between the industrial belt and the irrigation channel, while the part to riverward remained predominantly agricultural, with only early symptoms of piecemeal development. In the decade after UPA designation, the more developed sector stagnated, while the more agricultural urbanised rapidly, with well over 100 speculative schemes. The onward movement of the development frontier brings an initial burst of activity as owners put a sliver of paddy field on to the market to establish its urban value. Once that has been done, the remainder is retained in agricultural use to accumulate value.[33] This remaining urban agriculture is astonishingly resilient. Households do eventually quit farming, but as Gil Latz discovered in neighbouring Saitama prefecture, the wastage rate is actually higher in rural than in urban areas.[34]

A comparable strategy of land-holding can be seen in the land readjustment projects. The technique of land readjustment—*kukakuseiri*—is an increasingly important instrument of planning for the hard-pressed municipalities of the outer metropolitan area. The basic idea is derived from agricultural improvement techniques. Landowners combine into an association, regulated under public law, to exploit their holdings. The land is pooled, equipped with roads, parks and other infrastructure, and parcelled into building plots. Up to half the costs of subdivision may be covered by a land readjustment grant from the public purse. The larger the project, the more likely it is to be grant-aided. However, the majority of land readjustments are private affairs, done on a self-financing basis. Some of the plots are 'reserved' by the association for sale to cover the initial development costs, the remainder restored to the owners in proportion to their original holdings. The attraction of land readjustment to the farmers is that they are left with marketable building plots. Its attraction to city governments is that the cost of infrastructure provision is carried by the landowners and not the public at large. Even in grant-aided projects, grants cover at most only half the cost of roads and bridges, and a fifth of the cost of sewers. Over 15 per cent of the site area will be dedicated for public infrastructure.

However, land adjustment undoubtedly accentuates sprawl. A familiar spectacle in the outer periphery of any large city is a serviced set of building sites—with roads laid out and electricity poles erected—with only one in every ten plots occupied by a house. Local landholders, after an intensive bout of land trading when speculators buy into the farmland market in 1000 square-metre lots, have formed a land readjustment association and successfully pressed the local authority to initiate a project in an area as yet unripe for development, perhaps on productive agricultural land or a wooded hillside where a preliminary to development is the clearance of all existing ground cover. Once laid out, the sites will be sold off as gradually as possible, subject to the cash flow requirements of the association, in order to conserve their value. A purchased site may be left undeveloped for many years by its urban owner. It is a form of investment, or the first step in a self-build project that will take decades to complete. In a survey of projects around Nagoya, it was found that the average rate of building construction on completed land readjustment areas was only 3.2 per cent per annum. Completion of the residential area will take some 30 years, and—a final problem—even when the scattered, desultory landscape of the land readjustment project has finally been consolidated into a residential suburb, the resulting urban environment too often matches the lowest standard of commercial speculative subdivisions with straight roads, small lots (often 70–80 square metres), no mature trees and minimal park provision (normally three per cent). Farmer-proprietors successfully resist attempts by local authorities to accelerate the pace of development or improve the quality of public open space because they threaten the viability of the land readjustment technique, on which the local authorities depend to get urban expansion serviced without cost to themselves.

The city of Matsudo has used land readjustment on a very large scale, as Table 6.2 shows. Forty per cent of the area designated for urban development has been developed by this method. The streets are wide and safe, occupying 20 per cent of the land area.[35] The projects have yielded 69 hectares of parkland (over two-thirds of the city's total park area) without any cost to the municipality—a highly significant gain, since park-sites must otherwise be acquired at full market value. Only the use of readjustment can explain why Matsudo is relatively so well endowed with public facilities. Just under a third of the municipality is registered as public land, as against a tenth in neighbouring Kamagaya, where no land readjustment has so far been carried out.

Against the evident advantages of land readjustment must be set the drawback that it is a sluggish source of supply of urban land. Market forces and the fiscal environment encourage owners to delay the release of their developed plots for as long as possible. Far better to retain them as investment assets rather than sell them on for final users. The development pipeline in land readjustment areas is thus a long one, particularly in the smaller, privately-financed projects. Because of the protracted negotiations involved, it takes on average just under a decade to carry out the land site development, and building and sale to final users may not follow for another twenty years. Once the reserve plots have been sold to cover project costs, development rates in *kukakuseiri* projects fall dramatically.

In one land readjustment case study from the inner suburbs of Matsudo, 60 per cent of the private plots were developed within four years, after which the building rate tailed away to just over one per cent per year.[36] The commercial logic was quite straighfor-ward. Because the readjustment occurred in an area that was already partly built-up, more plots were needed to accommodate existing residents and displaced uses—in fact, a fifth of the site—and another fifth had to be reserved to the association for sale to finance the higher costs of project implementation: but once this had been done, there was all the greater incentive to landowners to hold the remaining land for investment purposes. In another Matsudo project on open land further out of town, the association had to reserve only 15 per cent of its 230 plots to cover costs. All but three of the reserve plots were promptly sold and built up, whereas three-quarters of the redistributed plots remained vacant, when we investigated eight years later.

In Japan, as in any market economy, the instruments of physical regulation available under planning law are ineffectual if unsupported by the price, subsidy and tax regimes. The failure of the planning system to consolidate development within urban promotion areas has a fiscal, if not a physical, explanation. Land hoarding is rewarded both by inflated agricultural subsidies, and by loopholes in the residential land taxation system. Though full value taxation of unbuilt land within UPAs was introduced in 1971, precisely to bring vacant land on to the market, most farmers continue to enjoy a 98 per cent exemption under the 'long-term farming continuous agricultural land system'. Exemptions are granted by the local tax authority, i.e. the mayor. Provided the owner undertakes to continue farming the plot for two decades (raised in 1991 to three), rice paddies or orchards—typically persimmon saplings—deep into the built-up area pay on the basis of agricultural rent rather than asset value. Paradoxically, the rather low productivity of urban farmland ensures that more than three-quarters of it falls into the lowest agricultural land tax bracket, even in the Tokyo metropolitan region where land prices are highest. The corporate sector also had little incentive, during the decade of the bubble economy, to bring urban land holdings into active use. Empty sites, being tradeable, were the most acceptable collateral against bank borrowing: cumulatively, landowners' willingness to leave sites idle enhanced the scarcity of building land and so boosted prices.[37]

The quantity of unbuilt land within Urbanisation Promotion Areas became a source of scandal as house prices rocketed in the late 1980s. Targeted first by domestic critics, it was seized on by US trade negotiators in their bilateral negotiations with the Japanese government over structural impediments to trade. The urban land issue, number two in the check list of six demands made by the Americans early in 1990, epitomised many grievances, being used both by Japanese exporters as collateral to boost their borrowing power, and by farmers to maintain over-protected and inefficient agriculture. Inflating land prices, it suppressed domestic demand and added to the difficulties of foreign firms seeking to enter the Japanese market.[38] 'No-one is advocating that Japan changes its culture in any sense of the term', wrote a vociferous critic, Chalmers Johnson. 'If the Japanese want to subsidise their farmers, keep the LDP [Liberal Democratic Party] in power forever, and accept artificially low levels of income for the people as a whole, that's their business. But it is important to ensure that the Japanese, and not their trading partners, pay for these preferences. This is where land utilisation enters the international economic equation.'[39]

A tighter tax on landholding in UPAs had, in fact, already been placed on the political agenda by prime ministers Nakasone and Takeshita before the Structural Impediments Initiative put it in the limelight. The LDP's tax specialists published firm proposals in 1990 for a five per cent tax on vacant sites worth more than 500 million Yen.[40] Intense lobbying by farmers and business groups got the rate down to 0.2 per cent and the threshold up to one billion Yen when the landholding tax came into operation in the 1992 financial year. The tax as enacted fell almost entirely on the corporate sector,[41] demonstrating once again the political power of the agricultural connection.

We now turn to the other side of the *sen-biki* system, the operation of the control areas. The official statistics on rates of development per unit area of UCA and UPA are somewhat misleading, for much of the land under the control designation is intrinsically unsuited by gradient or ground conditions for building of any kind. That is why the impact of UCA designation is best studied in municipalities on flat land to the east of Tokyo rather than, for example, in the Osaka-Kyoto-Nara triangle, which have similar growth rates but are physically much more constrained.

The city planning presumption against urban land development in control areas falls a long way short of the blanket restriction imposed by British green belts, or indeed of the concept of Preservation Zones originally proposed in the sixth report of the drafting committee for the City Planning Bill in 1967.[42] The City Planning Act of 1968 allowed a long list of categories of permitted development in UCAs, of which the most important were:

(a) 'Vested-right' or *kitokukea* developments by landowners and leaseholders who acquired land prior to the UCA designation and apply to develop it for their own house or business within five years of the designation;
(b) Developments on sites of over 20 hectares (reduced to five hectares after a deregulation in 1983) which do not interfere with any long-term plans for the area;
(c) Developments by prefectural or municipal governments;
(d) Agriculturally related developments, such as housing for members of farming households, or processing plants.

Subsequent amendments, all in the direction of greater flexibility, have enlarged the scope for construction on registered 'building lots' within or beside existing settlements in the UCA. Areas suffering unemployment may suspend *sen-biki* altogether. The degree of loosening of UCA control has been left to prefectural discretion, opening the way to competitive deregulation between areas.[43]

Chiba's towns have a substantial volume of development in their control areas. First, the agricultural exemption allows a steady build-up of good quality residences for members of farming households. An average of 16 units were being built yearly in the Matsudo control area in the 1980s. The 'building lot' exemptions expanded markedly, and in the mid-1980s were running at an average of 46 developments of 10–15 000 square metres a year, a contribution equivalent to as much as a fifth of the total residential output in the city's Urbanisation Promotion Area. The scattered development of so-called agricultural housing is also a marked feature of farmland designated under the Agricultural Promotion Areas Act of 1969. In characteristic Japanese fashion, these areas often overlap the City Planning Area Control Zone (UCA). Within them, permission is required from either the Ministry of Agriculture or the prefectural governor before farmland can be used for building. But the farming interest, well represented on the Prefectural Agricultural Committee which operates the exemption procedure, takes a lenient view of applications. The numerical volume of developments actually runs at a higher rate per hectare than in the promotion area. Nevertheless, these loophole developments are small-scale (typically around 275 square metres) and participation tends to be limited to the privileged existing residents of the area. The limited development opportunities for commercial developers are reflected in the market value of land. Figure 6.2 shows the reported prices over four years of a square metre of land on 70 sites in 18 cities in Chiba prefecture. Each dot on the graph represents a pair of sites more or less equidistant from the nearest railway station, one in a UPA and one in a UCA. None of the UCA sites is sewered and 43 per cent do not even have access to water mains. All but three of the UPA sites have piped water and 29 per cent are fully serviced—with water, sewerage and gas. Their different infrastructure endowments and planning status give UCA plots a value of between a third and a half of UPA land: the gap has narrowed since 1991. Differentials of this order may seem large to owners of plots on the wrong side of the line, but they are minor by comparative planning standards, indicating the good probability of winning building consents on protected farmland.

The modest differential has an important, though paradoxical, effect on the distribution of public investment projects. There is clear evidence that municipalities and other public authorities exploit the control area as a reservoir of relatively cheap land for schools, hospitals, industrial centres and similar facilities. Typically, public facilities will be located just inside the restraint zone, where land is cheaper, but close to the catchment populations of the built-up area. Of the many types of development which escape through the loopholes of UCA designation, public projects on large sites, with ample car parking, probably do most to undermine its supposedly non-urban character.

Professor Yorifusa Ishida, of Tokyo Metropolitan University, has carried out an instructive survey of a strip of rice paddy land along the banks of the Tsurumi Gana River near his home in Yokohama City. The land is doubly protected as Urbanisation Control Area under the City Planning Act, and as Exclusive Agricultural Area (*noyochi-kniki*) under the Agricultural Promotion Area Improvement Act. A sample square kilometre nevertheless contains 34 new developments, including an orphanage, a senior high school (with playing fields), a telephone exchange, a primary school, a police station, a Nokyo office, a ward office, apartment blocks for public utility employees, a railway electricity substation and a lavishly engineered dual carriageway road. The incidence of development may be unusually high because the area is traversed by a trunk road, but it fairly illustrates the way in which *sen-biki* may actually have encouraged *desakota*, by exerting a centrifugal pull on public facilities. UCA land is likely, for the time being, to be physically less encumbered and offer larger sites, and the price

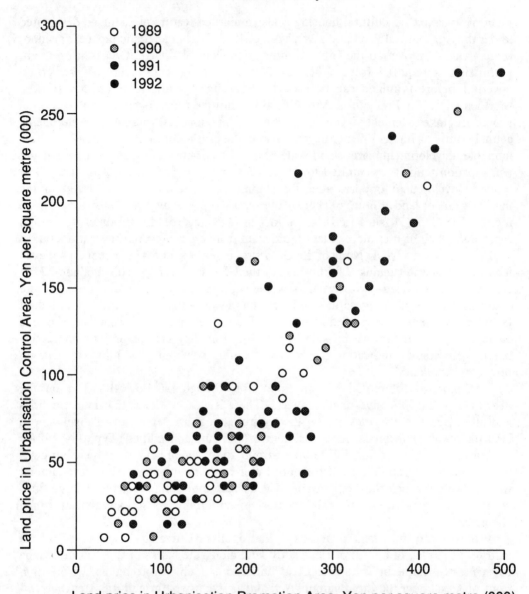

Fig. 6.2 Sample land prices in Chiba prefecture, 1989–1992 (source: National Land Agency data, compiled by Professor Hideo Nakai of Kinki University)

argument is compelling in a context where land acquisition costs absorb up to 70 per cent of the public works budget.

Figures 6.3, 6.4 and 6.5 offer, by way of synthesis, three views of a section of control area next to the town of Kashiwa. We see it first, on a 1971 map, as undeveloped farmland with a scattering of detached houses and one small residential estate. Figure

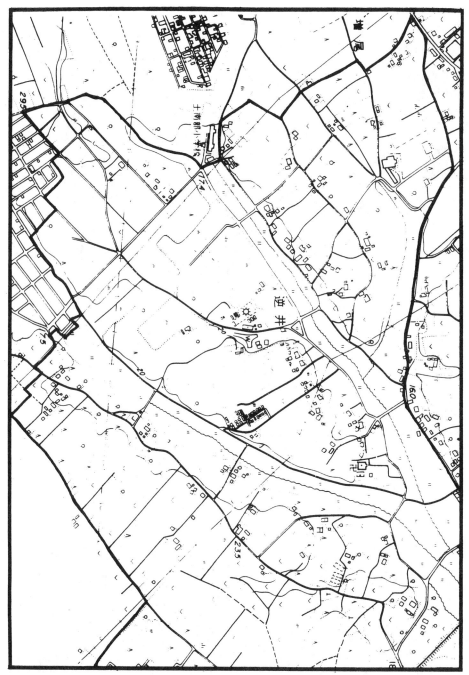

Fig. 6.3 Agricultural belt around Kashiwa, Chiba prefecture, 1971 (source: Hebbert, M. and Nakai, N., *How Tokyo Grows: Land Development and Planning on the Metropolitan Fringe* [Occasional Paper II], London, Suntory Toyota International Centre for Economics and Related Disciplines, London School of Economics, 1988, Fig. 5.23)

Fig. 6.4 Development in the Kashiwa Urbanisation Control Area, 1970–1987

Fig. 6.5 The Urbanisation Control Area today (source: by kind permission of Kanto Survey Division, National Geographical Survey Institute, Ministry of Construction)

6.4 distinguishes three categories of development over the subsequent years—the pre-existing, those built under 'vested-right' and 'building plot' exemptions, and the newly-built. Figure 6.5, a recent aerial photograph, shows the effects on the ground. What was farmland has become classic *desakota* landscape, in its intermingling of field, forest, homes and workplaces. Its UCA designation has not shielded this peri-urban area from the impact of Kashiwa's population growth (which was still running at 12 per cent in the five years 1985–90, after growth of 38 per cent, 86 per cent and 143 per cent in the three previous decades), but it has affected the nature of development. While densely-packed *danchi* press up to the UPA boundary, the control area combines spacious private houses, under the agricultural exemption, with institutional developments in extensive grounds. The effect of *sen-biki* has not been to prevent urban sprawl but rather to modify its character, in a manner quite favourable to farm households and public bodies, but less so to urban residents.

The cost of urban sprawl falls most heavily on private families in the outer metropolitan area, tied to the big city labour market with daily work-journeys of one-and-a-half hours each way, poor access to shops and facilities, and a chronic under-provision of the more discretionary public goods such as parks, libraries and children's playgrounds. The sporadic building process that leaves sites undeveloped gives families, at least for a while, 'smells of the soil' and deep nocturnal tranquility.[44] People willingly endure long work travel for the enjoyment of home ownership. But the pricking of the land price bubble has left many home buyers exposed. Discontent with the residential milieu was a significant element in the environmental politics of the 1970s and could become so again in the 1990s.[45]

Conclusion

The present chapter has looked at urban sprawl from its least flattering aspect, in the lee of a world city. Admittedly, for Ginsburg and McGee the essential *desakota* lies further from the gravitational fields of Tokyo, Nagoya and Osaka, in the dense infill that joins metropolitan areas into megalopolis. Like Gottmann in *Megalopolis*, their primary interest lies in the melding of agriculture, industry and services in an out-of-town or small-town context where the *sen-biki* system is at its weakest. The Japanese government has shown an increasing interest in *desakota*'s potential to counterbalance excessive concentration on Tokyo. In the Third and Fourth Comprehensive National Development Plans of 1977 and 1988, the National Land Agency tried to articulate a philosophy of multi-polar dispersal of growth to local towns and cities and their rural hinterlands. One of the preparatory reports, issued by the Agency in 1984, argued that traditional distinctions between urban cities and agricultural villages would tend to break down over the next few decades, not just through migration and integration of urban with rural functions, but physically through the emergence of 'areas where habitation and production coexist in harmony . . . in an agricultural environment'. The document discussed the question of what it called 'melting of housing and countryside'—a much more euphonious metaphor than scatteration or sprawl—underlining its potential benefits as 'a way to vitalise both urban cities and agricultural villages, and to make fruitful human life in an urbanised society'.[46]

The official valuation of *desakota* resembles Joel Garreau's American verdict on urban sprawl: 'Americans basically are pretty smart cookies who generally know what they're doing'.[47] The *sen-biki* system has not been used to impose a conventional—which is to say West European—image of the compactly planned city, efficiently serviced with infrastructure, set against a protected background of agricultural land. The ensuing *desakota* can be seen partly as an expression of distinctive cultural tradition and geography, but also as a political outcome of the entrenched power of the farming and landowning interest, linked to the big business axis via party-political and bureaucratic interests. The peculiarly Japanese combination of scatteration, small site development, limited infrastructure and high land values has served farmers and industrialists rather better than householders. Gottmann argued that the residents of the north-eastern seaboard of the United States should feel 'rightly proud' of their megalopolis.[48] Today, their Japanese counterparts are less sure.[49]

NOTES AND REFERENCES

1 Gottmann, J., *Megalopolis, the Urbanised Northeastern Seaboard of the United States*, New York, The Twentieth Century Fund, 1961, p. 9.

2 Hall, P. et al., *The Containment of Urban England*, London, Allen and Unwin, 1973, Vol. 1, pp. 46–58; Gottmann, J. and Harper, R., *Metropolis on the Move: Geographers Work at Urban Sprawl*, New York, J. Wiley, 1967, pp. 162–71.

3 Gottmann, J., 'Japan's Organisation of Space', *Ekistics*, **298**, 1981, pp. 258–66; Moon, S. N., *Japanese Cities: Urbanisation and Factorial Ecology*, Stockholm, Stockholm University Institute of Sociology, 1978.

4 Gottmann, J. and Harper, R., *Since Megalopolis*, Baltimore, The Johns Hopkins University Press, 1990, p. 9.

5 McGee, T. G., 'The Emergence of Desakota Regions in Asia' in Ginsburg, N., Koppel, B. and McGee, T. G., *The Extended Metropolis: Settlement Transition in Asia*, Honolulu, University of Hawaii Press, 1991, p. 7.

6 Ibid., p. 5.

7 Yamamoto, S. and Tabayashi, A. exploit the geographical potential of the data in 'The Structure of Rural Space in Japan: The Impact of Urbanisation and Off-Farm Employment on the Transformation of Japan's Rural Landscape and Economy', *Science Reports of the Institute of Geoscience*, University of Tsukuba, A,10, 1989, pp. 1–21.

8 McGee, T. G., 'Asia's Growing Urban Rings', United Nations University, Work in Progress, **13**, 1991, pp. 3: 9.

9 Unwin, R., *Town Planning in Practice*, London, Fisher Unwin, 1909, p. 154.

10 Haar, C. M., *The President's Task Force on Suburban Problems*, Cambridge, MA, Ballinger, 1974, p. 34.

11 Most readably, in recent years, by Joel Garreau in *Edge City: Life on the New Frontier*, New York, Doubleday, 1991. The pro-sprawl literature is usefully brought together by Ivonne Audirac and Maria Zifou in *Urban Development Issues: What is Controversial in Urban Sprawl? An Annotated Bibliography of Often-Overlooked Sources* (CPL Bibliography

247), Council of Planning Librarians, September 1989.

12 See, for example, the contributions to Breheny, M. (ed.), *Sustainable Development and Urban Form*, London, Pion, 1992.

13 Ginsburg, N. et al., op. cit., pp. xv–xvi.

14 Ishida, Y., 'Some Failings in the Transference of Western Planning Systems to Japan' (Paper to the Third International Planning History Group Conference, Tokyo, November 1988), pp. 9–10.

15 Smith, H. D., 'City and Country in England and Japan: Rus in Urbe versus Kyō ni inaka ari', *Senri Ethnological Studies*, **19**, 1986, p. 36.

16 Berqué, A., *Vivre L'Espace au Japon*, Paris, PUF, 1982.

17 English and Japanese approaches to urban growth are compared in Hebbert, M., 'Drawing the Line between Town and Country' in Bennett, R. J. and Estall, R. (eds.), *Global Change and Challenge*, London, Routledge, 1991, pp. 197–216.

18 Other summaries, putting city planning law respectively into the contexts of land policy and environmental policy, are Hebbert, M., 'Rural Land Use Planning in Japan' in Cloke, P., *Rural Land Use Planning in Developed Nations*, London, Unwin Hyman, 1989, pp. 130–51; and Barrett, B. and Therivel, R., *Environmental Policy and Impact Assessment in Japan*, London, Routledge, 1991, pp. 50–67.

19 See Chapter 4, 'Urbanisation Promotion and Control Areas' in Hebbert, M. and Nakai, N., *How Tokyo Grows: Land Development and Planning on the Metropolitan Fringe* (Occasional Paper 11), London, Suntory Toyota International Centre for Economics and Related Disciplines, London School of Economics, 1988.

20 Seoul and the seven other Korean cities surrounded by green belts offer an important exception to the Asian *desakota* thesis. The policy is briefly described in Mills, E. and Song, B-N., *Urbanisation and Urban Problems*, Cambridge, MA, Harvard University Press, 1979.

21 Hanayama, Y., 'Urbanisation and Land Prices: The Case of Tokyo' in Tsuru, S. (ed.), *Economic Growth and Resources: Problems Related to Japan* (Proceedings of the Congress of the International Economic Association, Vol. 5.), London, Macmillan, 1980, pp. 341–53.

22 See *Japan Economic Journal*, 2 December 1989, and Latz, G., 'The Persistance of Agriculture in Urban Japan' in Ginsburg, Koppel and McGee, op. cit., p. 220.

23 The recent ethnographic study by Eyal Ben-Ari (*Changing Japanese Suburbia*, London, Kegan Paul International, 1991) offers good insights into *danchi* development on pp. 63–109.

24 Yoshio, T., 'Chubu: A Valley between Kanto and Kansai' in Ito, Z. and Shionya, H. (eds.), *Climate and Society of the Chubu Region*, Nagoya, Chubu Region Development Research Centre, 1983.

25 Peter Hall succinctly summarises trends in the London region in *London 2001*, London, Unwin Hyman, 1989.

26 *Statistical Indicators of Social Life*, Tokyo, Government of Japan Statistics Bureau, 1984.

27 Allinson, G. D., *Suburban Tokyo: A Comparative Study in Politics and Social Change*, Berkeley, CA, University of California Press, 1979, p. 149.

28 See, for example, the reported figures for the size of floor area of new dwellings in square metres:

	Chiba	Tokyo	Japan
Rental			
1970	39.5	43.7	48.0
1982	50.2	48.2	54.9
Owned			
1970	82.4	89.5	99.2
1982	108.4	116.7	125.8

Source: *Statistical Indicators of Social Life*, 1984, pp. 124–25.

29 The literature is brought together in Andirac and Zifou, op. cit. See also Lynch, K.

A., *Theory of Good City Form*, Cambridge, MA, MIT Press, 1981, p. 403.

30 Kirwan, R. M., 'Urban Fiscal Policy and the Price of Land and Housing in Japan', *Urban Studies*, **24** (5) 1987, pp. 345–60.

31 Hebbert and Nakai, op. cit., pp. 90–91.

32 Ibid., pp. 84–88.

33 Ibid., pp. 101–04.

34 Latz, G., 'The Persistence of Agriculture in Urban Japan: An Analysis of the Tokyo Metropolitan Area' in Ginsburg, Koppel and McGee, op. cit., p. 228.

35 The average figure for the city area is 13.5 per cent. In the *minikaihatsu* area discussed above, roads occupied only 10.9 per cent, which is to say they are narrow, have no kerbed pavements, and pose a fire hazard.

36 Hebbert and Nakai, op. cit., pp. 104–11.

37 Noguchi, Y., 'Land Problem as an Unintended Industrial Policy: Its Mechanism and Limit', ESRC Japan Foundation Conference on Government-Industry Relations, 28–30 March 1988.

38 Sawa, Takamitsa, 'Doing What Must be Done', *Japan Times*, 19 March 1990.

39 From Yamamura, K. (ed.), *Japan's Economic Structure: Should It Change?*, WA, Society for Japanese Studies, pp. 113–1

40 *Japan Times*, 11 December 1990.

41 Big corporation payments accounted for 93.4 per cent of the tax yield in the first year (*Japan Times*, 26 February 1993).

42 Hebbert and Nakai, op. cit., pp. 44–45.

43 Ibid., Chapter 6.

44 Cybriwsky, R., 'Comments on Suburban Peace and Quiet' in *Tokyo: The Changing Profile of an Urban Giant*, London, Belhaven, 1991, p. 193.

45 Ben-Ari, op. cit., Chapter 5.

46 Bureau of Planning and Coordination, National Land Agency, *Interim Report on the Fourth National Comprehensive Development Plan*, Tokyo, November 1984.

47 Garreau, J., *Edge City: Life on the New Frontier*, New York, Doubleday, p. xi.

48 Gottmann, op. cit., p. 777.

49 See the concluding pages of David Kornhauser's study of *Urban Japan: Its Foundations and Growth*, London, Longman, 1976, pp. 149–54, where he hopes that the future Japan metropolis will take as its model the European compact city rather than the American urban sprawl.

ACKNOWLEDGEMENTS

The initial research for this chapter was supported by a core project grant from the Suntory Toyota International Centre for Economics and Related Disciplines (STICERD). The author records with gratitude help given by Ronald Dore, Yorifusa Ishida, Hazel Johnstone, Keiji Kamayama, Richard Kirwan, Hideo Nakai, Kanako Nakai, Norihiro Nakai, Sasumu Osada, Noriako Saito, Philip Shapira and Paul Waley in the preparation of the chapter. The usual disclaimers apply.

and Market and its Impact on
Housing and Urban Life

MICHAEL WEGENER

Tokyo is unsurpassed among the large cities of the world by its extraordinary land prices. During the last two decades, land prices in Tokyo have increased many times faster than consumer prices and much faster than in the rest of Japan. At the same time, despite its highly efficient public transport system, Tokyo also has the longest commuting times of comparable world cities, with work trips of one-and-a-half hours one-way being not uncommon.

These two phenomena are not unrelated. The long commuting times are the result of an unprecedented decentralisation of population during the last decades, stretching the city's boundaries to more than 50 kilometres from central Tokyo. At first sight, this rapid decentralisation is the unavoidable consequence of the growth of the Tokyo metropolitan area, which with a population of nearly 30 million now comprises almost a quarter of the population of Japan.

A closer look, however, reveals that the decentralisation of population has been much greater than in comparable cities, and that it has been to a large part a displacement process by which middle-class households have been forced to move farther and farther away from their still centralised workplaces. The reasons can be traced to twenty years of exaggerated land prices and a system of land ownership rewarding speculative land hoarding. Under the conditions of a distorted land market, urban planning has been either ineffective or, despite the best ambitions, has even contributed to aggravating the problems it tried to solve.

The organisation of the large Japanese city is both an outcome and an essential element of the organisation of Japanese society. High land prices and the displacement of large parts of the middle class from the city, the long working hours and commuting times, the restricted housing conditions and the organisation of family life, the situation of women and the education system: they all constitute a *coherent system*, the functioning of which has been an important precondition for the economic success of Japan. If one essential element of this system is changed, there are repercussions for other parts of the system. The urban land market is such a key element, although recent developments in the Tokyo land market have demonstrated that its impacts may be reduced by the ability of other aspects of modern Japanese society to accommodate and adjust to change without resulting in major transformation.

The Urban Development of Tokyo in Historical Perspective

In the seventeenth and eighteenth century, Edo, the predecessor of Tokyo, was one of the largest cities in the world. With its one million people it was larger than London and much larger than Paris. Its size had political reasons behind it. It rested in the regulation that Japan's feudal lords, or *daimyo*, had to hold residence with their family and retainers in the Shogun's capital. Edo consisted of two parts: the hilly areas to the north, west and south of the Shogun's palace (*Yamanote*) and the marshland areas to the north-east and east (*Shitamachi*). The *daimyo* lived on the Yamanote hills, while the merchants and craftsmen serving them lived in the Low City. The whole urban area measured not more than five kilometres in diameter, so housing conditions in the Low City must have been extremely crowded.[1] Being a castle town, its roads were intentionally kept narrow and winding (different from Kyoto). The castle was protected by layers of moats with few gates, and the Low City had a system of canals with arched bridges. Like in Venice, the most appropriate transport modes were boats, walking, carrying and being carried (by palanquin). There were also hand-drawn carts.[2]

With the Meiji Restoration of 1868, the *daimyo* and with them their large households disappeared, and the city's population was reduced to 600 000. It took twelve years to get the new Tokyo back to one million. The Meiji period (1868–1912) first brought the rickshaw and the horse-drawn carriage, later the trolley (1883) and finally the electric tramway (1903), but the narrow streets inherited from Edo were a bad fit for vehicles. This did not change much until the Great Kanto Earthquake of 1923, after which in the most damaged eastern part of the city new wider roads were built. The railways arrived in Tokyo in 1872, when the first train went to Yokohama. In 1890, the Chuo line going west from Tokyo was finished, and in 1891 the northern line started from Ueno. Intra-city rail travel started with the opening of the loop or Yamanote line in 1910, modelled after the Berlin *Ringbahn* (see Fig. 7.1).

At the end of Meiji, Tokyo had a population of 2.2 million. At this time, private railway companies like Keio and Seibu began the combination of railway and real estate business characteristic of Tokyo. To attract passengers for their (originally electric trolley) lines fanning out from the Yamanote ring to the west, these companies developed agricultural land along their lines as residential suburbs for the growing number of office workers of the burgeoning capital—comparable with the 'streetcar suburbs' of American cities or the garden city developments along rail lines outside London or Berlin. Within the Yamanote loop, electric tramways dominated until the first subway, the Ginza line, opened in 1929.

The terminals of the private railways along the Yamanote line developed into fast growing shopping and entertainment centres, Shinjuku and Shibuya being the most prominent. The railways established department stores at their terminals and so offered their passengers/tenants a total service for all needs of life. The growing of the urban area beyond the Yamanote loop marked the first phase of the separation of workplaces and residences, while at the same time Western-style apartments were built in the inner wards.[3] During the 1920s and 1930s the city grew by immigration and expansion to

Fig. 7.1 Central Tokyo

6.8 million. During the Second World War, half the houses in Tokyo were destroyed by air raids and its population decreased to 2.8 million.[4]

After the war, a special law for the reconstruction of Tokyo was enacted. However, its ambitious plans for land readjustment had to be scaled down because of lack of funds to pay the necessary compensations to landowners.[5] Only some six per cent of the planned readjustments were carried out, in contrast to many European cities, which took advantage of the bombings to reorganise their urban structure, or to another Japanese city heavily destroyed during the war, Nagoya, which today has one of the most efficient street layouts of Japanese cities.

At the same time, the return of people evacuated during the war, repatriates from the colonies, and growing rural immigration created an enormous need for housing which could not be met even by large public housing programmes, so low-standard wooden rental flats sprang up all over the city without much planning control. By 1955, Tokyo had a population of seven million.

In 1958, for the first time a regional plan for the National Capital Region covering an area of between 50 and 100 kilometres from Tokyo Station was announced. This plan, modelled after the Greater London Plan by Sir Patrick Abercrombie, aimed at structuring the metropolitan region into clearly articulated town areas (including new towns) divided by green belts. However, the plan was soon passed over by the explosive growth of Tokyo after the Korean War. During the years of rapid economic growth in the 1960s, the Tokyo metropolitan area grew by 600 000 persons annually, from 18 million to 24 million. The huge housing demand could only be met by moving farther and farther out into the suburbs. In these years, the first large high-rise housing estates were built by the Japan Housing Corporation. At the same time, private railway companies continued to develop low-rise housing areas at the outer ends of their commuter lines.

Infrastructure improvement concentrated on public transport in order to relieve overcrowding of rush-hour trains. From early after the war, Tokyo has continuously extended its subway system to its present 11 lines with 220 kilometres of track. Today public transport (including buses) accounts for 70 per cent of the 50 million daily passenger trips in the Tokyo metropolitan area. Road construction lagged behind. Still in 1960, most residential roads in Tokyo were unpaved. Only a few major thoroughfares had been widened after the war. Mass motorisation did not hit Japan until the 1960s. In the 1960s, Tokyo superimposed an extensive expressway system over its irregular street network. Today the expressways, despite their high toll fees, are heavily congested.

In the 1970s and 1980s, there were a multitude of government plans to promote a more balanced polycentric development of the country.[6] Among them, the Fourth Basic Plan for the Capital Region proposes a diversified urban structure built around five major business core cities within 30 kilometres of Tokyo.[7] Nevertheless, Tokyo continues to grow. Today the Tokyo metropolitan area has a population of almost 30 million, of which 11 million live in Tokyo itself. Its commuters come from an area extending over four prefectures within 50 kilometres from central Tokyo.

Urban Development and Land Prices in Tokyo

There has always been a very close association between transport infrastructure and land prices in Tokyo. Unlike in other countries, most notably the USA, the most important determining factor of land price is not the location in the highway network, but in the rail network expressed as travel time to central Tokyo and, on a more microscopic level, the distance to the next rail station. Therefore, land price maps typically show the areas of higher land prices extending finger-like along the radial railway lines, with small peaks around rail stations. This pattern has remained stable over time despite the enormous changes in price levels (see Fig. 7.2).

A comparison of the two maps in Figure 7.2 shows an average increase by a factor of 15 between 1969 and 1987. In fact, land prices in the six largest metropolitan areas in Japan grew by a factor of 155 between 1955 and 1989 (the peak year of the land price boom), compared with a consumer price index increase by only a factor of five. Also in 1989, a square metre of land in Tokyo cost ¥1 million ($7200) on average, which according to a study of the Japanese Association of Real Estate Appraisal was 99 times as much as in Los Angeles or 30 times more than in London or Frankfurt. It has been estimated that in the late 1980s the total real estate of Tokyo, at $7.7 trillion, was worth more than twice as much as all the land in the USA. At prime locations in the Ginza or Marunouchi areas, a square metre was traded for as much as ¥30 million ($215 000).

The exaggerated land prices were reflected in building rents. Retail space in the Ginza area rented for an average of ¥86 000 ($615) per square metre per month, more than in the Trump Tower in New York ($445). Office rents in the main business areas were around ¥10 000 ($70) per square metre per month, but much higher at choice locations. A choice location was the Kioicho Building opened in November 1989 (see Fig. 7.3). Space in one of its 17 office floors was let for between ¥14 000 ($100) and ¥17 500 ($125) per square metre per month. The six top floors of the Kioicho Building contain apartments. They were advertised for between ¥1.6 million ($11 000) and ¥2.4 million ($17 000) per month. These rents were not exceptional. Within the Yamanote loop it was hard to find a three-bedroom apartment for less than ¥500 000 ($3600) per month. This was more than the monthly income of the average worker household of ¥481 000 ($3435).

The gap between incomes and house prices was even more pronounced. This can be demonstrated using an example due to Hasegawa et al.[8] In Japan, it has long been a rule of thumb that a typical house should cost no more than 5.5 times the annual income of a household. In 1956, the average household could still buy a small house with a floor area of 66 square metres on a lot of 165 square metres near Ogikubo, two stations west of Shinjuku on the Chuo line, for 5.5 times its annual income. Due to price increases in construction and land, 5.5 times the average annual household income in 1985 could only pay for 55 square metres of floor space on 17 square metres of land. Another possible response was to settle down farther out where land prices were still lower. If the same household insisted on buying a house of 66 square metres on 165 square metres of land for only 5.5 times its annual income, then it would by 1986 have had to move as far

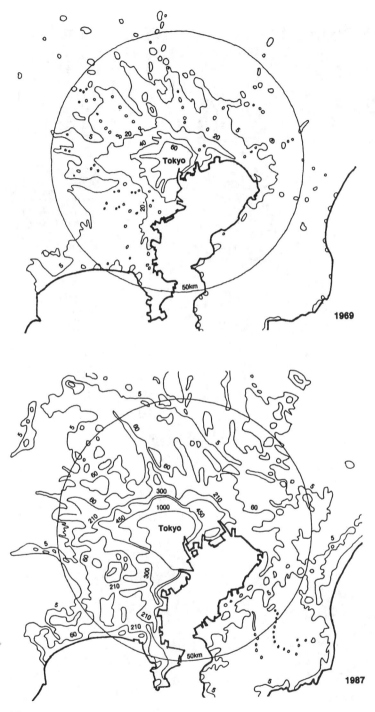

Fig. 7.2 Land prices in the Tokyo metropolitan area in 1969 and 1987, in ¥1000 per square metre (source: Tokyu Real Estate Corporation)

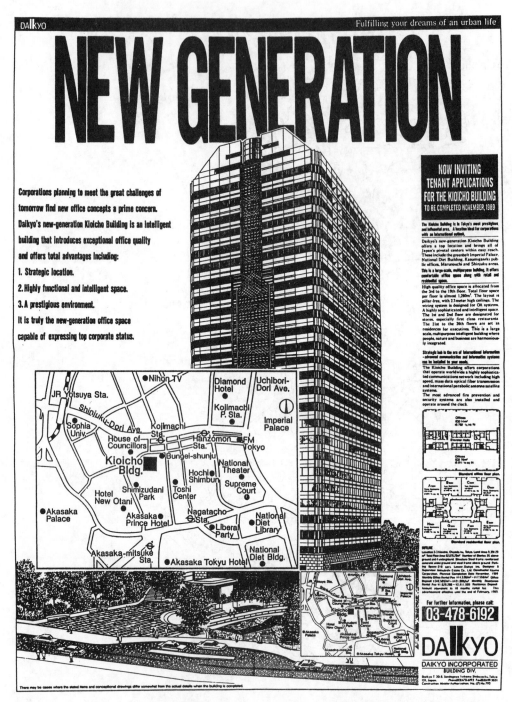

Fig. 7.3 Advertisement for the Kioicho Building, with location map enlarged (*The Japan Times*, 17 January 1989)

as 60 kilometres from Tokyo with nearly two hours' travel time. In Tokyo, the household would have had to spend more than ten times its annual income for a similar home. In 1987, the standard house in Tokyo had a floor area of 123 square metres on a site of 102.5 square metres and cost ¥85 million ($607 000); this translated into monthly payments of ¥557 607 ($3900) for a 25-year mortgage, or 123 per cent of the household's monthly salary.[9]

In 1989, for the first time land prices in Tokyo remained nearly stable, but continued to rise even more rapidly in Osaka and Nagoya. In 1990 they picked up again in Tokyo, though at a considerably lesser rate than in the 1980s. In 1991 and 1992 they fell again by between 30 and 40 per cent. This was enough to lead to the near failure of a number of Tokyo real estate firms and spectacular rescue operations by banks. It is said that half of the approximately one thousand major real estate companies in Tokyo are in difficulty. The Finance Ministry urgently advised banks to restrict loans to real-estate customers. At the Tokyo stock market, in 1990 real estate stocks went down by 60 per cent. It has been estimated that a decline of land prices by 30 per cent is equivalent to destroying assets equivalent to 25 per cent of Japan's annual GNP. In early 1993, 161 credit institutions, under the direction of the Finance Ministry, established a joint venture, the Cooperative Credit Purchasing Company (CCPC) to take over ailing real estate credits.

The consequences for recent home buyers are less publicised. Their mortgage payments carry on while the value of their property is dwindling away. Nor are prospective buyers better off. Although land and house prices have been declining, they are still twice as high as in the mid-1980s, and twenty times higher than in New York, London or Paris and, with increasing interest rates, still beyond the reach of the majority of households. Many families in Tokyo have given up the dream of owning a house and have turned to vigorous buying of consumer goods, according to the 1988 White Paper on National Life by the Economic Planning Agency. The recent 'gourmet boom' in basement floors of department stores has also been related to the purchasing power of frustrated would-be home owners. Young people, singles or newly-weds move into very modest flats in run-down inner city apartment buildings. The majority, however, value home-ownership highly. In a survey conducted in 1988, when asked whether they preferred a detached house requiring long commuting time or a flat with a short commuting time, 54 per cent said they preferred the detached house.

This choice behaviour is also one factor behind the extreme degree of decentralisation of population in the Tokyo metropolitan area. That population is indeed extremely decentralised is shown in Table 7.1, which has been adopted from Kakumoto.[10] Three metropolitan areas of (in 1980) similar size were compared: Tokyo, New York and Paris. Each city was subdivided into a core and an inner-ring zone in an attempt to make the subdivisions as similar as possible. It is immediately observable that the core of Tokyo had many more workplaces and much less population than the cores of the two other cities. Nine out of ten employees working in the core were commuters. In New York only 71, and in Paris only 53 per cent of all core employees lived outside the core. More than half of the commuters in Tokyo were long-distance commuters, i.e. they lived outside the inner ring. The same proportion was 32 per cent for New York and 38 per cent for Paris.

Table 7.1 *Comparison of Tokyo, New York and Paris: area, population, employment, and commuting*

		Core*	Inner ring	Total[†]
Tokyo (1980)	Area (km²)	59	533	592
	Population[‡]	638	7669	8352
	Employment[‡]	2406	3828	6234
	Commuters[‡]	2111	1144	3255
New York (1980)	Area (km²)	57	725	782
	Population[‡]	1428	5644	7072
	Employment[‡]	1949	1351	3300
	Commuters[‡]	1379	291	1670
Paris (1975)	Area (km²)	105	656	761
	Population[‡]	2300	3977	6277
	Employment[‡]	1918	1640	3558
	Commuters[‡]	1016	500	1516

*Tokyo: Chiyoda, Chuo, Minato, Shinjuku; New York: Manhattan; Paris: City of Paris.
[†]Tokyo: Tokyo (23 wards); New York: New York City; Paris: Paris, Seine-St Denis, Val-de-Marne and Hauts-de-Seine.
[‡]in 1000s.
Source: Ohta, K., 'The Spatial Structure and Transportation System of the Tokyo Metropolitan Region', *The Wheel Extended*, 18, 1989, pp. 43–49.

If one looks at the area outside the inner ring, one is surprised by the scattered pattern of development. Between 15 and 30 kilometres from central Tokyo, one can frequently find clusters of houses surrounded by small fields still in agricultural use, and the proportion of non-developed land becomes larger as one gets farther out.[11] Even in some of the outer wards of Tokyo such as Nerima a surprisingly large share of the total area is still used for scattered agriculture.[12] Yet despite this seemingly easily developable land, which is frequently in close proximity to rail stations, residential development occurs at the same time in areas much more distant from Tokyo. Because of this continuing urban sprawl, decentralisation of population in the Tokyo metropolitan area is much greater than in comparable cities.

The reasons for this are also related to high land prices. Agricultural land ownership in Japan is fragmented—a heritage from the land reform after the Second World War—and protected, as long as the land is used for agriculture. Moreover, it is taxed as low-value agricultural land instead of by its much higher market value as residential land. Even in areas not zoned as residential, frequent zoning changes in the past have nourished the expectation that eventually the land will become residential. All this makes it profitable for small landlords to sell as little land as possible and to hoard the rest in the expectation that suburban land prices in the long run will continue to rise. It follows that it is not lack of land that is at the core of high land prices, but unavailability of existing land.

It has also been argued that the low-density urban-rural mixture now characterising

Tokyo's suburbs may be environmentally and socially more acceptable than many forms of crowded city housing or mono-functional suburban subdivisions.[13] These ideas deserve serious consideration. However, this model would require a consistent and effective policy of decentralisation of employment.

Employment in Tokyo, however, is highly concentrated in the core, and this concentration is increasing due to the still growing importance of Tokyo as a financial centre. Why foreign and domestic companies insist on a location on a few square kilometres of central Tokyo in a time of computer networks and telecommunications remains 'a riddle wrapped in a mystery inside an enigma' (Winston Churchill), but is aptly summarised in the advertisement for the Kioicho Building, where the little map shows what the text calls a 'strategic location and prestigious environment': National Diet, Liberal Democratic Party, House of Councillors, and the Hotel New Otani and the expensive restaurants in Akasaka where the receptions and luncheons take place which are so important for business. As long as they are important, the concentration of office space in central Tokyo is not likely to be reduced.

The problem is that each new office building is likely to displace more of the small houses still existing in central Tokyo, and that their residents, willingly or not, have to become commuters. If trends continue, the urban area will expand further even beyond the 50-kilometre radius around central Tokyo.

A Distorted Land Market

It is by no means natural that urban land is in private property. In the Middle Ages in many cities in Europe, all land was public and was only given away to individual citizens on a leasehold basis, say for 99 years. From the point of view of urban planning, the land market has only one function: to bring about the most efficient allocation of urban land.

Land prices are the capitalised revenue that can be derived from a piece of land by economic activity. If demand for land is higher than supply, scarcity rents appear to match demand and supply. In a price-quantity diagram, the demand curve slopes downward, i.e. demand decreases if prices go up. The supply curve slopes upward, i.e. if prices go up, so does supply. Market clearing occurs at the quantity and price where demand equals supply. These simple mechanisms become distorted if there is land speculation. Land speculators are firms or individuals who buy land not to use it but to resell it for a profit. For large-scale land speculation to occur, two conditions must prevail: the availability of money and the expectation of rising land prices.

Both conditions were ideally met in the Tokyo metropolitan region until recently. Since the Plaza Accord in 1985 and before the increases of the prime rate by the Bank of Japan after 1988 and again today, Japan has been a country with very low interest rates and large amounts of floating money looking for investment opportunities and with unbroken confidence in the great future of the Japanese economy and the continued growth of Tokyo. Many firms and private investors therefore turned to the domestic real estate market as an attractive alternative to investment abroad or in Japanese stocks.

These investors are not interested in the revenues from lease or rent but in the far higher profits from reselling buildings or land at higher prices.

The problem is that land speculation disrupts the connection between land prices and land revenues. Once land prices reach a certain level, the return on land investment can no longer be generated from rent or lease income, but only from speculative gains. From then on, there is in principle no limit on the speculative cycle. Even worse, speculative investors develop a bidding behaviour which under normal market conditions would be considered perverse: they prefer objects that promise to increase in price in the near future, and these tend to be those that have shown price increases in the recent past. In other words, they buy expensive rather than cheap and so accelerate the land price escalation.

Another deviation from 'normal' market behaviour is mentioned by several authors.[14] The small landowners already referred to have an emotional relationship with their land and sell only if they need money for building a house or for the wedding of a daughter or the education of a son. That implies that they do not behave as profit maximisers but target a certain sum of money, and under a regime of rising prices, sell *less* if market prices rise.

In a land market in which, with rising prices, demand increases and supply decreases, the pressure on untapped land reserves must become excessive. This was until recently especially felt by the still existing small land and house owners in the inner Tokyo wards. It is well known that they were harassed almost daily to sell by representatives of banks or real estate firms or by 'land sharks' frequently associated with the *yakuza*.[15] Sooner or later, many of them yielded to this pressure or to the seduction of a large sum of money. But even if they resisted until their death, the inheritance tax forced their children to sell the house, and so opened the way for its demolition, thus helping to destroy another part of the small-scale variety of Tokyo's inner city neighbourhoods.

In either case, population became more decentralised and commuting increased. The costs of this are still today being carried partly by the public in the form of construction costs and subsidies for transport infrastructure, partly by employers in the form of commuting allowances, and partly by commuters in the form of long commuting times. If the causal analysis relating decentralisation and long commuting times to high land prices is correct, this result contains a large degree of unfairness, because high land prices benefit only a relatively small number of land sellers, whereas the much larger number of land users continue to pay throughout their lifetime through a heavy financial burden and long commuting times.

Urban Structure and Society

The spatial organisation of cities fundamentally determines the life and life opportunities of the people who live in them. At the same time, this organisation is not random but the result of economically and culturally determined decisions about the allocation of space. It can be hypothesised that the present Japanese city, too, including its distorted land market, is not accidental but both an outcome and an essential element of the organisation of present Japanese society. If this hypothesis is true, it has implications for the likely success of policy alternatives. In the following section, a few conjectures on the relationship between city structure and society in Japan based on personal observations and referring to studies such as Nakane,[16] Hijiya-Kirschnereit[17] and Neuss-Kaneko[18] are proposed. Figure 7.4 is an attempt to visualise this relationship in an admittedly highly reductionist diagram.

The point of departure is provided by the long travel times and small dwellings. The long commuting times without doubt determine the rhythm of life of the majority of white-collar workers in large cities in Japan. In conjunction with the (compared with other countries), long working hours, they leave little margin for self-determined activities.

The result is the typical lifestyle of the male Tokyo *salariman,* who leaves his home early and returns home towards midnight. Even his after-work free time is spent more often with colleagues or customers than with his wife or children. His after-work social contacts take place near his workplace and more often than not are off-limits for his wife, irrespective of the fact that it would be too far for her to come into the city. On the other hand, his home would be too far away to invite his friends or acquaintances there.

Besides, in many cases the flat would be too small. The smallness of the flat is another

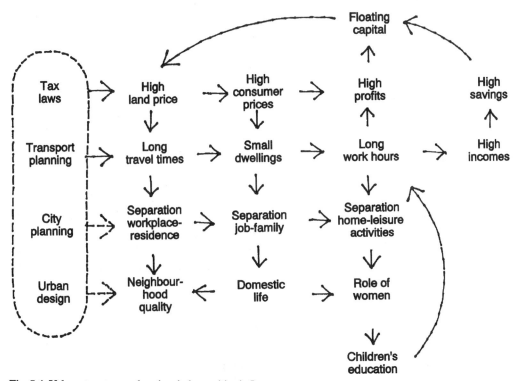

Fig. 7.4 Urban structure and society in large cities in Japan

reason for the late return of the husband; he might be in the way. Of course, the small flat is not the principal reason for his long working hours, but certainly contributes to his willingness to stay late in the office and demonstrate his relentless identification with his company.

This is good for the family income but also good for the company, because the hard work of its employees is the key to its success. High salaries imply high consumer prices, but these are also a result of high land prices, which in Tokyo constitute a substantial share of total product costs. High consumer prices, in turn, restrict the housing budget of households and so contribute to the small size of the dwellings. High company profits and the traditionally high savings rate are the basis for the large amount of floating capital searching for investment opportunities, the real source of land speculation and hence exaggerated land prices.

The extreme spatial separation of workplaces and residences, and hence of job and family, essentially determines the situation of the wife. As, after her marriage, she has in most cases given up her job, she is confined to the household. As the husband is absent during the day, women have to take care of neighbourhood problems, but given the lack of a counterpart on the side of the local administration, improvements are not easily achieved. The main responsibility of the married Japanese woman is the education of her children. Without an alternative to an education system geared to conformism rather than to self-determination, she inevitably educates her children after the model of the absent father, and so lays the foundation for the perpetuation of the system.

This system of interlocking mechanisms was not planned or deliberately designed; it has developed historically over a long time and has displayed a surprising degree of stability. The important fact is that it seamlessly blends into the all-encompassing orientation of present Japanese society, the primary objective of which continues to be long-term economic expansion. The spatial organisation of the large Japanese city is ideally suited to maintaining the readiness of the population for hard work and to prevent its degeneration into the individualism and hedonism of Western leisure societies.

If this hypothesis is only partially correct, it is easy to understand why all attempts to reform the current practice of urban land markets have not achieved very much. The politicians and bureaucrats, who personally do not suffer under high land prices (and frequently as landowners benefit from them), have no reason to pursue the matter with urgency. The real victims, the families, who are deprived of the right to a dwelling conforming to the affluence of their country, and the workers, who spend a disproportionate amount of their best years in crowded commuter trains, have been trained to sacrifice without questioning the need for their suffering and will continue to do so as long as the system offers them sufficient surrogates in the form of consumer goods, travel and career opportunities.

The Role of Urban Planning

Urban planning in Tokyo is by no means without power to halt or at least slow down the displacement of inner city residential neighbourhoods by commercial and office developments. Japan's planning legislation is largely modelled after the German *Bauleitplanung*, a two-tier system of local plans consisting of a more general preparatory land use plan (*Flächennutzungsplan*) and a more specific building plan (*Bebauungsplan*). The Japanese District Planning Law of 1980 is in effect a Japanese version of the *Bebauungsplan*.[19] In addition, as early as in 1919, the first Japanese urban planning law introduced a system of land readjustment modelled after the German *Umlegung*, including effective provisions for land expropriation in cases of eminent domain, i.e. the need to acquire land for public purposes. In summary, Japan's planning legislation has all the instruments necessary for effectively controlling and guiding the physical development of a city. Unfortunately, however, they are not used.

There are several reasons for this. First, because of high land prices, it is almost impossible to buy the land required for public infrastructure or land readjustment projects, in particular where individual landowners use all legal possibilities to delay a sale in the expectation of further land price increases.

Second, the planning departments of Japanese cities are not capable of fully using the control privileges afforded to them by the law. For instance, to apply effectively the District Planning Law, each ward of Tokyo would have to have hundreds of skilled planning officers, who do not, however, exist. Therefore, today only a fraction of all urban developments are subject to any form of planning coordination or control.

A third, and probably most important, reason is that there is no public demand for such planning coordination or control. The same Japanese who, when travelling in Europe, admire the Place Vendôme, the Piazza di Spagna or the market square of Rothenburg, do not seem to see any reason why at home a public authority should interfere in the economic exploitation of urban land by an individual owner—although this may be changing with more and more Japanese spending their holidays abroad.

The result is the well-known clutter of disparate structures of different height, shape, orientation, and purpose found all over Tokyo—picturesque at best but in most cases simply uneconomical, impractical and unsightly. The result is the 'pencil buildings', the unlit courtyards, the obstructed windows and balconies, the ubiquitous waste bins, parking lots, billboards and electricity wiring characteristic of the Japanese city-scape.

There are defenders of all this who celebrate it as the 'hidden order' of Tokyo[20] or admire the 'subtle transition between private and public spaces' in Japanese cities.[21] However, this typical architects' jargon only testifies to a remarkable lack of sensitivity for the simple requirements of a harmonious and practical living environment. It is true that nowhere other than in Japan do architects enjoy so much freedom to express their ideas. Indeed, in Tokyo there are innumerable examples of exciting, sophisticated and beautiful modern office buildings and houses, which would probably have no chance to pass the scrutiny of, say, a German planning permit official. Unfortunately, they are difficult to find among the much more frequent examples of thoroughly commercialised cheap or bombastic architectural staple food found everywhere.

Under these circumstances it is almost a miracle that so many of the old residential neighbourhoods still exist. Their human scale and sophisticated layout built on mutual consideration, respect and cooperation, their economical use of urban space and efficient methods of car restraint make them examples worth studying for Western planners. Unfortunately, they are more and more difficult to find. It seems that during the rapid urbanisation process, the harmony and economy of the traditional Japanese house, which once stimulated the *avant-garde* of the modern movement of world architecture, such as Frank Lloyd Wright, Mies van der Rohe or Walter Gropius, has largely been forgotten. The rediscovery and revitalisation of these qualities could be a challenging task for modern affluent Japan.

Policy Alternatives

The Metropolitan Government expects the population of Tokyo to grow to 12.3 million in the year 2005, 3.7 per cent more than in 1985. However, including commuters into Tokyo from outside the metropolitan boundaries, the city's day-time population will reach 14.8 million, 5.6 per cent more than in 1985. That means that the 'commuter gap' between the day-time and night-time populations will increase from 2.18 million in 1985 to 2.52 million in 2005. Of the inbound people, 1.46 million will be coming to the four central wards of Tokyo (see Table 7.1), 23 per cent more than in 1980. Moreover, not only is it predicted that there will be 500 000 new residents who will need housing, but also that the 11.8 million already living in Tokyo will want to improve their housing conditions as Japanese society becomes more affluent. The additional housing demand thus generated will put enormous pressure on the land market and stimulate further land price increases.

There have been numerous proposals on how to cope with the problem of high land prices and long commuting times. They can be roughly classified into eight groups.

POLICIES TO DECENTRALISE EMPLOYMENT

If the concentration of jobs in the inner wards of Tokyo is the main cause behind the spatial separation of employment and population in the Tokyo metropolitan area, policies to decentralise employment would be the most rational solution to the city's problems. There is in fact a long tradition of such policies. After the 1923 earthquake, the first major industrial plants were relocated from inner city locations to newly created industrial areas along Tokyo Bay, and this was continued in the post-war reconstruction period, partly using land reclaimed from the Bay (see below). Decentralisation of office activities is proceeding more slowly. Only during the 1980s have excessive land prices in central Tokyo spurred the development of secondary office centres throughout the region, many of them waterfront developments around Tokyo Bay. However, a recent slump in demand for office space has again retarded the process. The new office and exhibition centre, Makuhari, on the east side of Tokyo Bay near Chiba, for instance, is reported to suffer from lack of tenants at this remote location. The plans for a decentralised National Capital Region, just like the government's periodically renewed pledge to move the national government out of Tokyo, conflict with its stated goal of making Tokyo a 'global city' and the related tendency of high-level office functions to concentrate in central Tokyo, and therefore are not likely to become effective before well into the next century.

POLICIES TO CREATE NEW LAND

These policies aim at increasing the supply of land by creating new land underground, on the water, or in the air. The most substantial land gains are expected from land reclamations from Tokyo Bay. In the northern part of the Bay, housing for 60 000 people and workplaces for 110 000 people are planned on several artificial islands. More than a hundred other schemes have been proposed. These projects have one thing in common: because of their high construction costs, their financing schemes work only under the prospect that the land they create can be sold after completion at market prices. So these projects cannot be expected to bring land prices down, even though they may take some pressure from central Tokyo. The effect on commuting time depends on the number of residences that will eventually exist in the new developments.

POLICIES TO MOBILISE UNTAPPED LAND SUPPLY

These policies aim at making it less attractive for landowners to hold vacant land. The greatest impact is expected from abolishing the tax privilege of farming landowners in suburban areas.[22] If the property tax on suburban agricultural land could be made equal to that on residential land, most farmers would be forced to sell or develop their land. Depending on the amount of supply released, land prices should go down. This would lead to shorter commuting times. However, the new property law which went into effect in 1992, has again failed to solve this problem as it retains the privileges of suburban farmers. The effects of an increase in the tax on capital gains from land sales are difficult to predict. In the case of speculative land transactions, the effect on price formation is likely to be minimal. Other proposals include an increase in the city planning tax or compulsory inclusion in land readjustment schemes.[23] Increasing the city planning tax would have a similar effect as the property tax, except that it would also increase the tax load of residential lots. Land readjustment actually reduces the amount of residential land, although the new lots have a higher use-value and may carry more dwellings, so commuting times would decrease. Land prices are likely to go up.

POLICIES TO INCREASE HOUSING SUPPLY

One way to protect households from the financial burden of high land prices and rents is to subsidise housing construction. In the Tokyo metropolitan area there have been extensive housing projects both by the Japan Housing Corporation and by local government. Being in general high-rise developments, these projects have helped to fight urban sprawl. However, as land for them had to be bought at market prices, they have not contributed to a reduction of land prices. Because of high land prices, the housing projects of the Japan Housing Corporation in particular have tended to be at distant locations and have thus effectively contributed to the increase in commuting times.

POLICIES TO SUBSIDISE HOUSING DEMAND

Besides subsidising housing projects, housing subsidies can be given to households in the form of housing loans or allowances. Housing loans from public loan corporations have lower interest rates than private bank loans, but not everybody is eligible. With rising land prices, not only has the number of households finding themselves in debt grown considerably, but the share of their income required for monthly instalments and the duration of repayment have also increased.[24] Housing loans create demand at market price, and hence stimulate land price development. Many large corporations, in particular foreign firms, are giving housing allowances to their employees to make it possible for them to live in Tokyo. Housing allowances frequently exceed salaries. Clearly, they create demand in the high-price sectors stimulating rent increases. In fact a special market for luxury apartments and houses has developed in the south-western suburbs of Tokyo to cater for the growing number of such households.

POLICIES TO SUBSIDISE COMMUTING

Practically all firms subsidise the commuting expenses of their employees through commuting allowances. While it is fair that at least the financial burden of long commuting is taken from commuters, it has the undesirable effect that, when choosing a residence, they consider only travel time. If they had to pay for commuting from the same budget as for housing, many households would probably opt for a closer but smaller house. The government supports this system of wrong incentives by tax-exempting expenditures for commuting allowances by employers up to a limit of ¥50 000 per month, good for 100 kilometres of commuting. To abolish the tax exemption of commuting allowances would be a first but unpopular move to discourage long commuting. Another certainly even more unpopular policy would be to raise public transit fares. While this would be highly effective in reducing average commuting distances, it would do so at the expense of those who are the least to blame for the long commute.

POLICIES TO REDUCE COMMUTING TIME

The most direct way to reduce long commuting times is to provide faster transport. On existing commuter rail lines this can be achieved through higher train speeds, shorter stops and more frequent trains. In fact all of these measures have been extensively applied to produce the impressive efficiency of the public transportation system in Tokyo. Therefore, dramatic further reductions in door-to-door journey times are not likely. The greatest impacts will occur where entirely new lines open up land at the periphery of the metropolitan area for commuting. The irony is that such a transport improvement, under the conditions of a speculative land market, may contribute to its extension. With an upward sloping demand curve, the additional land supply does not help to bring land prices down; instead, through the land price increase along the line, it forces many households to move farther out. The benefits of the new line largely go to developers and landowners, while the households, through higher land prices and longer commuting times, are in a worse situation than before. A similar phenomenon in the Munich metropolitan area was described by Kreibich.[25]

POLICIES TO RECLAIM TRANSPORT COSTS

These policies were originally discussed to open up new channels of financing transport infrastructure in the face of rising construction costs and land prices using the principle of value capture.[26] However, some of these measures also serve to distribute the benefits and burdens of transport improvements in a more equitable way between landowners and land users. If, for instance, landowners along a new rail line are charged a higher property tax in proportion to the increase in price of their property due to the new line, a fairer distribution of benefits would result. Apart from the difficulties of objectively imputing the benefits to individual lots, the problem is that nothing can prevent landowners passing these extra costs on to their tenants or buyers, in which case the value capture measure would contribute to justifying further land price increases. A positive effect would result in the case of speculative land hoarding, as it would make it more expensive to withhold vacant land from the market.

COMPARISON OF POLICIES

Summarising the policies reviewed so far, it is possible to give an overview of their most likely impacts (see Table 7.2).

Probably the most rational solution to Tokyo's urban problems would be a consistent policy of decentralisation of employment. However, this conflicts with the stated goal of making Tokyo a 'global city'. There are a number of policies which might mobilise suburban land presently withheld from the market, but only few policies in which the additional supply would also lead to reductions in land prices. Of these, raising agricultural land taxation to the level of residential land, thus creating a land holding tax, would probably be the most successful.

All sorts of financial assistance to households, be it in the form of loans or allowances, improve their housing situation, but at the same time create demand at market

Table 7.2 *Impacts of policies on the land market and commuting in Tokyo*

Policy		Likely impact on:		
	Land supply	Land prices	Commuting time
(1) Job decentralisation		− −	− −
(2) Land reclamation	+ +	−	−
(3) Land holding tax	+ + +	− −	− − −
Capital gains tax		−	
City planning tax	+ +	−	−
Land readjustment	+	+	−
(4) Public housing			+
(5) Housing loans		+	
Housing allowances		+ +	
(6) Commuting allowances			+ +
Fare increases			− −
(7) Faster trains		+	−
New lines	+ +	+	+ +
(8) Value captures	+	+	

Legend: +/++/+++ small/medium/large increase.
       −/−−/−−− small/medium/large decrease.

conditions and thus reinforce high land prices and long commuting. To increase public transport fares would reduce commuting times, but at unacceptable social costs. Faster trains would do the same, but would induce land price increases likely to outweigh that benefit. Transport investments will make commuting faster, but may contribute to further land price increases, even where they make new land supply at the periphery of the urban area accessible. In that case, they may even make commuting times longer.

In short, besides decentralisation of employment and the land holding tax, there is no single policy that would achieve the two objectives of lower land prices and shorter commuting times without negative side effects. These two policies, however, seem to be the most difficult to implement because they collide with vested political interests.

Conclusions

It has been shown that the extreme decentralisation of population in the Tokyo metropolitan area is a consequence of high land prices and fragmented land ownership. These exaggerated land prices, however, are less the result of land scarcity than of large-scale speculation and withholding of land due to imbalances in the property tax system. It has also been shown that transport investments, under the conditions of a speculative land market, may contribute to increasing land prices and even commuting times. The review of policies addressing the two objectives of reducing land prices and commuting times showed that decentralisation of employment and increasing the property tax, making withholding of agricultural land in suburban areas more expensive, would be most effective.

However, it was also suggested that the present spatial organisation of large Japanese cities, including high land prices, small dwellings and long commuting times, are elements of a coherent system, the functioning of which has been an important precondition for the economic success of Japan. If one essential element of this system is changed, the whole system may be transformed. It has been demonstrated that the urban land market is such a key element.

There are two ways to draw conclusions out of this. The first would be that the problems of Tokyo are not genuinely urban problems but have their cause in the one-dimensional growth orientation of Japanese society, and so cannot be solved by urban planning at all. If this view is correct, only a thorough transformation of the financial and economic system of the country can put an end to the destructive impacts of land speculation on the city. An alternative view would hold that reform policy in Japan would be in the first place urban policy, and that changing the Japanese city would trigger a long-term process of redirection of societal goals. From a Western perspective, the example of Tokyo can be used to help fight similar harmful tendencies now already in full force in New York and Los Angeles, London and Paris, but also beginning to appear in lesser cities such as San Francisco and Boston, Brussels, Madrid, Munich or Berlin.

The recent developments in the Tokyo land market have demonstrated the ability of modern Japanese society to absorb shocks while deflecting major system transformation. Since the 1990 peak, land prices in Tokyo declined by between 30 and 40 per cent through to the end of 1993. However, all predictions that the bursting of the land price bubble would result in a sudden collapse have so far been proved wrong. While land prices have declined and many financial institutions and developers have suffered deep losses, the concerted actions of government and the financial sector have prevented a broader crash.

Yet, it remains to be seen for how long this rearguard effort can be sustained. In the history of urban land booms, there has not been a single case in which exaggerated land prices have been gracefully reduced to a *normal* level. In all cases, an eventual collapse occurred, with disastrous consequences such as failed banks, lost investments, and crippled communities.[27] As and when this happens in the Tokyo land market, the adjustment process will not be pleasant. Though the main victims will be the big speculators, many thousands of small buyers will find themselves in debt for the rest of their lives for property worth only a fraction of what they bought it for. For urban planning, this situation will be both a relief and a new challenge. On the one hand, it will be possible again to acquire land for badly needed infrastructure. On the other hand, planning authorities may be faced with demands for more spacious housing hitherto artificially constrained by the high costs of land—a demand that, if satisfied, would fundamentally change the Japanese way of life.

NOTES AND REFERENCES

1 Seidensticker, E., *Low City, High City*, Tokyo, Charles E. Tuttle, 1983.

2 Matsuba, K., Jinnai, H. and Fujimori, T., 'A Historical Perspective of Tokyo', *The Wheel Extended*, **18**, 1989, pp. 3–9.

3 Cassim, M. and Negoro, M., 'Lebensformen in Tokyo' ['Lifestyles in Tokyo'], in Herold, R. (ed.), *Wohnen in Japan* [*Housing in Japan*], Berlin, E. Schmidt Verlag, 1985, pp. 231–50.

4 Hanayama, Y., *Land Markets and Land Policy in a Metropolitan Area: A Case Study of Tokyo*, Boston, Oelgeschlager, Gunn & Hain, 1986.

5 Ibid.

6 Wegener, M. and Shibasaki, R., 'Urban and Regional Planning in Japan and West Germany: A Comparison' in *Regional and Urban Planning and Geographical Information Systems*, Tokyo, Department of Civil Engineering, University of Tokyo, 1989, pp. 1–14.

7 Ohta, K., 'The Spatial Structure and Transportation System of the Tokyo Metropolitan Region', *The Wheel Extended*, **18**, 1989, pp. 43–49.

8 Hasegawa, T., Tanaka, K. and Iwamatsu, S., 'Symposium on Land Problems', *Observations*, **1**, 1988, pp. 1–15.

9 Hayakawa, K. and Hirayama, Y., 'The Impact of the *minkatsu* Policy on Japanese Housing and Land Use', *Environment and Planning D: Society and Space*, **9**, 1990, pp. 151–64.

10 Ohta, op. cit.

11 Hebbert, M., 'Urban Sprawl and Planning Failure: Some Reflections on the Japanese Case' in Masser, I. (ed.), *Japanese Urban Planning: Some British Perspectives*, Sheffield,

Department of Town and Regional Planning, University of Sheffield, 1985, pp. 29–53.

12 Hanayama, op. cit.

13 Hebbert, op. cit.

14 Hanayama, op. cit. and Flüchter, W. and Wijers, P. J., 'Bodenpreisprobleme im Ballungsraum Tokyo' ['Land Price Problems in the Tokyo Agglomeration'], *Geographische Rundschau*, 42, 1990, pp. 196–207.

15 Hayakawa and Hirayama, op. cit.

16 Nakane, C., *Japanese Society*, Berkeley, CA, University of California Press, 1970.

17 Hijiya-Kirschnereit, I., *Das Ende der Exotik* [*The End of Exoticism*], Frankfurt, Suhrkamp Verlag, 1988.

18 Neuss-Kaneko, M., *Familie und Gesellschaft in Japan* [*Family and Society in Japan*], Munich, C. H. Beck, 1990.

19 Wegener and Shibasaki, op. cit.

20 Ashihara, Y., *The Hidden Order. Tokyo through the Twentieth Century*, Tokyo/New York, Kodansha International, 1989.

21 Greenbie, B. G., *Space and Spirit in Modern Japan*, New Haven/London, Yale University Press, 1988.

22 Hanayama, op. cit.

23 Ibid.

24 Shitara, K. and Sugimoto, T., 'Die wirtschaftlichen Grundlagen des Wohnens' ['The Economic Foundations of Housing'] in Herold, R. (ed.), *Wohnen in Japan* [*Housing in Japan*], Berlin, E. Schmidt Verlag, 1985, pp. 129–55.

25 Kreibich, V., 'The Successful Transportation System and the Regional Planning Problem', *Transportation*, 7, 1978, pp. 137–45.

26 Hayashi, Y., 'Issues in Financing Urban Rail Transit Projects and Value Captures', *Transportation Research A*, 23A, 1989, pp. 35–44.

27 Meier, R. L., 'The Japanese Land Super-Bubble' (unpublished working paper), Berkeley, CA, University of California at Berkeley, 1989.

Chapter 8

The Institutional Context of Japanese Planning: Professional Associations and Planning Education

IAN MASSER and TAKAHIRO YORISAKI

A constantly recurring theme in discussions of Japanese urban planning is the extent to which the institutional context governing planning differs from Western models. It is recognised that planning in Japan is the product of very different historical and cultural traditions from those of Western Europe and North America, and it is also clear that Japan has experienced economic growth and urbanisation over the last forty years which have no parallel in the developed economies of the West, but relatively little is known about the impact that these and other factors have had on the development of urban planning practice.

This chapter explores some aspects of the institutional context which underlies Japanese urban planning, with particular reference to their impact on the nature of the professional association that represents the interests of planners, the City Planning Institute of Japan and on the provision of planning education. The choice of professional associations and education reflects the interest in these issues shown by British and American scholars in recent years. In both countries the development of professional associations and associated training programmes has been an important feature of the institutional context of twentieth-century industrial capitalist society. Under these circumstances, as Friedson points out:

> Occupations seeking a secure and privileged place in the economy of these countries could do no more than seek State support for an exclusionary shelter in the open market where they had to compete with rival occupations. They had to organise their own training and credentialling institutions, since the State played a passive role in such affairs.[1]

The development of the town planning profession in Britain is a particularly good example of such developments. It can be regarded both as a product of the institutional context which gave rise to the emergence of planning as a predominantly local government activity, and also as a force in its own right which has had a marked impact on the evolution of urban planning practice through the control that the professional association, the Royal Town Planning Institute, has exercised over the provision of planning education. In Healey's view:

The planning profession has probably been at its most effective in expanding the educational provision for planners and converting training into a graduate form. However, by pursuing a narrowly defined generalist curriculum for planning training, and by ensuring that planning education occurred in distinct planning schools, professionalisation has tended to isolate the knowledge base for planning from the built environment and social science disciplines which should feed it.[2]

With these considerations in mind, this chapter examines the activities of the City Planning Institute of Japan, and the provision of planning education in Japan in relation to the historical and cultural context within which planning operates in that country. At each stage in the discussion, the findings of the analysis of Japanese experience are compared with those of Britain. In this way, the paper not only draws attention to some distinctive features of Japanese urban planning practice, but also highlights some of the unique qualities of British planning.

The discussion is divided into two main parts. The first of these describes some of the main features of the Japanese urban planning system, while the second considers the activities of the City Planning Institute of Japan and the provision of planning education. At the end of each of these parts, there is a comparative evaluation of Japanese experience in relation to that of Britain. The concluding section of the chapter summarises the main findings of the analysis and identifies some potentially fruitful areas for further research.

Urban Planning Practice in Japan

THE EVOLUTION OF JAPANESE PLANNING

At the time of the Meiji restoration in 1868, Japan was essentially an agricultural society. In the half century that followed the restoration, the Meiji government sought to create 'a wealthy nation and a strong army' (*fokuku kyohei*) based on institutions derived from Western models, and the Imperial capital was moved from Kyoto to Tokyo. The central portions of the new capital were laid out on similar lines to those of the major cities of the West.[3] With this in mind, the first piece of urban planning legislation in Japan, the Tokyo City Improvement Ordinance, was enacted in 1888.

From the turn of the century, the pace of industrialisation and urbanisation began to accelerate in Japan. By the end of the First World War, public concern about conditions in the new industrial areas resulted in the City Planning Act and the Urban Building Act of 1919. The former introduced a fairly comprehensive planning system which combined traditional city improvement programmes with new techniques such as zoning, building line control and land consolidation.[4] In the first instance, this Act applied only to six urban areas, but its provisions were subsequently extended to cover the whole country. The City Planning Act of 1919 remained the central component of Japanese planning legislation until it was superseded by the 1968 City Planning Act.

Alongside these developments, the Japanese government also introduced land readjustment procedures based on German models to facilitate the consolidation of land holdings and the provision of infrastructure in the Arable Land Consolidation Act of 1899.[5] The application of these techniques to urban land management problems was given a boost by the Great Kanto Earthquake of 1923. This destroyed large parts of Tokyo and Yokohama and necessitated a large-scale urban reconstruction programme.

During the Second World War, Japan's economy was almost completely destroyed and its cities devastated by intensive bombing. In the immediate post-war period under the American occupation, economic revival and urban reconstruction were given the highest priority. The need for reconstruction on a massive scale gave another boost to the application of land readjustment methods. In Nagoya, for example, a quarter of the entire urban stock was flattened by bombing, and the population of 1 600 000 reduced to less than half. To deal with these circumstances, a massive project was launched which involved the replanning of 3450 hectares of inner city land. This involved negotiations with 40 000 landowners and took until 1981 to be completed.[6]

Previous legislation relating to land readjustment was consolidated and extended by the 1954 Land Readjustment Act so that government subsidies were made available to assist in the preparation and implementation of projects. During the post-war period, schemes utilising these procedures became the dominant mode of urban land development in Japan, accounting for 30 per cent of all land in Japan's Densely Inhabited Districts in 1980.[7] In this year alone, it has been estimated that land readjustment schemes accounted for 43 per cent of all land brought into urban use.[8]

Since the Second World War, Japan has experienced a period of sustained economic growth which has been accompanied by urbanisation on a massive scale. The population living in urban areas nearly trebled between 1950 and 1980 from 27 to 80 million, and the proportion of urban dwellers in the population as a whole rose from 32 to 68 per cent during this period.[9] Urbanisation and urban growth in Japan has been particularly concentrated in the three main urban agglomerations centred on Tokyo, Osaka-Kobe and Nagoya respectively. In 1980, these three areas alone accounted for nearly a third of Japan's population.[10]

At the national level, urban planning became the responsibility of the Ministry of Construction (MOC), which was established in 1948. In 1954, the National Land Development Act laid the foundations for national urban policy with a view to securing balanced development between different regions. This culminated in the approval of the first of a series of National Comprehensive Development Plans in 1962 which paralleled the National Economic Plans formulated by the Economic Planning Ministry.

The basic framework for urban planning at the local level in Japan at the present time is laid down by the 1968 City Planning Act. This devolved plan-making powers to the prefectural and municipal levels and established a hierarchy of municipal (metropolitan), prefectural and national plans. The central feature of this Act is the sub-division of city planning areas into Urbanisation Promotion Areas (UPAs) and Urbanisation Control Areas (UCAs) to stimulate and restrict development respectively. By 1984, the provisions of the 1968 Act had been applied in 349 city planning areas involving 874 municipalities, accounting for three-quarters of the total population.[11] In 324 of these, a division into UPAs covered a quarter of the total land area involved, with the other three-quarters allocated to UCAs.[12]

COMPARATIVE EVALUATION

From this brief description of the legislative framework of Japanese planning, it can be seen that Japan has been going through a major city building phase ever since the Meiji restoration. This has shown no signs of slackening since the Second World War and, as a result, recent thinking about planning has been dominated by physical development considerations and great emphasis has been given to large-scale infrastructure provision and construction projects. There are many parallels between recent Japanese experience and that of the developing countries where rapid urbanisation is also taking place,[13] and there are more similarities between conditions in Britain before the First World War than those associated with the post-war period within which the modern British planning system has come into being.

For a variety of reasons, Japanese urban planning is also much less of a local government activity than planning in Britain. In the first place, this is due to the relatively weak position of local government in Japan. Japan's 47 prefectures and over 3000 cities, towns and villages constituted as local public bodies are generally portrayed as being part of a system designed to enhance the dominance of central government 'to the extent that although nominally autonomous the prefectures are conventionally understood to be subordinate to the centre (most of their functions are centrally delegated ones), and the cities, towns and villages are likewise portrayed as subordinate to the prefectures'.[14]

Secondly, the range of statutory duties given to Japanese local authorities by the 1968 City Planning Act and related legislation is relatively restricted by comparison with those given to British local authorities by the 1947 Town and Country Planning Act and subsequent legislation. This is particularly the case in relation to strategic planning, where the tendency to concentrate on physical development considerations is reinforced by the widespread utilisation of land readjustment procedures within both the public and private sectors and by the proliferation of project-oriented agencies in the public sector. According to Samuels,[15] more than one hundred agencies of this kind are currently operating at the national level, of which the most important from the standpoint of urban planning are the National Land Agency, the Japan Housing and Urban Development Corporation, and the Japan Regional Development Corporation. In addition to these national agencies, there are also more than 3000 public local corporations funded by the localities through grants and investment which act as 'private organisations of central government'.[16]

Because of this, urban planning practice in Japan is far more diverse in character than is the case in Britain, where a survey carried out in 1988 showed that local government positions accounted for 65 per cent of the corporate membership of the Royal Town Planning Institute.[17] No directly comparable statistics are available for Japan, but some indication of the spread of planning activities is given by the job destinations of first degree graduates from the Department of Urban Engineering at the University of Tokyo between 1976 and 1985.[18] On the basis of a crude distinction between 'planning' and 'non-planning' jobs according to the type of employer rather than the nature of the post to which graduates were appointed, and omitting 'non-planning' jobs from the analysis, only 14.9 per cent of all graduates entered positions in local government during this period. By comparison, nearly twice as many (26.3 per cent) entered positions in central government, and an even higher proportion (47.5 per cent) took up posts in the private sector in planning consultancies, construction companies or real estate firms. The corresponding figures from the 1988 RTPI survey are 11 per cent for central government and 19 per cent for the private sector.[19]

The comparative evaluation of Japanese and British urban planning highlights the degree to which urban planning in these countries is the product of very different stages of urban development, and the extent to which this is reflected in the strong physical project orientation of Japanese planning, which contrasts with the emphasis placed on social and environmental considerations in British planning. At the same time, although the analysis inevitably begs the question as to what constitutes 'a planner', the predominant role of local government in British planning is not evident in Japan, where both central government and private-sector involvement in plan making and project formulation is much greater than is the case in Britain. With these considerations in mind, it is now possible to explore in greater depth the activities of the City Planning Institute of Japan and the provision of planning education.

Professional Associations and the Provision of Planning Education in Japan

THE CITY PLANNING INSTITUTE OF JAPAN

The nearest organisation in Japan to a professional planning association is the City Planning Institute of Japan (CPIJ), which was founded in 1951 by Yoshikazu Uchida and others who had worked for the improvement of planning legislation. Under Article 4 of its constitution, the objectives of the CPIJ are set out in the following terms:

> to act as a forum for the publication of members' research, the exchange of information and the encouragement of contact among members and with other appropriate bodies, and to promote the progress and dissemination of learning relating to city planning.

Since its foundation, the membership of the CPIJ has grown steadily from 157 ordinary members and 22 student members in 1952 to 3249 ordinary members and 209 student members in 1985. In the latter year, there were also 31 honorary members and 207 corporate members resulting in a total membership of 3696 as against 179 in 1952.

The City Planning Institute of Japan is generally regarded as the most authoritative body in the planning field, and it has played an important part in the development of urban planning in Japan since its foundation, but it functions more like a learned society than a professional association. This is reflected in the relatively high proportion of academics and researchers who together account for about a third of its membership, while the other two-thirds are divided more or less evenly between central and local government officials on the one hand and planners from the private sector on the other.

A high proportion of members have undergraduate or postgraduate degrees in architecture or engineering, and the overwhelming majority live in one of the three largest urban areas, particularly Tokyo.

The overall status of planning as a professional activity in Japan is relatively weak in comparison, for example, with professions such as architecture. Whereas the CPIJ was not established until 1951, the Japan Society of Architects (*Zoka Gakkai*) was founded as early as 1886. From the outset, this body and its successor, the Architectural Association (*Kenchiku Gakkai*), acted as a learned society for the discussion of matters relating to architecture, while a different organisation, the Japan Association of Architects (*Nihon Kenchikushikai*) took on the role of a professional body, dealing with matters such as registration, until the Architects Act came into operation in 1952.

The weakness of urban planning in professional terms by comparison with architecture can also be seen from civil service grades and descriptions. Even though planning is increasingly becoming a specialist occupation in central government ministries and organisations such as the National Land Agency, there are still no appointments bearing the title 'Urban Planner', and applicants wishing to work in this field are placed in the disadvantageous position of being compelled to take the civil service examinations for the post of, for example, 'Architect'.

The development of specialist professional associations such as the CPIJ is hindered by the principle of lifetime employment, which assumes that people will work within the same organisation throughout their careers and that they will be promoted largely on the basis of their length of service. Under this system, organisations rely heavily on on-the-job training at the workplace to develop their staff's skills, and members of the elite who will occupy positions of leadership are likely to experience a variety of postings for two or three years at a time to broaden their range of experience.

Under these circumstances, there is a strong likelihood that the acquisition of narrowly defined professional skills may clash with career development within the organisation. This is especially the case with central or local government officials working in organisations where no clear line can be drawn between urban planning tasks and other tasks relating to urban development or project management.

As a result, the main source of pressure for the establishment of a strong professional body to represent urban planning interests comes from those working in the private sector, particularly in the planning consultancy field where organisations are continually changing in response to the immediate needs of the market. This can be seen, for example, from the findings of a survey of private-sector members of the CPIJ which was carried out in 1977,[20] which showed that 60.9 per cent of those responding felt that there should be a professional body for planners. Among the reasons given by respondents for their views were the need to raise levels of competence and skills, the desire to raise the social status of planning as an activity, and the importance of obtaining independence from other organisations.

THE PROVISION OF PLANNING EDUCATION

Throughout its existence, the CPIJ has been interested in planning education in general terms but has made little attempt to lay down guidelines for course development. As a result, there is great diversity in educational provision at all levels, even though urban planning is generally viewed from the standpoint of architecture and engineering, and there are relatively few social science-based courses. This reinforces the strong physical development and project planning component of urban planning practice in Japan that was noted earlier in the chapter.

The range of courses currently available at both the undergraduate and postgraduate levels can best be illustrated by reference to concrete examples from the courses provided by the Department of Urban Engineering at the University of Tokyo and the Department of Social Engineering at the Tokyo Institute of Technology.

The Department of Urban Engineering at the University of Tokyo was established in 1962 within the Faculty of Engineering. It enjoys an independent status in the Faculty, alongside the Departments of Architecture and Civil Engineering. It provides both urban planning and sanitary engineering courses at the undergraduate and postgraduate levels. The basic aim of the urban planning course is 'to train the physical planner who has comprehensive knowledge and ability in basic engineering fields (i.e. civil engineering, architecture and building science, sanitary engineering etc.), social sciences, quantitative approach, and theory and methodology of the urban community'.[21]

In the mid-1980s, the Department of Urban Engineering had 15 full-time faculty, over 110 undergraduate students and about 60 postgraduate students enrolled on its books. Masters' degree students comprised about three-fifths of the postgraduate complement, with the balance made up of doctoral candidates and foreign research students. Like virtually all university courses in Japan, the formal undergraduate curriculum is very general in nature. The greater part of the two junior years is devoted to general introductory courses in a very wide range of academic disciplines and attaining a competence in foreign languages. Consequently, the urban planning dimension does not figure prominently in the teaching curriculum until the third or fourth senior years.

After graduation, about a quarter of the undergraduates from this course enter the Masters' course for more specialised training in the urban planning field. The remainder of the students go directly into public or private employment, but not necessarily into planning jobs. The ratio between the two sectors ranges generally from 40:60 to 50:50.

Graduates from the undergraduate course make up about a third of the total entry to the postgraduate course. The remainder of the entrants come from other departments at the University of Tokyo, especially architecture and civil engineering, as well as from other universities. This is typical of other postgraduate courses in Japan in the planning field, which provide both specialist training for undergraduates from planning courses as well as performing a conversion role for graduates from other disciplines.

The architectural and engineering tradition of the Department is clearly evident in the emphasis that is given to studio work in the curriculum. Lectures are restricted to morning sessions so that the afternoons can be devoted to studio sessions which provide 'all students with the common system in which they have to learn how to plan and shape building complexes, districts, communities, and regions, as well as how to carry out investigations, analyses, projections, plan making and presentations'.[22]

Like the Department of Urban Engineering at the University of Tokyo, the Department of Social Engineering at the Tokyo Institute of Technology is a separate department in the Faculty of Engineering which was established in the early 1960s. It also provides a full range of undergraduate and postgraduate courses for its students and is broadly similar in size with respect to both numbers of staff and students enrolled on undergraduate courses and Masters' and doctoral programmes.

The main difference between the two departments is in terms of the range of topics covered in the curricula. The Department of Social Engineering regards itself as 'a combination of social sciences and engineering technologies. Emphasis is placed in this department on socio-economic planning and on urban-environment planning and design based on the mastery of applied mathematics and computer technology'.[23] Consequently, the Department sees itself as embracing a wide range of planning activities within the broad urban field. For this reason, the six Chairs in the Department are allocated to specific fields: social systems, planning methodology, city planning, regional planning, resource allocation and environmental planning, and economic and transportation planning.

Like the University of Tokyo, the first and second undergraduate years of such courses are very general in character. At the Tokyo Institute of Technology, the first year is devoted largely to liberal arts and foreign languages. Only one-sixth of the total time is spent on courses relating to a cluster of architectural, civil engineering and urban planning topics. Students are not expected to choose their specialist field of study until the second year, and even at this stage social engineering courses occupy only one-third of the total curricula time. It is not until the senior years that more than half the time is actually spent on specialist subjects.

In this case, over half the entrants to the Department's Masters' programme come from the undergraduate programme itself. The remainder, like the University of Tokyo, come from other Departments at the Institute or from other universities in Japan or elsewhere. The Masters' programme combines more specialist training with a strong interdisciplinary emphasis, and specialist teaching from other Departments is brought into the Department to teach topics such as social psychology, logic, statistics and the history of science and technology.

These descriptions demonstrate the extent to which the boundaries between town planning and other activities associated with urban and regional development are blurred in Japan. Although the Departments of Urban Engineering and Social Engineering are separate entities within their respective universities, the content of the courses given does not clearly distinguish between town planning and fields such as urban design, landscape design, resource management and regional economics. It is also worth noting that staff in the Architecture and Civil Engineering Departments in these institutions have specialist research interests in the urban and regional planning fields and provide courses on these subjects.

There are few signs that this lack of identity seriously worries Japanese planners. If anything, the trend is to develop even more broadly-based urban studies curricula with a view to overcoming what are seen to be the traditional disciplinary biases produced as a result of the present educational system.[24]

COMPARATIVE EVALUATION

Both in terms of professional associations and planning education, there are marked contrasts between the two countries which highlight some of the distinctive features of the institutional context underlying urban planning in both Britain and Japan. There are few similarities between the City Planning Institute of Japan and the British Royal Town Planning Institute. Founded in 1914, the latter has regarded itself from the outset as an association which has the objective of promoting the development of planning as a professional activity, and it has modelled itself on the professional associations of its initial members, who were drawn largely from architecture, civil engineering or surveying. Consequently, it took on the role of a qualifying association which devised its own curriculum and conducted its own examinations for entry to the profession.

The status of planning as a profession in Britain was secured following the 1947 Town and Country Planning Act, which established planning as a bureaucratic activity within local government and created a demand for suitably qualified personnel. As a result, membership of the Royal Town Planning Institute increased from 900 in 1939 to over 4000 by 1960.[25] Subsequently, membership levels had continued to rise to the extent that there were over 12 500 members of the RTPI in 1980, of which 7744 were ordinary corporate members and 4752 were student members.[26]

The difference between Britain and Japan in terms of the size of their respective professional associations is considerable, particularly when it is borne in mind that Japan roughly outnumbers Britain by two to one in terms of population. As against 7744 ordinary members of the RTPI in 1980, the CPIJ had only 2765 ordinary members in 1982 and 3249 in 1985. In terms of student membership, the differences are even more extreme, with 4752 RTPI members in 1980 as against only 209 CPIJ student members.

There are also very marked differences between the two countries with respect to the provision of planning education. Because of the criteria laid down in Britain by the RTPI for entry to the profession, planning education is relatively homogeneous in nature. Both undergraduate and postgraduate courses seeking professional accreditation must conform to the Institute's guidelines and are subject to inspection by a visiting board of the Institute every five years. The 1982 guidelines cover a large number of matters ranging from the resources available to the subjects that must be covered in the curriculum. In the latter respect, particular importance is attached to the content of the core curriculum that must occupy at least one-third but no more than two-thirds of all the teaching time involved.[27] In its current form, this covers three main subject areas: planning methodology (i.e. theory, methods and techniques of plan making and implementation), the physical environment (i.e. land development processes and their consequences), and the administrative context (i.e. planning law and public administration).

Not only is the heterogeneity of Japanese planning courses of the kind described in the previous section very striking when compared with the homogeneous nature of British provision, but there are also major differences in content which draw attention to the different circumstances within which planning operates in the two countries. This can be seen if the syllabuses of the two Japanese courses described in the previous section are evaluated from the standpoint of the 1982 guidelines laid down by the RTPI for Britain. In both courses, it would appear that matters relating to planning methodology and the physical environment are dealt with to a greater or a lesser extent, but little time in either of these courses is devoted to a discussion of the administrative context. Consequently, it is unlikely that either of these courses would meet the criteria laid down by the RTPI for professional recognition

What this demonstrates is the importance that is attached to a view of urban planning as a bureaucratic activity in Britain as against Japan. Less obviously, it also draws attention to the strong social science tradition that has been built up in British planning as against the strong architectural and engineering tradition that is evident in Japan

Conclusions

The findings of this analysis draw attention to some important differences in the institutional context which underlies urban planning in Japan and Britain. In some ways, the countries represent polar extremes from the standpoint of professionalism and the provision of planning education, and these differences are reinforced by the strong physical project emphasis in Japanese urban planning as against the social and environmental thrust of much British planning.

There are obvious strengths and weaknesses in both countries' approaches. The flexibility of Japanese planning education is envied by British planners, concerned about the isolation of the knowledge base of British planning brought about by the imposition of a narrowly defined generalist curriculum on planning schools by the Royal Town Planning Institute. On the other hand, Japanese planners who are worried about the low status of planning as an activity look with some awe at the achievements of the Royal Town Planning Institute in this direction.

The findings of the analysis also raise some interesting questions which need further investigation. High on the list of these is the need for research on the values and attitudes of Japanese urban planners. Research of this kind is likely to be potentially fruitful in the light of the emphasis given to physical development issues in Japan, and it would also be useful to explore the extent to which greater private-sector involvement in planning is reflected in planners' attitudes. In the United States, for example, the findings of the studies carried out by Howe and Kaufman[28] indicate that environmental and social issues are given high priority by American planners, and this is coupled with hostility to private developers. Similar characteristics can also be seen in British studies carried out by Healey and Underwood[29] and Knox and Cullen,[30] despite the predominantly middle-class backgrounds of the groups they investigated.

Given the extent to which the institutional context of urban planning in Japan differs from that of the United States or Britain, a cross-cultural comparison of attitudes and values could be very revealing. A useful model for such a study can be found in Kaufman's comparative analysis of the attitudes of American and Israeli planners.[31] This demonstrated the extent to which the latter were even more hostile to private developers than the American planners and more favourably disposed to expressing their personal values in their work.

Research on planners' values and attitudes might also throw some light on the reasons why, as Alden, Hirohata and Abe's chapter in this book shows, inner city problems of the British type apparently do not exist in Japanese metropolises, despite the speed at which social change has been occurring over the last forty years as a result of economic growth and urbanisation. Such studies might be coupled with more general investigations of environmental perceptions and housing satisfaction, given the relatively low standards of Japanese cities that were noted by the OECD urban policy review.[32]

Another issue which needs more detailed investigation is the role of local government bodies in urban planning. The findings of the analysis indicate the relative weakness of planning as a local government activity in Japan within the context of a highly centralised system of government. However, the evidence from Reed's[33] analyses of policy making in three Japanese prefectures and Samuel's[34] study of the regional policy process associated with the Tokyo Bay bridge construction project, indicates that local government bodies in Japan have a greater degree of discretion than was previously thought.

In the light of this new evidence, there is a pressing need for a more detailed investigation of urban planning at the local government level in Japan. Case study research on particular localities is also likely to provide insights into public/private-sector relations and the operation of public project organisation, given that the municipality is typically the arena within which much of the detailed discussion of planning and development issues takes place.

Finally, the findings of this study demonstrate the value of adopting a specifically comparative perspective to highlight key features of the institutional context which governs Japanese urban planning. The present study has looked at Japan essentially from a British perspective, and there is a need for further research which looks at Japanese urban planning from different cultural and developmental perspectives. A useful starting point for such research is the series of studies by authors from developing countries that is brought together in the United Nations Centre for Regional Development volume on 'The transferability of development experience.[35] In terms of professional associations and the provision of planning education, a great deal might be learnt by evaluating Japanese experience against the perspectives of countries such as France, where there are no strong traditions of professionalism in fields such as urban planning, and the role of central government in organising both training and employment is much stronger than in Britain or the United States.[36]

NOTES AND REFERENCES

1 Friedson, E., 'The Theory of Professions: State of the Art' in Dingwall, R. and Lewis, P. (eds.), *The Sociology of the Professions*, London, Macmillan, 1983, p. 24.

2 Healey, P., 'The Professionalisation of Planning in Britain: Its Form and Consequences', *Town Planning Review*, 56 (4) 1985, pp. 492–507 (at pp. 502–03).

3 Watanabe, S. I., 'Metropolitanism as a Way of Life: The Case of Tokyo, 1868–1930' in Sutcliffe, A. (ed.), *Metropolis 1890–1940*, London, Mansell, 1984, pp. 403–29.

4 Watanabe, S. I., 'Planning History in Japan' in *Urban History Yearbook*, Leicester, Leicester University Press, 1980, pp. 63–75 (at p. 65).

5 Nishiyama, Y., 'Western Influence on Urban Planning Administration in Japan: Focus on Land Management' in Nagamine, H. (ed.), *Urban Development Policies and Programmes: Focus on Land Management*, Nagoya, UN Centre for Regional Development, 1986, pp. 315–55, especially pp. 329–33.

6 Mano, M., 'Urban Development and Improvement: A Case Study of Nagoya' (Paper prepared for the International Seminar on Urban Land Policies), Nagoya, Nagoya City Government and the UN Centre for Regional Development, 1982.

7 Nishiyama, op. cit., p. 32.

8 Ibid.

9 Organisation for Economic Cooperation and Development, *Urban Policies in Japan*, Paris, OECD, 1986, p. 17.

10 Ibid., p. 35.

11 Ibid., p. 53.

12 Ibid.

13 See, for example, Gedik, A., 'The Spatial Distribution of Population in Post War Japan (1944–1980): Implications for Developing Countries' in Friedrich, P. and Masser, I. (eds.), *International Perspectives on Regional Decentralisation*, Baden Baden, Nomos, 1987, pp. 86–118.

14 Samuels, R. J., *The Politics of Regional Policy in Japan: Localities Incorporated?*, Princeton, Princeton University Press, 1983, p. xix.

15 Samuels, op. cit., p. 38.

16 Ibid.

17 Nadin, V. and Jones, S., 'A Profile of the Profession', *The Planner*, 26 January 1990, p. 20.

18 *Department of Urban Engineering Handbook*, Tokyo, Faculty of Engineering, University of Tokyo, 1986, p. 14.

19 Nadin and Jones, op. cit.

20 City Planning Institute of Japan, 'The Realities and Opinions of Planners', *Toshi Keikaku*, 99, 1977, pp. 25–41.

21 University of Tokyo, *Information on the Faculty of Engineering, 1984–1985*, Tokyo, University of Tokyo, 1984, p. 19.

22 Ibid.

23 Tokyo Institute of Technology, *General Catalogue*, Tokyo, Tokyo Institute of Technology, 1985, p. 79.

24 See, for example, National Institute of Research Advancement, *Proposal for a System of Integrated Urban Research: Discussion of a New University for Education and Research on Cities*, Tokyo, NIRA, 1986.

25 Cherry, G. E., *The Evolution of British Town Planning: A History of Town Planning in the United Kingdom during the 20th Century and the Royal Town Planning Institute, 1914–1974*, Leighton Buzzard, Leonard Hill, 1974, p. 241.

26 Amos, F. J. C., Davies, M., Groves, R. and Niner, P., *Manpower Requirements for Physical Planning*, Birmingham, Institute of Local Government Studies, 1982, Table 1.

27 Royal Town Planning Institute, *Guidelines for Planning Schools*, London, RTPI, 1982.

28 Howe, E. and Kaufman, J., 'The Ethics of American Planners', *Journal of the American Planning Association*, 45, 1979, pp. 243–55; Howe, E., 'Role Choice for Urban

Planners', *Journal of the American Planning Association*, **46**, 1980, pp. 398–409; and Howe, E. and Kaufman, J., 'The Values of Contemporary American Planners', *Journal of the American Planning Association*, **47**, 1981, pp. 226–78.

29 Healey, P. and Underwood, J., 'Professional Ideals and Planning Practice', *Progress in Planning*, **9**, 1978, pp. 73–127.

30 Knox, P. and Cullen, J., 'Planners and Urban Managers: An Exploration of the Attitudes and Self-Image of Senior British Planners', *Environment and Planning A*, **13**, 1981, pp. 885–98.

31 Kaufman, J., 'American and Israeli Planners: A Cross Cultural Comparison', *Journal of the American Planning Association*, **51**, 1985, pp. 352–64.

32 OECD, op. cit.

33 Reed, S. R., 'Is Japanese Government Really Centralised?', *Journal of Japanese Studies*, **8**, 1982, pp. 133–64; and *Japanese Prefectures and Policy-Making*, Pittsburg, University of Pittsburg Press, 1986.

34 Samuels, op. cit.

35 Okita, S. (ed.), *Transferability of Development Experience: Case Studies on Japan*, Nagoya, UN Centre for Regional Development, 1984.

36 See, for example, Ben David, J., *Centers of Learning: Britain, France and the United States*, New York, McGraw Hill, 1977.

ACKNOWLEDGEMENTS

The study described in this chapter formed part of the Anglo-Japanese research project on planning systems in metropolitan areas, funded by the Toyota Foundation. The authors are also indebted to the Mori Foundation for Social Engineering, which provided the financial support which enabled Professor Masser to carry out field work in Japan at Hitotsubashi University. They would like to express their appreciation to all those who helped in this research, and in particular to Mr Shunichi Furukawa, Professor Sachihiko Harashina, Dr Yasuyoshi Hayashi, Professor Hidemitsu Kawakami, Professor Yoshinobu Kumata, Dr Koji Mizushima, Professor Noboru Sakashita, Mr Moriyuki Sawamoto and Professor Chushichi Tsuzuki. They are also grateful to their colleagues on the Toyota project, particularly Dr Shunichi Watanabe, for their instructive comments, to Professor Patsy Healey for her comments on an early draft, and to Graham Healey from the Centre for Japanese Studies at the University of Sheffield who translated and interpreted Japanese texts for Professor Masser. Needless to say, the interpretation of issues and the opinions expressed in the article remain the sole responsibility of the authors.

Chapter 9

Planning for Technology Development and Information Systems in Japanese Cities and Regions

DAVID W. EDGINGTON

The purpose of this chapter is to review Japan's urban and regional programmes for technology-based industrial and commercial growth. A comprehensive framework for regional development planning was established in Japan soon after the end of the Pacific war. During much of the post-war period, regional development was closely linked to national economic planning, reflecting an overall orientation to maximise economic growth.[1] In the 1950s the emphasis focused on developing Tokyo and the other core cities (Osaka and Nagoya) in order to maximise efficiencies associated with economies of scale in production. This approach changed sharply in the early 1960s due to problems of urban congestion and pollution, rural population decline and regional income disparities. Growth pole strategies for peripheral areas were pursued in the first Comprehensive National Development Plan (CNDP) of 1962, and involved the designation of new industrial cities and special areas to decentralise 'smokestack' industry from large cities.[2] Subsequent CNDPs in the late 1960s and mid-1970s encouraged this process through further industrial relocation schemes, controls on factory development, and the build-up of a wider array of social and community facilities in small-to-medium regional cities.[3]

During the 1980s, progress in science and technology in Japan advanced remarkably. This arose from national imperatives to restructure the economy following the 1970s 'oil shocks', causing the country to move away from its traditional raw materials processing industries (e.g. steel and petrochemicals) to new technologies, education and scientific research.[4] More recently, the revaluation of the yen after mid-1985 (*endaka*) provided a further push to restructure, as the assembly operations of even technology-based industries—such as integrated circuits (ICs)—were relocated overseas.[5] As Japan entered the 1990s, it was widely agreed that it had reached the technological levels of other advanced countries and so needed to turn its attention to more and more on more basic and creative research and the creation of an 'information society'.[6]

Parallel to this shift into a more technologically focused stage of development, urban and regional policies have emerged aimed at addressing directly the provision of infrastructure for 'knowledge'-based industries and information-based services.[7] As this chapter will show, national strategies for developing new technologies have involved specific and complementary programmes for cities and regions since the late 1970s. This concept received further support from the Fourth Comprehensive Land Development Plan (*Yonzenso*), published in 1987, which envisaged high-technology development as a means to make the spatial economy more balanced as well as more efficient.

The chapter proceeds by first describing recent developments (as at 1992) at the nationally supported Science Cities—Tsukuba in Eastern Japan, which is now functioning fully, and the Kansai Science City, currently being established. The following section then outlines the Ministry of International Trade and Industry's (MITI) 'technopolis' programme, focusing on some distinctive features associated with this type of project. The fourth section looks at recent policies of other national ministries which are designed to introduce new information technologies (optical fibre, cable TV, local computer networks and so on), together with special research infrastructure, into a number of 'model cities'—usually, although not always, in peripheral areas. Section five examines the new large-scale waterfront redevelopment projects in Japan's largest cities—Tokyo, Yokohama and Osaka—which are directed at improving the levels of technology and information-related infrastructure in core metropolitan areas. The chapter concludes with some comments on these strategies in terms of equity and efficiency concerns, as well as the role of the government in economic development.

Science Cities

TSUKUBA SCIENCE CITY

Tsukuba Science City was constructed in the 1970s to improve the nation's public research and development (R and D) effort.[8] The ability of Japan to generate high-level original research was hampered in the immediate post-war period by crowded and poor facilities scattered unsystematically throughout the larger metropolitan areas. The decision to construct a new academic town in the Mount Tsukuba area, 60 kilometres north of Tokyo, was undertaken by the national government in 1963. Such a bold move combined the physical improvement of the nation's R and D facilities with the reform of research institutes, and the creation of a new national university along Western collegiate lines. Unlike previous attempts at new town planning, Tsukuba represented the first true Japanese satellite city which combined both living and working facilities together.[9] Planned for a final target population of about 100 000, the construction phase of the new town was approved officially during the economic boom of the 1960s. Total expenditure to date has been in the order of $20 billion, and since its commencement in 1979 it has functioned as a unique agglomeration of public research institutes (comprising about 40 per cent of the nation's total).[10]

In the early 1980s, major issues arose related to the city's liveability and its ability to attract private research investment.[11] For example, the 'city' was spread initially over a vast area, yet lacked either a central shopping centre or cultural facilities. Another problem was the poor interaction between Tsukuba's public research and scientific establishments and academic institutes on the one hand, and nationwide private-sector enterprises on the other hand, leading to a lack of joint research and other 'spin-off' activities.[12] This in part was due to the poor physical access to the city from Tokyo. In 1985, however, the situation rapidly improved following the national government-sponsored Tsukuba Science Expo held in that year, which acted as a great spur to public and private investment. An expressway linking Tsukuba to central Tokyo was completed and large department stores and hotels were built to cater for the 20 million visitors to Expo, helping make Tsukuba a more tolerable place to live and work.[13] In response to these and other changes, the pace of entry of private research enterprises also accelerated in the late 1980s. Several of Japan's major companies built laboratories on the former Expo site where relatively inexpensive land was available, or on adjoining industrial parks established by the local prefecture government. Private sector industrial parks were also developed close to Tsukuba in Japan's so-called 'bubble' economic boom period of 1987–1990, often comprising research institutes, as well as factory space, information centres, sports and cultural facilities (see Fig. 9.1).

Of even greater importance than providing more industrial land has been the instigation of certain reforms directed at maximising the utilisation of Tsukuba's substantial research infrastructure. First, greater interaction between the public and private sectors has been encouraged. Although national institutions have always been open to the public, up to the mid-1980s researchers at Tsukuba had been severely limited in their relationship with private companies due to the specifications of the National Public Service Law. As a result of the 1987 Research Exchange Promotion Act, these limitations have been relaxed and the legal status of researchers altered to allow public-private collaborative work. Second, in 1987 the four existing towns and one village in the area were merged to form a single Tsukuba City. This merger allowed local government to expand its role as a supplier of critical infrastructure needed for technology development, such as additional industrial parks, office space and recreation facilities. Third, in an effort to bring together government, industry and academic representatives, the national government set up a Tsukuba Research Support Centre in 1989, composed of 55 major firms. This was intended to provide core facilities for open laboratories and research exchange, together with 'incubators' for start-up firms, exhibition halls, information services and in-house training programmes.[14]

Companies have been attracted to locate at Tsukuba by the concentration of research institutes, favourably priced land when compared with Tokyo, and the relatively good road accessibility to the capital (about one hour) on the newly constructed Joban Expressway. Currently, the Tsukuba area contains some 120 private research establishments including international majors such as Du Pont, ICI, Intel and Texas Instruments. Tsukuba city data show that since 1985, the number of company researchers and their support staff has risen dramatically to 5000—close to the number (6700) of government researchers.[15] In 1989, the 'New Tsukuba Plan' was announced by the National Land Agency in order to make the science city even more attractive to private-sector investment. It foreshadowed a new Joban rail line linking Tsukuba directly to central Tokyo in fifty minutes, and a new highway link to Narita International Airport.[16]

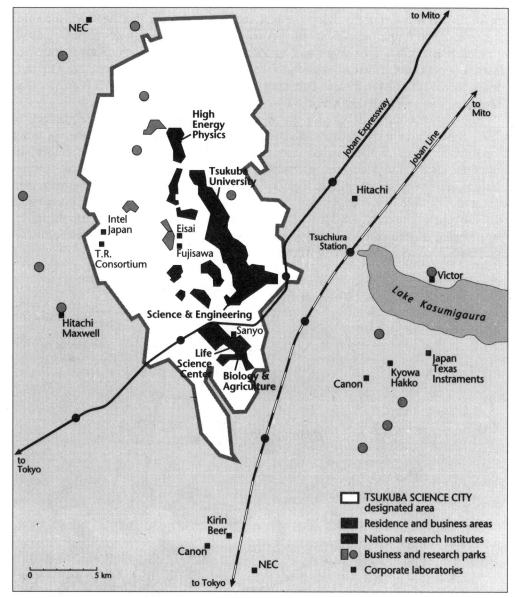

Fig. 9.1 Tsukuba Science City and environs (source: Housing and Urban Development Corporation, *Tsukuba*, Tokyo, HUDC, 1985)

KANSAI SCIENCE CITY

Kansai Science City (KSC) is being constructed on a scale comparable with Tsukuba, to provide a similar focus for science and technology in Western Japan (the Kansai region). It is situated in the Keihanna hills, an area which extends over three prefectures and within a 20–30 kilometre radius of Kyoto, Osaka and Nara. Upon completion, KSC will have a population of nearly 400 000. Planning for the new science city began in 1978 under special legislation involving the National Land Agency together with the three prefectures and four cities concerned.[17] After a 15 000 hectare site was chosen in 1980, detailed preparations took place and in 1986 a special agency—the Kansai Research Institute—was established to oversee the full-scale construction of the city. The total development area now includes 12 clusters totalling 3300 hectares, which is greater than Tsukuba Science City's domain of 2700 hectares (see Fig. 9.2 and Table 9.1).

Experience with the development of Tsukuba has been reflected in the planning of KSC, although there are some significant departures. Thus, unlike Tsukuba, its aim is not only to promote the natural sciences in public research institutes; rather, its functions encompass wider but interrelated activities in the fields of science, culture, design and the humanities. Also, given the generally tighter national government budgets of the late 1980s, the private sector has played a larger role in development than was the case at Tsukuba. KSC therefore is not merely a national government initiative, but is being implemented together with the region's private companies and industry, academic institutions and local government.

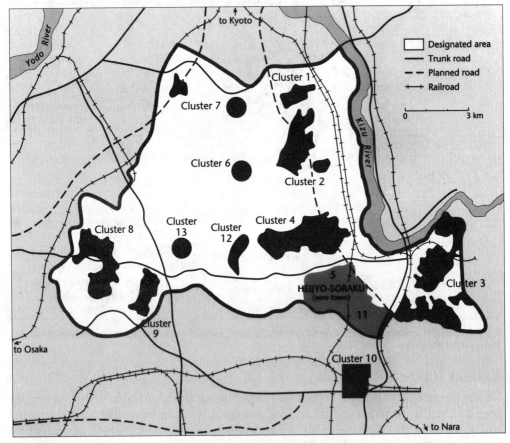

Fig. 9.2 Kansai Science City (source: Kansai Research Institute, *Kansai Science City*, Kyoto, Kansai Research Institute, 1990)

In addition, compared with Tsukuba, there is more attention given to the issues of staging, nature conservation and flexibility. For instance, the science city is being structured around a dozen cultural and scientific zones, linked together by transport and information systems. Around these zones the landscape is green, topographically varied and rich in historic associations—Kyoto having been the home of the Japanese emperors from 794 to 1868. The division of the area into small districts has allowed more sympathetic development in harmony with existing local communities and the most to be made of the natural environment. Moreover, each district is being developed with a particular theme, and in this way, a step-by-step plan of development is to be realised (Fig. 9.2 and Table 9.1). The cluster arrangement allows both flexibility in implementation and a wide spectrum of private, public and academic agencies to be involved.[18]

More than 40 research institutes belonging to national or local enterprises are either scheduled for siting inside KSC, or are already under construction. Public and private research institutes presently operating include the National Institute of Advanced Studies of the Ministry of International Trade and Industry (MITI), the Advanced Telecommunications Research Institute of Nippon Telegraph and Telecommunications Limited (NTT), the Ion Engineering Institute (which conducts research on new materials), and the engineering and science faculties of the Doshisha University—a major private university from Kyoto. KSC also has a number of new residential areas, including Kintetsu New Town, and private commercial centres such as Keihanna Plaza.[19]

Since it is being constructed in a region steeped in Japanese history, greater emphasis is placed on cultural activities, such as special memorial parks and gardens. In this regard, the Kansai branch of the national Diet library is already planned, together with research facilities for the preservation and restoration of the historic Heijo palace site. Another feature of KSC is the promotion of research into software and design. For example, a 'Hi-Touch Research Park' opened in 1990 within the Heijo-Soraku district (Fig. 9.2). This is a novel operation, constructed and managed entirely by a cooperative of thirteen small-to-medium companies engaged in Kyoto's traditional and contemporary manufacturing and service activities. Participating enterprises include those from the textiles, textile dyeing, kimono, green tea, music, scientific education, housing, advertising displays, electrical goods and publishing sectors.[20]

The Technopolis Programme

The technopolis programme was initiated by the Ministry of International Trade and Industry in the early 1980s. The major concepts have been well documented elsewhere and will not be covered here.[21] In essence, they propose that regional development should be based upon the creation of high-tech communities, modelled in part on California's Silicon Valley, but founded upon the three pillars of 'high-tech industry, academia and housing'. A major difference exists between the technopolis programme and previous regional development policies in Japan in that the technopolises have been

Table 9.1 *Kansai Science City: plan of development*

Prefecture	No.	Cultural and scientific research districts	Area (ha)	Population (1000s)	Completion time	Facilities to be prepared
	1	Tanabe	100	—	Completed	Education and research facilities
	2	Minami Tanabe-Komada	338	19	2000	Facilities for the creative and fundamental application research, facilities for research on the aged
	3	Kizu	740	40	2000	Facilities for the creative fundamental and application research on natural science
Kyoto	4	Seika-Nishi-Kizu	494	25	1995	Facilities for creative fundamental and application research, facilities for advanced research on culture and art, facilities for furnishing information
	5	Heijo-Soraku	264	30	Completed	Facilities for research and development related to living
	11	Fugenji (Kyoto prefecture)	Undecided	Undecided	Undecided	Facilities for test and research on agricultural systems, etc.
		SUBTOTAL	1936	114	—	—
	6	Himuro-Tsuda	65 (area will be extended after adjustment of conditions)	3	1995 (temporary goal)	Facilities for research and education related to frontier technology, facilities for research for common use
Osaka	7	Kiyotaki-Mirioke	340	3	Beginning of 21st century	Promotion of Cultural Greenery Park Project, facilities for education and research
	8	Tawara	127	10	1995	Facilities for the study, training and research related to living culture as health, etc.
		SUBTOTAL	532	16	—	—

Table 9.1 continued

Prefecture	No.	Cultural and scientific research districts	Area (ha)	Population (1000s)	Completion time	Facilities to be prepared
	9	Heijo Palace Site	142	1	Beginning of 21st century	Preservation and restoration of Heijo Palace Site, special historic remains, and Suzaku Oji Street comprehensive facilities for research on cultural properties and archaeology
	5	Heijo-Soraku (Nara prefecture)	362	38	Completed	Facilities for research and development related to living, information, etc., and their related facilities
Nara	10	Takayama	45 (area will be extended after adjustment of conditions)	—	1993 (temporary goal)	Advanced Institute of Science and Technology Exchange Centre for Advanced Science and Technology (tentative name), private research institutions
	12	Kita Tawara	Undecided	Undecided	Undecided	Facilities for research institute of culture and science related to the functions of Takayama District
		SUBTOTAL	504	39	—	—
		TOTAL	2972	169	—	—

Note 1. Area and estimated population are the total value excluding those of pending districts at the planning stage of construction.
Note 2. The expansion and decision of area will be made for Fugenji, Himuro, Takayama and Kita Tawara Districts after their preparation conditions are arranged.
Cf. also Figure 9.2.
Source: Kansai Research Institute, *Kansai Science City*, Kyoto, KRI, 1991.

financed principally by local communities. The prefectures have established substantial technopolis funds, supported by loans, taxes and corporate donations, while the national government has restricted its involvement largely to providing guidance and overall coordination, and only supplementary financial support.[22] By the end of the 1980s a total of twenty-six locations had been designated in regions covering nearly all prefectures outside the three major metropolitan areas—Tokyo, Osaka and Nagoya (see Fig. 9.3). Following designation, each prefecture concerned took the lead in planning technopolis zones, and each was at relative liberty to develop its own goals and ideas. Consequently, the motives for technopolis designations vary considerably from place to place, and there are also significant differences between individual technopolis plans, particularly with respect to size.

From a survey of ten technopolis sites made by the author, it was clear that a number of distinctive features had emerged:

1. The original image for the technopolis programme in the early 1980s was of a satellite city of around 50 000 persons which would integrate three formerly diverse elements—R and D, educational facilities, and production facilities for high-technology industry.[23] In the main, however, the technopolis zones have not turned out as academic new towns along the lines of Tsukuba, but in some respects mirror the layout of Kansai Science City. The physical activities of most technopolises can best be described as clusters of inter-linked activities (e.g. industrial parks, new housing estates and research facilities) lying in a rural setting just outside an existing 'mother city'. In most cases, the designated technopolis areas comprise a sizeable zone, often as large as 1000 square kilometres. Within this zone, some new housing, research and commercial activities have been established which are rather distant from each other as well as from the mother (regional) city. Thus a new residential area may be separated by several kilometres from an industrial park or university campus. This reflects a pattern of *ad hoc* and incremental land acquisition by in-coming factories and housing authorities, which have been compelled to procure land wherever it was suitable and available. There is, however, a strong functional connection between airport developments and new industrial estates, especially those occupied by producers involved in silicon chip assembly.[24] This aspect, together with the dispersed layout of new physical infrastructure and its relationship with the mother city, is well represented by the Nagasaki technopolis zone.[25]

2. In some cases, the technopolis was set up more along the lines of a conventional satellite new town (e.g. at Ube in Yamaguchi prefecture, at the Hiroshima technopolis, and at Nishi-Harima technopolis in Hyogo prefecture). Some of these new towns, such as the Nishi-Harima technopolis, have been planned and constructed at great cost by the prefecture government alone. In other cases, the technopolis designation is seen as a means of reinforcing existing new town programmes commenced by the nationwide Japanese Regional Development Corporation in the 1970s (e.g. Nagaoka New Town, Kibi Highland City, Kamo Academic Town).[26]

3. Each technopolis has chosen key types of technologies for their focus.[27] Yet in most cases there was no 'magnet' infrastructure[28] or 'leading edge' research technology which

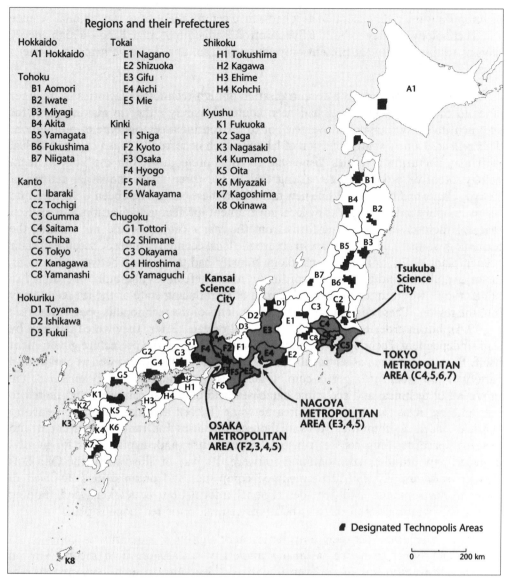

Fig. 9.3 Designated technopolis areas and the three largest metropolitan regions (source: Japan Industrial Location Centre, *Present Circumstances of Regional Development in Japan*, Tokyo, JILC, 1992)

could, by itself, either attract—or in the long term retain—footloose high technology firms. The competitive advantage of many technopolis areas is often related only to the relative cheapness of land and the availability of unskilled or part-time labour when compared with Tokyo, Osaka and Nagoya.[29] This represents a distinct drawback to the programme, especially as Japanese firms are now more inclined to place industrial plants in overseas locations to combat the effect of the high-valued yen. Nishi-Harima technopolis was a clear exception as it had a firm commitment from the national Science and Technology Agency to build a Synchrotron Radiation Storage Ring—a high energy physics testing facility (at present only found in Tsukuba) to serve firms in Western Japan.[30]

4. With some exceptions, the decentralisation of high-technology factories from larger cities to the technopolis zones had been confined mainly either to making parts for shipment to Tokyo, Osaka or overseas, or to the routine assembly type of production. This reflected a new spatial division of labour which occurred in Japan over the 1980s, with manufacturing activities dispersing to rural prefectures, but the bulk of technology-intensive production remaining tied to the three major industrial centres of Tokyo, Osaka and Nagoya. While new firms from these centres had been welcomed into the technopolis industrial parks by local government, prefectural governors also realised that, by themselves, in-coming firms from the major centres would not provide the technology transfer necessary to restructure the local economy. Indeed, because of their branch plant status, very little technology transfer had taken place between in-coming factories and local industries.[31] Accordingly, most prefectures had built, or planned to build, their own 'technopolis centre', aimed at introducing state-of-the-art technology into the region. These centres were key components of the technopolis programme (see Fig. 9.4), but in order to involve fully the local private sector, they were often run by semi-independent Technopolis Foundations rather than by the prefecture government itself. Each centre acted as an 'incubator' for small firm start-ups, as well as providing a variety of resources for larger in-coming factories. Its functions usually included: the provision of technical and economic databases held on a host computer and linked to surrounding firms through a local area network (LAN); accommodation for start-up ventures, such as computer software houses; facilities for renting equipment and meeting space; training courses run by the prefecture; and display areas for locally-designed new products and computer software. By way of illustration, the Oita Soft Park in southern Kyushu accommodated companies and organisations involved in software development, and provides regional information, educational and training facilities, laboratories, and other associations central to the technopolis plan.[32]

5. Close cooperation between universities and high-tech industries is common in Europe and North America, as many university researchers hold second jobs in industrial firms as consultants or even executives.[33] By contrast, such cooperation is rare in Japan. Indeed, except for special cases such as the Nagaoka University of Science and Technology (NUST), which has been instrumental in drawing up Nagaoka's technopolis plan), this type of relationship is virtually unknown.[34] Rather, it has been the prefectural technical laboratories—often located in the technopolis zone—which provide the vital link between university research and industrial application (Fig. 9.4). Besides conducting contract work for technopolis producers, they also carry out joint venture R and D projects involving the short-term secondment of both university and industry staff to work in the technopolis laboratory itself.

6. Hard infrastructure in the designated zones has not been ignored. Each technopolis

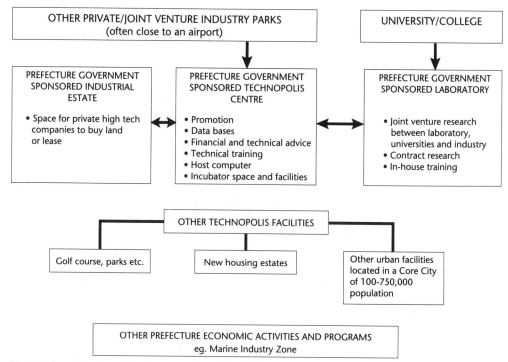

Fig. 9.4 Generalised model showing technopolis activities

has prepared twenty-year development plans, expected to cost in the region of $1 billion each to complete, and much of this has been funded locally. New infrastructure included upgrading of regional expressways and airports, additional university and laboratory facilities, technology centres and industrial/research parks (Fig. 9.4).

SUCCESS OF THE TECHNOPOLIS

As already noted, *endaka*, the rapid revaluation of the yen against the US dollar, threatened to undermine the technopolis strategy initially, due to the pressure for even high-tech firms to produce in overseas locations.[35] After 1987, however, the programme benefited from the wave of investment associated with Japan's 'bubble' economy boom period. Thus, in its first review of the technopolis programme, conducted at the end of the 1980s, MITI was satisfied with the overall rate of investment and the number of firms from the major metropolitan areas placing factories or research laboratories in technopolis areas. The programme was deemed a success in that it was able to attract high-tech industry to those local rural areas which would not have been expected to secure such industry. The MITI data show that over 2500 new factories had located in the original 14 technopolis areas between 1984 and 1989, and that by 1989 the rate of increase in new factory formation exceeded the national average.[36] However, since the collapse of the 'bubble' economy in 1991, the success rate of industrial attraction efforts appears to have worsened, as many companies have cut back or postponed their expansion or relocation plans.

Apart from new industries, all technopolis areas reported the establishment or expansion of new research institutions, colleges and universities, and these have strengthened the capacity to conduct independent research and train staff. Various cooperative research projects are now being undertaken by local universities or colleges, public research institutions and business enterprises. By the end of 1990 these ranged from biotechnology research on local dairy products in the Do-o technopolis (Hokkaido), to new optical technologies in Hamamatsu (Shizuoka prefecture), and robot-produced printed circuitry in Kumomoto.[37]

MITI was less satisfied, however, with the progress in technology transfer between the larger in-coming high-tech firms, new or enlarged colleges, public testing and research laboratories, and the many existing local small- to medium-scale industries (often called *jiba sangyo*). For instance, high technology industries, by comparison with other sectors such as the automobile industry, were found to use far fewer local subcontractors. Accordingly, as noted earlier, linkages between new firms and existing business have tended to be weak, and the spin-off effects on local economies rather small.[38]

Another manifest difficulty with the programme is that the apparent success of the technopolis programme has not been distributed evenly throughout Japan. Thus, those technopolis zones which benefited most from the technopolis designation, and so attracted significant private investment, were those which either had a long history of enterprising local industries (*jiba sangyo*) (such as Nagaoka in Toyama prefecture), or were well located along the Tokaido industrial belt between Tokyo and Osaka (such as Hamamatsu) (see Fig. 9.3), or were well connected to Tokyo by expressway (such as Nagaoka),[39] or, alternatively, had a successful record of capturing decentralising firms in the 1970s, such as Oita. By way of illustration, the five technopolises in Kyushu (Fig. 9.3), dubbed 'silicon island' due to its past success in attracting integrated circuit (IC) factories, gained a further round of investment in the 1980s amounting to 268 new factories between 1984 and 1987.[40] By contrast, Hakodate technopolis in Hokkaido, which is one of the most peripheral locations (see Fig. 9.3) with a weak industrial base, had only 27 companies open up in the zone following its designation in 1984, with the majority coming from the Tokyo area and only providing a small number of jobs.[41] Other studies confirm that new plant formation remained highest in those technopolis zones having greatest accessibility to Tokyo.[42]

Further measures were taken by MITI in 1990 in order to rectify these problems. Thus a new information network (called a 'techno-network') was planned to be established between local enterprises, newcomer factories and prefectural government laboratories, in order to support technical joint ventures and information exchange systems. Moreover, in 1992, second-phase proposals were made to extend the range of technopolis facilities, and to include cultural activities (e.g. museums, art galleries etc.) to make peripheral areas more attractive to potential investor companies and their employees.[43]

Other National Government Programmes

KEY FACILITIES CONCEPT

Since the mid-1980s, it has generally been recognised that within Japan, industrial sectors with the greatest growth potential were not those engaged in production itself, but rather activities such as software, information services, design, and engineering— 'brain' sectors, as the Japanese express it. This trend has accelerated now that more Japanese companies are committed fully to a global production strategy in the 1990s.[44] Of concern to Japanese regional planners has been the increasing concentration of these service activities in the major cities (the *daitoshi*), particularly Tokyo, as this was seen as a threat to the provinces.[45] To overcome such problems, MITI developed new plans to support the growth of service sector firms in peripheral regions (e.g. research laboratories, design studios, software houses etc.), and in 1988 the Japanese government enacted the Key Facilities Law (the formal title is the Law to Promote the Group-siting of Designated Types of Business Contributing to More Sophisticated Local Industrial Structures). This allowed the government to construct special facilities for information services in designated peripheral areas (including research parks and 'intelligent' buildings), and to give tax relief and other financial benefits to the operation of these new ventures. Twenty-two key facilities were designated by the end of 1992. In many ways, this programme has similar goals to the technopolis programme, although different economic sectors are to be targeted (see Table 9.2 for a listing of major national

Table 9.2 *National Japanese programmes for technology infrastructure*

Programme	Function	Responsible ministry	Date started
Technopolis	To increase the level of high-tech production and research in local rural regions	MITI	1980
Telétopia	To introduce new computer-based information systems in mainly rural towns	MPT	1985
Research Core	To establish incubator systems for venture business in major urban areas	MITI	1985
New Media Community	To introduce new computer-based information systems in mainly rural towns	MITI	1986
Intelligent City	To promote optic fibre and intelligent build principles in urban redevelopment	MOC	1986
Information Future City	To introduce advanced information systems to urban redevelopment schemes	MITI	1986
Greentopia	To promote the introduction of CATV systems in rural towns	MAFF	1987
Key Facilities	To support the growth of information services and related firms in peripheral regions	MITI	1988

government programmes). In the Key Facilities programme, third-sector organisations are being established to mediate between the major companies and smaller local concerns.[46]

The first 'key facility' site developed under the new legislation was at Hachinohe in Aomori prefecture (the Hachinohe Intelligent Plaza). This research park, which contains no factories, was planned as the location of R and D and other business enterprises necessary to support the nearby Aomori technopolis, and to bolster the restructuring of existing 'smokestack' industries in Hachinohe itself. Work on the site commenced in 1989 by the Japan Regional Development Corporation, and the project has to date been very successful at attracting both local research and software engineering firms, as well as decentralising firms from Tokyo. In 1992 an extension was being planned.[47]

NEW MEDIA COMMUNITY

Parallel to the high-technology and producer service focus of technopolis and the Key Facilities programmes, MITI has also promoted information-oriented business through rapid introduction of new media systems, such as two-way CATV (community access television) and videotex. These services are based on the merging of computing and communications technologies, with the overall aim of providing networking links between small-scale private companies in regional towns throughout Japan.[48] The New Media Community (NMC) programme, similar to technopolis and most of the other programmes considered in this section, is a 'model town' development which the government hopes will provide an incentive to others.[49] Although it is directed at small-sized centres outside the *daitoshi*, districts such as Yokohama's 'future port' MM21 complex (described later) are also included. In sum, the policy has three major objectives: first, to assist local regions to bridge the information gap with the large metropolitan areas; second, to help small- to medium-scale firms in industries impacted most by *endaka*; and third, to encourage the Japanese electronics industry to develop innovatory information systems for commercial application.

In operation, the model towns are expected to develop proposals for NMC designation themselves, in conjunction with local industries. For instance, Nishiwashi City, in Hyogo prefecture, formed a joint venture company with local clothing wholesalers in order to establish a new information system. Kainan City in Wakayama prefecture engaged in a similar project for assisting its firms in the sanitary and kitchenware industries. Both of these types of firms were hit hard by *endaka* in the mid-1980s, and so required a boost to their productivity in order to survive. Fifty per cent of the funding for the programme has been provided by a direct grant from MITI. Technical assistance comes from major Tokyo- and Osaka-based electronics firms, such as Fujitsu and NEC. They form part of MITI's NMC selection committees and give advice on the systems engineering aspects of each successful proposal. Of course, many of them hope to win the contract for system implementation later on.[50]

MITI recognises two types of new media communities. First, there are 'model areas' which are being developed by local initiatives; second, there are 'application development areas', directed towards the more active promotion of information systems development. Up to 1990, 21 model areas and 60 applications areas all over Japan had been designated.[51] The Ministry has also sponsored a plan aimed at introducing HDTV (high definition TV system) into 19 local cities through special investment and loan programmes. The objective here is to improve local government services and revitalise local industries.[52] Yet another MITI initiative is the 'New Media Centre' programme to promote software development in regional centres.[53]

TELETOPIA

Not to be upstaged by MITI, the Ministry of Posts and Telecommunications (MPT) in 1983 commenced a parallel programme to NMC called Teletopia. It is similar in its operation, except that it is more oriented toward assisting the public use of new information services in areas outside the larger cities. Teletopia programmes have been classified by the MPT under eleven broad types, such as disaster forecasting agricultural technology, hospital and medical care systems, tourist accommodation reservations and so on.[54] The intent here is to try and eliminate major differences in access to innovative information services between the *daitoshi* and the rest of Japan.

Unlike the NMC programme, more than one type of system can be introduced into any model Teletopia city. By the end of 1990, 198 systems were in operation in 78 model towns.[55] For example, in Obihiro City, Hokkaido, dairy farmers received laboratory analysis of their milk production by computer link from a central research laboratory. Other towns have established tourist information programmes, remote medical care systems and teleshopping facilities. Besides setting up new media centres at which the public can access data, efforts have been made under the programme to use public terminals located at train stations and post offices.[56]

In 1989, the MPT began to promote a new generation of programmes designed to develop local cities through new forms of telecommunications. One scheme, called the Hi-Vision City Plan, aims to provide high definition television (HDTV) broadcasting services to 24 local cities for use in public facilities, such as city halls, museums and libraries. Another scheme, the Telecommunications Town Plan, emphasises the promotion of information service enterprises in eight regional cities, such as Sapporo and Niigata, through the provision of advanced information technologies such as fibre optic circuits and satellite communication.[57] Other regional development programmes designed by MPT include the 'Telecom Research Park' and 'Telecom Plaza' projects. These also endeavour to promote R and D and the utilisation of new communications technology in Japan's more peripheral areas.[58]

GREENTOPIA

One more concept based around new information technologies was initiated in 1987 by the Ministry for Agriculture, Forestry and Fisheries, which moved to set up its own programme (on similar lines to those above) for rural areas. Greentopia is designed to utilise the latest information systems to assist in both the production and distribution of agricultural produce.[59] By 1990, 53 areas had been designated as 'greentopia'.[60] In the Tohaku area of Tottori prefecture, the greentopia project focuses on a local agricultural information centre. The centre collects data on soil and pest conditions as well as marketing information, and distributes these and others to farmers through a personal computer network. In addition, a CATV network is used to watch over and control the work of local irrigation facilities.[61]

INTELLIGENT CITY PROGRAMME

This low-cost model city programme of the Ministry of Construction (MOC) was set up in 1986 to advise both small cities, as well as large metropolitan areas, on the standards to use for pre-wiring their redevelopment areas with optic fibre networks. The objective is to maximise the potential for encouraging 'intelligent building' forms in new city projects. To be called 'intelligent', buildings must generally have advanced information and communication facilities, an advanced building management system—incorporating sophisticated security and air conditioning and so on—and assured communications lines linked to outside information networks.[62] Fifty-three cities had been so designated by the end of 1990.[63]

Local prefectures and cities are expected first to make their plans for redevelopment of commercial areas, and then pass these to the MOC for approval. To obtain the involvement of the MOC, and hence its substantial technical expertise and banking, three conditions have to apply. First, there have to be plans for an agreed local area communications network (LAN) within the redevelopment area. Second, where more than one redevelopment is considered, full telecommunication links between them must be possible (i.e. wide area network, or WAN). Finally, the city must be capable of attracting and promoting construction of office developments which can take advantage of the programme.

Again, as with most of the programmes discussed in this section, local government is expected to do most of the work in conjunction with private consultants. The MOC's role is to coordinate and facilitate development. Use is made of MOC optical fibre capable boxes at key positions such as highway interchanges. MOC officials report that it is intended to extend the concept over time to multi-function 'intelligent complexes' involving offices, hotels, schools, hospitals and so on.[64]

INFORMATION FUTURE CITY

Allied to the 'intelligent building' concept is the Information Future City programme initiated by the MITI in 1986.[65] Up to 1990, nine areas had received this designation, including waterfront redevelopment schemes at Tokyo, Osaka and Yokohama (covered below), Chiba's Makuhari business centre, Osaka's Rinku Town project, and development areas in Nagoya, Hiroshima and Sendai. The MITI initiated the programme to facilitate development of support information systems for 'smart card' security systems, household information systems, automatic garbage collection, and other advanced urban facilities.

RESEARCH CORE

In order to overcome the problems associated with the diffusion of technology to small- to medium-sized firms (experienced at both Tsukuba and with the technopolis programme), MITI has developed plans for a number of public research centres equipped with special facilities for small businesses wanting to locate close-by. The intention is to induce the exchange of research findings with the private sector and assist product innovation, new software, information processing and related industries. To maximise the opportunities for technology transfer, each research core complex has venture business incubators, training components and special joint venture research facilities. Similar to the technopolis programme, the research core programme encourages the collaboration of local governments and the private sector in funding, planning and construction. The national government commitment is limited to tax incentives, special credits, and insurance guarantees.[66] Thirty-three locations have been proposed since 1986. From these plans, eight locations have been developed, all near large metropolitan areas. These include Senri New Town, close to Osaka; Kurume Techno Park, a technopolis site near to Fukuoka in Kyushu; Eniwa Research Business Park close to Sapporo in Hokkaido; and the Kawasaki Research City in Kanagawa prefecture, close to Yokohama.[67]

Metropolitan Redevelopment Programmes

Since the early 1970s, laws designed to alleviate pollution and congestion problems have prevented the expansion of large-scale production within Japan's largest metropolitan areas (Tokyo, Osaka and Nagoya). Accordingly, both national and local planners have targeted the future role of these cities at the management and research end of industrial and technological growth. State-of-the-art infrastructure which supports these white collar activities is therefore vital for the competitive position of each city. In this context, the 1980s deregulation of the Japanese finance and telecommunication sectors led to a surge of inter-city rivalry concerning teleport programmes[68] and associated urban redevelopment schemes, often involving the reclamation of waterfront land, and generally planned by local governments jointly with private industry.

The projects described below are designated to upgrade communications and information services for the metropolitan areas concerned. They all rank among the largest redevelopment projects currently under way in Japan, and are supported by the Japanese government under its 'Information Future City' programme, discussed above.[69]

TOKYO TELEPORT TOWN

The Tokyo Metropolitan Government (TMG) is developing a reclaimed island (Tokyo Teleport Town) in Tokyo Bay as a teleport-based sub-centre of some 450 hectares, located some six kilometres away from the downtown area (see Fig. 9.5). While the eastern side of the reclaimed land will be retained for harbour uses, the heart of the new district will be a high-level telecommunications centre with information oriented business accommodation capable of twenty-four hour operation. The Tokyo Port Bridge, to be completed in 1993, will give direct access to the island from the mainland to the first stage of development, to be built later in the decade; and a new transportation system, including a light rail system and underground express highway, will be provided to service subsequent phases up to the year 2000. In conjunction with the new teleport will be a complex of intelligent office buildings, cultural and convention facilities to serve a working population of about 100 000 persons and a residential population of about 60 000. The development plan includes around 320 000 square metres of housing space and 150 000 square metres of commercial and cultural facilities. Waterside restaurants, shops, sports and recreation features will complement the technology-intensive infrastructure and so make for a densely-built multi-function urban area.[70]

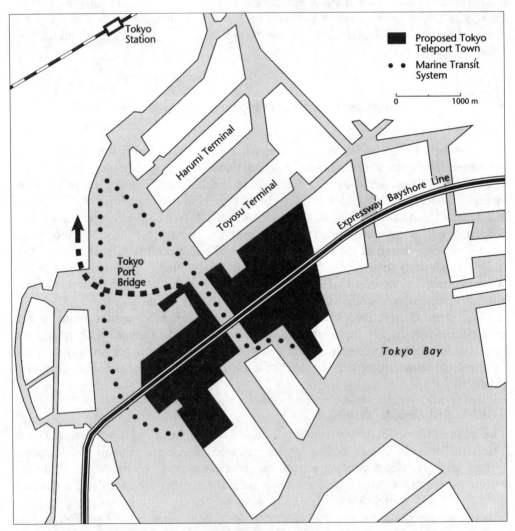

Fig. 9.5 Location of Tokyo Teleport (source: Tokyo Metropolitan Government, *Tokyo Teleport Town: Metropolitan Waterfront Subcentre*, Tokyo, TMG, 1990)

YOKOHAMA MINATO MIRAI 21

Minato Mirai (MM21) is translated from Japanese into English as 'the new port city for the twenty first century', and comprises a large-scale coastal redevelopment plan scheduled to be complete by the year 2000 (see Fig. 9.6). MM21 is being developed currently as a new business centre for Yokohama, 30 kilometres south of Tokyo, and extends over 180 hectares of existing and reclaimed land. The new centre is located on an area used until the mid-1980s as a railway marshalling yard, a dock, and a shipyard. An international exposition held on the development site in 1989 provided the catalyst for the initial clearing of land, provision of infrastructure and the opening of a new Yokohama Art Museum.

During 1992, the first stage of MM21 was completed with the introduction of a waterfront park, together with an international hotel and convention facilities, the latter ranking as the largest in Japan. Later stages include a 70 storey 'Landmark Tower' located at 'Block 25', and an Eastern Japan headquarters of the Sumitomo Corporation at 'Block 26' (Fig. 9.6). The former will be Japan's tallest building and is scheduled for completion in 1993. MM21 will also contain modern shopping complexes and hotels, together with parks and other open space covering twenty-five per cent of the site. It is predicted that the district will support a day-time population of 190 000 while its residential area will house just 10 000 persons. The housing will consist of modern apartments for single business people; families are not expected as the project contains no schools. Originally, MM21 did not include any housing, but as a '24-hour city' concept was promoted, the designers decided to include a modest amount of residential space.[71]

OSAKA TECHNOPORT

Since the Second World War, Japan's second largest metropolis—Osaka—has lost its relative share of commerce, finance and industrial strength to the nation's capital, and is now planning to revitalise its economy and stem the outflow of the key administrative and economic control functions to Tokyo.[72] Osaka must encourage new cosmopolitan and information-intensive activities in order to reinforce its role as a trade, technology-based production and finance centre. Fortunately, a host of large-scale projects—such as the nearby Kansai International Airport and Kansai Science City—promise to help the city attain these goals, and boost its infrastructure capacity to attract and retain knowledge-intensive industries.[73] The largest of these undertakings is the Osaka Technoport, based on three vast coastal reclamation areas totalling 775 hectares.[74] Together, these areas will form a new type of urban centre combining communications, research and advanced technology industries, as well as cultural and international trade activities. These large areas are set to be constructed in stages, but in its entirety, Technoport Osaka is scheduled to be completed around the year 2010 with a planned population of 60 000 residents and 92 000 commuters. Together with visitors, the day-time population is scheduled to be 200 000.

The reclaimed islands are ten kilometres from downtown Osaka and are called Nanko (South Port) and Hokko (North Port, comprising two islands) (Fig. 9.7). Of

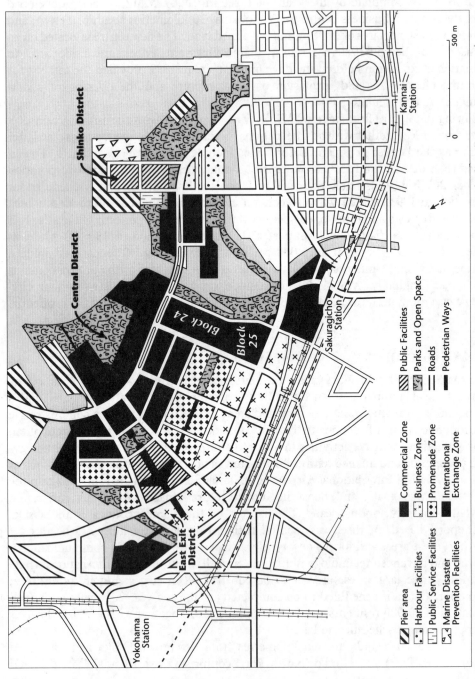

Fig. 9.6 Plan of Yokohama's Minato Mirai 21 (source: Yokohama Minato Mirai 21 Corporation, *Minato Mirai 21: A Leading Urban Development Project Representing Japan*, Yokohama, Yokohama Minato Mirai 21 Corporation, 1990)

these two areas, Nanko is presently being developed. It already contains the Osaka Port Town (a high-density residential redevelopment project for forty thousand persons), Japan's only functioning teleport, a software park, and 'Intex Osaka'— a major trade show and exhibition facility. Under construction in the immediate vicinity are the Osaka World Trade Centre, an International Trade Mart, an Asia/Pacific Trade Centre, and an air cargo terminal for the forthcoming Kansai International Airport. As for the other two islands, the Hokko North district is being planned currently as a 'sports island', and will become the city's largest athletic centre. Reclamation of the Hokko South island is still under way, and this district will be planned in detail at the beginning of the next century (Fig. 9.7). An express road to these islands from the mainland was already completed in 1989; during the 1990s an underground rail link will be developed to bring the Technoport complex closer to downtown Osaka and the new Kansai International Airport. To extend the communications functions of the Technoport, Osaka has established a public-private joint venture (the Osaka Media Port) to lay optic fibre cables from the teleport site to the downtown area and beyond, utilising the existing subway network.[75]

Evaluation

National economic planning in Japan has long involved specific and complementary programmes for cities and regions. These have been designed to make the spatial economy more efficient in order to foster overall economic growth.[76] Since the early 1980s, the Japanese government has again appeared determined to develop new forms of economic infrastructure; this time to promote innovation and technology into all facets of society—from national science cities and farming areas to downtown redevelopment schemes.

The logic of the programmes discussed in this chapter can be analysed on a number of different levels. First, technopolis and similar programmes are an attempt to counteract the magnetism of Tokyo and diffuse technology to local industries and areas. In Japan's mainstream of technology development, concentrated mainly around the major centres, the programmes of MITI and the other branches of government have often been found to operate at the margin, especially compared with the sizeable R and D effort by Japan's principal companies.[77] This has not been the case, however, for small- to medium-sized industry and for *jiba sangyo* firms in peripheral regions; and it is here that technopolis and the other projects are most supportive. Second, they may be seen as evidence of the ongoing ritual of administrative rivalry, in which MITI, the MPT, the National Land Agency and other ministries compete with each other for dominance in regional development policy as well as strategies to promote a high-tech economy and an information rich society.[78] Third, the programmes described in this chapter can be interpreted as part of the new balance between central and regional power, and a tentative move by local cities and towns to project their own regional interests. Thus, technopolis and the other programmes have been financed and implemented essentially by local bodies, whereas previous regional development was led

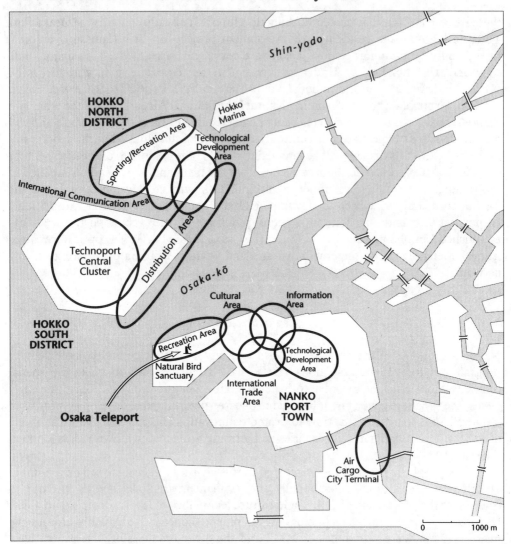

Fig. 9.7 Plan of Technoport Osaka (source: Ports and Harbour Bureau, City of Osaka, *Technoport Osaka: An Innovative Urban Development Scheme at the Port of Osaka*, Osaka, Ports and Harbour Bureau, City of Osaka, 1990)

primarily by central government. Finally, it is clear that shifts in the national economy favouring information-intensive services have fostered greater inter-city rivalry among the *daitoshi* for new investment. Sapporo, for instance, a city with about one million population at the nation's northern periphery, has established successfully its own Technopark aimed at providing an incubating environment for small computer firms.[79]

Despite the enthusiasm for regionally-based technology development, many commentators have argued that, to date, they have generated few direct 'spin-offs' for local firms (noted earlier), and that the net result of the programmes has been to reinforce the existing urban hierarchy.[80] This raises important issues of whether locally-based

Table 9.3 *Conceptual model of programmes for high-technology development in Japanese cities*

Level and scale	Programme	Responsibility
INTERNATIONAL	Tokyo and Osaka Teleport and related bayside developments	National Government/Tokyo Metropolitan Government/Osaka City Government
NATIONAL	Tsukuba Science City	National Government
	Kansai Science City	3 x Prefectures/National Government
LOCAL	26 x Technopolises	National/Prefectural Governments
	Teletopia	Ministry of Posts & Telecommunications
	RESEARCH CORE	MITI
	New Media Community	MITI
	Intelligent City	Ministry of Construction
	Information Future City	MITI
	Greentopia	Ministry for Agriculture, Forests and Fishing
	Key Facilities	MITI
	Minato Mirai 21	Yokohama City Government
	Numerous City Science Parks	City Governments

technology initiatives—such as technopolis and the 'key facilities' concept—can ever be successful in arresting the existing concentration of R and D, important information services, and associated technology-intensive production in Japan's large metropolitan areas, particularly greater Tokyo.[81] For example, to what degree do government plans for national science and technology cities at Tsukuba and Keihanna, and the encouragement of ambitious programmes at each core area for further development, compete for investment funds to promote regional decentralisation and make Tokyo, Osaka and Nagoya less favoured?

In practice, these projects are indeed in competition, yet to a large degree they are also complementary to each other within a broader national framework. Table 9.3 shows that the current Japanese strategies and projects can be structured into a hierarchy comprising three levels. At the highest level, Tokyo and Osaka, because of their scale and direct links with other countries, can be seen to operate as *international* level 'technopolises'. This pattern was affirmed by the Fourth Comprehensive National Development Plan (*Yonzenso*)[82] in which Tokyo, and to a lesser extent Osaka, were seen as Japan's international gateways, and therefore important contributors to the development of the nation's bid to internationalise in such fields as finance, information and technology. They will continue to be critical to the organisation of advanced technology firms throughout the country, largely due to the high density of opportunities they provide for personal informal contacts in production and marketing. At the second level, the government's Tsukuba Science City can be viewed as a *national* level technopolis,[83] together with the proposed Kansai Science City in Western Japan. Tsukuba and KSC will have the highest concentration of national research facilities, and, as long as open access by the private sector is maintained, they will be important resources providing 'seeds' for the future of industry for Japan as a whole. Finally, at a lower level in the hierarchy, the 26 designated areas of the technopolis programme, together with those newer programmes of MITI and the other ministries, and similar initiatives in other cities, are more local in their scale and impact. These programmes will provide important support services for local industry and small firms.

Notwithstanding this sense of hierarchy, which favours overall Tokyo and the *daitoshi*, local cities and regions have an important role to play under the Comprehensive Development Plan through upgrading their own R and D and information processing industries, as well as their local manufacturing activities. To the extent that they are successful in implementing these aims, programmes such as technopolis will be essential to *Yonzenso*'s goal of a multi-polar spatial structure and more decentralised development. The danger lies in a lack of differentiation between the large number of locations chosen for assistance. Accordingly, each city and region should continue developing a tightly targeted set of technology development objectives. Only in this way can national efficiency be maximised without zero-sum inter-prefectural competition for mobile high-technology firms. If this and other potential problems mentioned above can be overcome, then in the long run the local programmes will provide important counter-weights to the growth of Tokyo's congestion.[84]

NOTES AND REFERENCES

1 See Abe, H. and Alden, J. D., 'Regional Development Planning in Japan', *Regional Studies*, **22**, 1988, pp. 429–38.

2 Glickman, N. J., *The Growth and Management of the Japanese Urban System*, New York, Academic Press, 1979.

3 National Land Agency of Japan, *Sanzenso: The Third Comprehensive National Development Plan*, Tokyo, NLA, 1979; Kawashima, T., 'The Regional Pattern of the Japanese Economy: Its Characteristics and Trends' in Association of Japanese Geographers (ed.), *The Geography of Japan*, Tokyo, Teikoku-Shoin, 1980, pp. 390–414.

4 Japan External Trade Organisation, *Softnomics, the Service-Oriented Economy of Japan*, Tokyo, Jetro, 1984; Itakura, K., 'The "Soft" Sector of Japanese Industry', *Science Reports of Tohoku University, 7th Series (Geography)*, **34** (1) 1984, pp. 1–12.

5 Sargent, J., 'Industrial Location in Japan with Special Reference to the Semi-conductor Industry', *Geographical Journal*, **153**, 1987, pp. 72–85.

6 'Japanese Technology Survey' (Supplement), *Economist*, 2 December 1989, pp. 1–18; Ichikawa, S. et al., *Science and Technology Research in Japan's Future*, Tokyo, Foreign Press Centre, 1990.

7 Terasaka, A., Wakabayashi, Y., Nakabayashi, I. and Abe, K., 'The Transformation of Regional Systems in an Information-Oriented Society', *Geographical Review of Japan (Series B)*, **61**, 1988, pp. 159–73; Cheung, C., 'Regional Innovation Strategies and Information Society: A Review of Government Initiatives in Japan', *Asian Geographer*, **10**, 1991, pp. 48–49; Infocom Research, *Information and Communications in Japan, 1992*, Tokyo, Infocom Research Inc., 1992.

8 Onda, M., 'Tsukuba Science City Complex and the Japanese Technopolis Strategy' in Smilor, R. W., Kozmetsky, G. and Gibson, D. V. (eds.), *Creating the Technopolis: Linking Technology Commercialisation and Economic Development*, Cambridge, MA, Ballinger, 1988, pp. 51–68; Public Relations Committee, Tsukuba Science City, *Tsukuba Science City: A Bilingual Introduction to Research Institutes and Universities*, Tsukuba, Tsukuba Press, 1990.

9 For previous attempts at new town planning in Japan, see Kikuchi, S. and Inouchi, N., 'New Towns in Japan', *Geoforum*, 7, 1976, pp. 1–12; and Nagamine, H., 'New Town Development in Japan: An Experience of Muddling Through' in Phillips, D. R. (ed.), *New Towns in East and South East Asia: Planning and Development*, Hong Kong, Oxford University Press, 1987, pp. 170–201.

10 For a description of Tsukuba's early development, see Bloom, J. L. and Asano, S., 'Tsukuba Science City, Japan Tries Planned Innovation', *Science*, 212, 1981, pp. 1239–47; Takahashi, N., 'A New Concept in Building: Tsukuba Academic New Town', *Ekistics*, 289, 1981, pp. 302–06; and Edgington, D. W., 'Japan's City of Brains: Tsukuba Academic New Town', *Royal Australian Planning Institute Journal*, 21, 1983, pp. 130–32.

11 See Edgington, op. cit.

12 Taketoshi, M., *Explanatory Note on Tsukuba*, Mito, Ibaraki prefecture, 1984 (mimeo); Tatsuno, S., *The Technopolis Strategy*, New York, Prentice-Hall, 1986, p. 112.

13 Gregory, G., 'Science City: The Future Starts Here', *Far Eastern Economic Review*, 28 March 1985, pp. 43–48.

14 'Tsukuba Becoming a World Science City', *Shimizu Insight*, 2 (4) 1988, pp. 1–3.

15 Swinbanks, D., 'Tsukuba Science City, Success Coming – But Only Slowly', *Nature*, 345, 31 May 1990, pp. 378–79.

16 Public Relations Committee, Tsukuba Science City, op. cit. *Nikkei Weekly*, 1 June 1991.

17 Kansai Research Institute, *Kansai Science City*, Kyoto, Office of Science City, Public Works and Construction Department, Kyoto Prefectural Government, 1987; Kyoto Prefectural Government, *Kansai Science City*, Kyoto, Office of Science City, Public Works and Construction Department, Kyoto Prefectural Government, 1987; Kansai Research Institute, *Kansai Science City*, Kyoto, Kansai Research Institute, 1990. *Jetro*, 'Kansai Science City: Research Parks in Japan (12)', July 1991, pp. 5–7.

18 Personal communication with H. Monden, Planning Manager, Kansai Research Institute, Kyoto, June 1992.

19 Kansai Research Institute, op. cit., 1990. Note that shortage of funds for research 2institutes and the high cost of housing remain important obstacles for the implementation of KSC (see *Nikkei Weekly*, 27 June 1992).

20 *Jetro*, 'Hi-Touch Research Park: Research Parks in Japan (10)', March 1991, pp. 6–9.

21 See, for example, Japan Industrial Location Centre, *Technopolis Concept, Technology Integrated City*, Tokyo, JILC, 1981; Edgington, D. W., 'High Technology as a Regional Catalyst in Japan', *Royal Australian Planning Institute Journal*, 21, 1983, pp. 6–8; Japan External Trade Organisation, *Technopolis*, Tokyo, Jetro, 1983; Onda, op. cit.; Tatsuno, op. cit.; Masser, I., 'Technology and Regional Development Policy: A Review of Japan's Technopolis Programme', *Regional Studies*, 24, 1990, pp. 41–53; and Tatsuno, S. M., 'Building the Japanese Techno-State: The Regionalisation of Japanese High Tech Industrial Policies' in Hilpert, U. (ed.), *Regional Innovation and Decentralisation: High Tech Industry and Government Policy*, London, Routledge, 1991, pp. 219–36.

22 Japan Industrial Location Centre, *Present Situation of Technopolis and Techno-Network*, Tokyo, JILC, 1989; Japan Industrial Location Centre, *Technopolis Constructing Plan in Japan*, Tokyo, JILC, 1990 (mimeo); and Japan Industrial Location Centre, *Technoparks*

Manual: Development and Management, Tokyo, JILC, 1991 (mimeo).

23 See, for example, Edgington, 'High Technology as a Regional Catalyst in Japan', 1983, op. cit.

24 As noted by Nishioka, N., 'High Technology Industry: Location, Regional Development and International Trade Friction', *Aoyama Journal of Economics*, **36** (2–4) 1985, pp. 295–341; and Sargent, op. cit.

25 See Edgington, D. W., 'New Strategies for Technology Development in Japanese Cities and Regions', *Town Planning Review*, **60** (1) 1989, pp. 1–27.

26 Japan Regional Development Corporation, *Your Guide to Investment in Japan's Industrial Parks*, Tokyo, JRDC, 1984.

27 See Tatsuno, 1986, op. cit., pp. 273–76; and Masser, op. cit.

28 Blakely, E. J., Roberts, B. H. and Mandidis, P., 'Inducing High Tech: Principles of Designing Support Systems for the Formation and Attraction of Advanced Technology Firms', *International Journal of Technology Management*, **2**, 1987, p. 337–56.

29 Note that skilled labour still remains in relatively short supply in most of Japan outside the major centres, or *daitoshi*, and most firms relocating to technopolis zones are expected to provide their own.

30 'Nishi-Harima Technopolis', *Look Japan*, March 1987, pp. 13–15.

31 This point is argued by Nishioka, op. cit., p. 310; Fujita, K., 'The Technopolis: High Technology and Regional Development in Japan', *International Journal of Urban and Regional Research*, **12**, 1988, pp. 566–94; and Takeuchi, A., 'Spatial Conflicts Arising from the Restructuring of Japanese Industry' in Rich, D. C. and Linge, G. J. R. (eds.), *The State and the Spatial Management of Industrial Change*, London, Routledge, 1991, pp. 58–74.

32 *Jetro*, 'Oita Prefectural Soft Park: Research Parks in Japan (13)', October 1991, pp. 6–7.

33 See, for example, Segal, N. S., 'The Cambridge Phenomenon: Universities, Research and Local Economic Development in Great Britain' in Smilor, R. W., Kozmetsky, G. and Gibson, D. V. (eds.), *Creating the Technopolis: Linking Technology Commercialisation and Economic Development*, Cambridge, MA, Ballinger, 1988, pp. 81–90.

34 Higashi, C. and Lauter, G. P., *The Internationalisation of the Japanese Economy* (second edition), Boston, Kluwer Academic, 1991, p. 307.

35 National Land Agency, *Outline of the FY 1986 White Paper on National Land Use*, Tokyo, Foreign Press Centre, Japan, 1987.

36 Japan Industrial Location Centre, 1990, op. cit.

37 Tatsuno, 1986, op. cit.; Japan Industrial Location Centre, 1990, op. cit.

38 See also Japan Industrial Location Centre, 1989, op. cit.; Tatsuno, S. M., *Created in Japan: From Imitators to World-Class Innovators*, Cambridge, MA, Harper Business, 1990, p. 97.

39 Masser, op. cit.

40 Note that even the IC assembly factories relocating to Kyushu were mainly branch plants, with few R and D functions and high-technology subcontracting. R and D in the semiconductor industry has always remained firmly centred in the capital region. See Sargent, op. cit.

41 Personal communication with O. Sakaguchi, Technology Division, Hokkaido Prefectural Government, March 1988. Since then, another 13 companies were expected to open plants; personal communication with P. Shapira, February 1993.

42 Stohr, W. and Ponighaus, R., 'Toward a Data-based Evaluation of the Japanese Policy: The Effect of New Technological and Organisational Infrastructure on Urban and Regional Development', *Regional Studies*, **26**, 1992, pp. 605–18.

43 Japan Industrial Location Centre, 1989, op. cit.; *Nikkei Weekly*, 9 May 1992; personal communication with S. Iijima, Executive Director, Japan Industrial Location Centre, Tokyo, June 1992.

44 Morris, J. (ed.), *Japan and the Global Economy: Issues and Trends in the 1990s*, London, Routledge, 1991; Edgington, D. W., 'The Globalisation of Japanese Manufacturing Companies', *Growth and Change*, **24**, 1993, pp. 87–106.

45 According to MITI figures, in the 1980s the Tokyo metropolitan area had about 25 per cent of Japan's population and only 23 per cent of its plants and factories, but 46 per cent of private laboratories and 56 per cent of employees in the information service sectors (Japan Industrial Location Bureau, *Research Core and Key Facilities Siting Concept*, Tokyo, JILC, 1989, p. 26).

46 For their locations, see Industrial Location and Environmental Protection Bureau, MITI, *Regional Economic Policies in Japan*, Tokyo, MITI, 1990 (mimeo); Cheung, op. cit.; Infocom Research, op. cit.; and *Nikkei Weekly*, 18 July 1992.

47 Japan Industrial Location Bureau, 1991, op. cit., p. 27; personal communication with S. Iijima, op. cit.

48 For locations see Cheung, op. cit.

49 Personal communication with H. Ono, Machine Information Industry Division, Ministry of International Trade and Industry, March 1988.

50 Ibid.

51 Cheung, op. cit.

52 Infocom Research, op. cit.

53 Cheung, op. cit.

54 Ministry of Posts and Telecommunications, *Outline of Telecommunications Administration*, Tokyo, MPT, 1986.

55 For locations see Cheung, op. cit.

56 Ministry of Posts and Telecommunications, op. cit.

57 Infocom Research, op. cit.

58 Cheung, op. cit.

59 Advanced Information Congress, *Kinki New Media Map '87*, Osaka, Advanced Information Congress, 1987 (in Japanese).

60 For locations see Cheung, op. cit.

61 Ibid.

62 See Lipman, A. D., Sugarman, A. D. and Cushman, R. F., *Teleports and the Intelligent City*, Homewood, IL, Dow Jones-Irwin, 1986; *Science and Technology in Japan* (Special Feature on Intelligent Cities), **6** (22) 1987, pp. 6–17.

63 For locations see Cheung, op. cit.

64 Personal communication with T. Inui, Urban Policy Division, Ministry of Construction, March 1988.

65 Cheung, op. cit.

66 Kawashima, T. and Stohr, W., 'Decentralised Technology Policy: The Case of Japan', *Environment and Planning C*, **6**, 1988, pp. 472–92.

67 For locations see Cheung, op. cit.; and Industrial Location and Environmental Protection Bureau, MITI, op. cit.

68 Teleports are information bases, usually integrating earth satellite stations with overland optic fibre network systems; see Lipman, Sugarman and Cushman, op. cit.; and Noothoven van Goor, J. M. and Lefcoe, G. (eds.), *Teleports in the Information Age*, Amsterdam, Elsevier Science Publishers, 1987.

69 Personal communication with H. Ono, op. cit.

70 Otsuka, S., 'Tokyo Teleport' in Noothoven van Goor and Lefcoe (eds.), op. cit., pp. 307–12; Tokyo Metropolitan Government, *Tokyo Teleport Town: Metropolitan Waterfront Subcentre*, Tokyo, TMG, 1990.

71 Yokohama Minato Mirai 21 Corporation, *Minato Mirai 21: A Leading Urban Development Project Representing Japan*, Yokohama, Yokohama Minato Mirai 21 Corporation, 1990; Edgington, D. W., 'Economic Restructuring in Yokohama: From Gateway Port to International Core City', *Asian Geographer*, **10**, 1991, pp. 62–78.

72 Edgington, D. W., 'Managing Industrial Restructuring in the Kansai Region of Japan', *Geoforum*, **21**, 1990, pp. 1–22.

73 Morita, K. and Hiraoka, H., 'Technopolis Osaka: Integrating Urban Functions and Science' in Smilor, Kozmetsky and Gibson, op. cit., pp. 23–49.

74 Ports and Harbour Bureau, City of Osaka, *Technoport Osaka: An Innovative Urban Development Scheme at the Port of Osaka*, Osaka, Ports and Harbour Bureau, City of Osaka, 1990.

75 Ibid.; Ihda, K., 'Osaka Teleport as the Hub of the Technoport Osaka Development' in Noothoven van Goor and Lefcoe, op. cit., pp. 133–40; Edgington, D. W., 'Osaka and the Kansai Region of Japan' in Blakely, E. J. and Stimson, R. J. (eds.), *New Cities of the Pacific Rim*, Berkeley, Institute of Urban and Regional Development, University of California at Berkeley, 1992, pp. 10-1–10-22.

76 Glickman, op. cit.

77 See, for example, Friedman, D., *The Misunderstood Miracle: Industrial Development and Political Change in Japan*, Ithaca, Cornell University Press, 1988.

78 Johnson. C., 'MITI, MPT, and the Telecom Wars: How Japan Makes Policy for High Technology' in Johnson, C., D'Andrea Tyson, L. and Zysman, J. (eds.), *Politics and Productivity: The Real Story of Why Japan Works*, Cambridge, MA, Ballinger, 1989, pp. 177–241.

79 Sapporo City Government, *Sapporo Electronics Centre, Sapporo Techno Park*, Sapporo, Sapporo City Government, 1988; personal communication with S. Ikeda, Chief, Long-term Planning Section, City of Sapporo, Sapporo, July 1992.

80 These arguments are also set out in Nishioka, H. and Takeuchi, A., 'The Development of High Technology Industry in Japan' in Breheny, M. J. and McQuaid, R. (eds.), *The Development of High Technology Industries: An International Survey*, London, Croom Helm, 1987, pp. 262–95; Douglass, M., 'The Transnationalisation of Urbanisation in Japan', *International Journal of Urban and Regional Research*, 12, 1988, pp. 425–54; Glasmeir, A. K., 'The Japanese Technopolis Programme: High-tech Strategy or Industrial Policy in Disguise', *International Journal of Urban and Regional Research*, 11, 1987, pp. 268–84; Miyakawa, T. and Wada, N., 'Functions of Corporate Headquarters: Concentration in Tokyo', *Japanese Economic Studies*, XV (4) 1987, pp. 3–37; Sassen, S., *The Global City: New York, London, Tokyo*, Princeton, Princeton University Press, 1991; and Cheung, op. cit.

81 For a more optimistic viewpoint, see Tatsuno, 1991, op. cit.

82 National Land Agency, *The Fourth Comprehensive National Development Plan*, Tokyo, National Land Agency, 1987.

83 Taketoshi, op. cit.

84 For an interesting review of contemporary planning problems in the Tokyo metropolitan area, see Fuji, N., 'Directions for Growth', *Japan Echo*, 14, 1987, pp. 12–19; 'Rebuilding the Capital', *Japan Echo*, 15, 1988, pp. 5–33. Yasuda, Y., 'Tokyo On and Under the Bay', *Japan Quarterly*, 35 (2) 1988, pp. 118–26; Togo, H., 'Prospects for the Metropolitan Policy of the Twenty-First Century: Focussing on Tokyo', *The Wheel Extended*, 18 (3) 1989, pp. 17–23; and Cybriwsky, R., *Tokyo: The Changing Profile of an Urban Giant*, London, Belhaven, 1991.

ACKNOWLEDGEMENTS

The author wishes to acknowledge the valuable assistance of Professor Yuzo Kato, Faculty of Arts, Yokohama City University, during the summer of 1992 when this research was carried out. Financial support was provided by a Yokohama City Fellowship Award.

Chapter 10

Industrial Restructuring and Economic Development Strategies in a Japanese Steel Town: The Case of Kitakyushu

PHILIP SHAPIRA

Over the past decade, the traditional heartland manufacturing regions of North America and Western Europe have been transformed by industrial restructuring. In the US Midwest, Northern England, the Ruhr, Northern France, and other older industrial regions, industries producing steel, ships, textiles, machinery, and vehicles have undergone rationalisation, plant shutdowns, employment cutbacks, and fundamental changes in patterns of production and work.[1] For these regions, restructuring has invariably resulted in adverse consequences for affected workers and communities, with the decline of well-paid and unionised industrial jobs, unemployment, loss of income, and community disruption and decay being the usual aftermath.[2]

The challenges of industrial restructuring, regional decline, and economic revitalisation, so common in Europe and North America, have also been experienced in Japan despite the latter's impressive overall economic and technological growth. In the 1960s, coal mining regions suffered major employment losses through the switch to oil and cheaper imported coal.[3] The 1970s saw decline in Japan's textile producing areas.[4] Most recently, it has been the turn of heavy industries, such as shipbuilding, steel, and other metal-working sectors. These industries first began to face problems in the 1970s, with higher energy prices and the general slowdown of Japanese economic growth. Excess capacity and declining profits led to transfers of some existing employees to other companies, reductions in new hires, and cutbacks in temporary workers.[5] In the mid-1980s, a far deeper phase of restructuring was initiated following the growth of protectionism in export markets, shifts in domestic demand patterns, over-capacity, and much intensified competition from developing countries. The sharp increase in the value of the yen (*endaka*) after 1985 compounded the problems facing Japan's heavy industries, raising the relative costs of production in Japan *vis-à-vis* other countries. In the late 1980s, the fortunes of many Japanese heavy industries were lifted by unexpectedly strong domestic growth fuelled by increased construction and land values, an expanded financial sector, and higher public spending. But, in 1991, this so-called 'bubble-economy' collapsed, and through to 1994, many Japanese industries faced difficult conditions in their traditional core businesses in both domestic and export markets.

To respond to these changes in the economic environment, Japanese heavy industries have cut excess capacity and increased offshore sourcing and production, as well as introducing new technologies at home and diversifying into new business areas. Employment in parent companies and suppliers has been reduced. Unionised workers have largely been spared from involuntary redundancies, but they have experienced early retirement and transfers to other companies and locations. Non-union and subcontract workers have had far less protection. Unemployment has increased in traditional heavy industry regions, especially in the more peripheral parts of Hokkaido, Northern Honshu, and Kyushu. A string of one-industry towns built on steel, shipbuilding, and also coal mining have seen these industries phased out. Out-migration has increased from these areas to Tokyo, Osaka, and other cities in Japan's more prosperous central core, where high technology and advanced service industries have clustered.

Japan's older industrial regions thus face problems which planners in similar areas in the Atlantic economies would readily recognise. There are, of course, some important differences. Joblessness, while high by Japanese standards, has not reached the massive levels seen in the older regions of the United States, Britain, France and Belgium during the restructuring of their heavy industries in the 1970s and 1980s. Moreover, the worst fears in the period immediately following *endaka* about the demise of Japanese manufacturing industry and the 'hollowing out' of the economy have not been realised.[6] Nonetheless, at both central and local levels of government, it is now acknowledged that Japan's traditional heavy industry areas need assistance and a range of programmes have been introduced to develop new sources of employment and more diverse types of enterprises and economic activities.

This chapter examines the experience of one of these traditional heavy industrial areas—the city of Kitakyushu, located in the northern part of Kyushu (the most western of the four main islands of Japan). With a population of just over one million people, Kitakyushu's economy has long depended on metal, chemical, and other heavy industries. In particular, the city is home to the huge Yawata steel works, originally built by the Japanese government at the turn of the century and now owned by Nippon Steel, the world's largest steel company. Nippon Steel has been rationalising steel production and is diversifying into new industries. There has been a regional tilt to the company's restructuring programme, with steelmaking cut most in peripheral areas such as Kitakyushu. Steelmaking employment at the Yawata works and in associated sub-contractors has declined. The company's commitment to long-term employment for its unionised workers has avoided mass unemployment. Nonetheless, Kitakyushu's economic base has waned as a result of the phase-down of the Yawata works and other heavy industry plants. To address this problem, a series of new initiatives have been launched in the city to promote high-technology, small business, and tourism. Nippon Steel is involved in some of these efforts, most noticeably through building a huge space theme park on the site of former blast furnaces.

The chapter explores the processes, effects and responses to restructuring in a Japanese industrial region using Kitakyushu as a case study. After an overview of Kitakyushu's development and economic situation, there is a focus on the growth and decline of the city's Yawata steel works, Nippon Steel's restructuring strategy and its effects on Kitakyushu, and the employment adjustment process used at the works and among contractors. This is followed by a discussion of public and private projects to promote new forms of economic development in the city. The chapter offers an assessment of the likely effectiveness of these efforts.

Kitakyushu City: Regional and Industrial Context

Kitakyushu City spreads itself, in an elongated fashion, alongside the strait separating Northern Kyushu from the southern tip of Honshu, Japan's largest island (Fig. 10.1). The city's boundaries actually extend 32.5 kilometres east to west and 33.5 kilometres north to south, but much of the southern part of the city is taken up by low, non-developed, mountain ranges. To the north and east are flatlands, facing the sea. Heavy industrial and port facilities have been developed in the northern coastal zone, often on reclaimed land. The residential sector lies between the coastal industrial zone and the mountains to the rear, stretching in a narrow east-to-west line. Kitakyushu City was established in 1963 through the merger of five older and smaller cities: Kokura, a seventeenth-century castle town; the port city of Moji, once the main gateway to the island of Kyushu; the industrial city of Yawata; the coal port of Wakamatsu; and the industrial city and port of Tobata. Kokura is the main commercial hub, with smaller commercial districts found in the cores of the four other formerly independent cities and in the newer suburbs which have developed to the south and west.

The area's industrial development dates back to 1901, when the Japanese government established Japan's first integrated iron and steel plant at Yawata, then a small fishing village. Yawata's coastal location was convenient for using coal from the nearby Chikuho mines and iron ore shipped from China. By 1913, the Yawata works was making 85 per cent of Japan's steel. As the work's material needs and usable by-products grew, and aided by the development of infrastructure, energy resources, an industrial labour-force and culture, and government and corporate policies, metal-working and machinery companies and suppliers, chemical plants, cement and glass works, refractories, and other heavy industries were located nearby. Iron and steel, machinery, and materials-processing industries continue to dominate Kitakyushu's industrial structure, although most of these heavy industries have seen significant employment declines over the last two decades (Table 10.1).

Today, Kitakyushu is the heart of the North Kyushu Industrial Zone—one of Japan's four major industrial regions, the others being Keihin (Tokyo-Yokohama), Hanshin (Osaka-Kobe), and Chukyo (Nagoya). In recent years, the North Kyushu Industrial Zone has declined in importance due to the faster growth of the other three, more centrally-located, industrial areas, and the emergence of industrial areas elsewhere in Japan, including other cities and greenfield technology centres in Kyushu. A generation ago, Kitakyushu was the largest employment and population centre in Kyushu. But, over the last two decades, the prefectural capital of Fukuoka City,

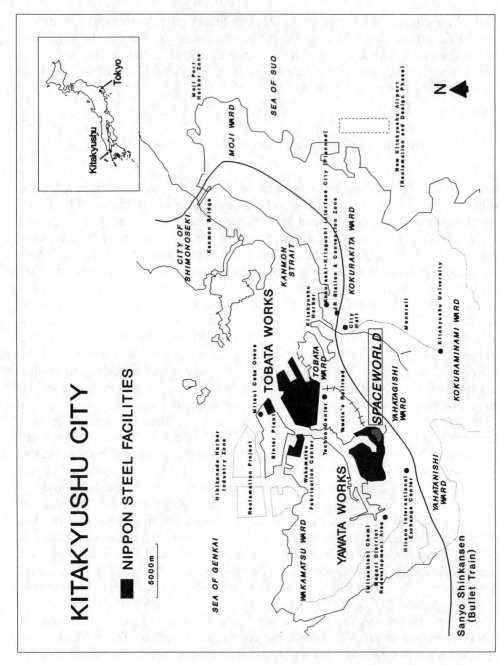

Fig. 10.1 Kitakyushu City

Table 10.1 *Kitakyushu City, manufacturing employment, 1965–1988*

Industry	Employment by industry class			Employment change		Average annual percentage change	
	1965	1985	1990	1965–90	1985–90	1965–90	1985–90
Iron and steel	47 263	21 993	14 953	−32 310	−7040	−4.5	−7.4
Fabricated metal products	12 784	6861	7885	−4899	1024	−1.9	2.8
Chemicals	11 234	6339	6158	−5076	−181	−2.4	−0.6
Food processing	10 645	5697	7802	−2843	2105	−1.2	6.5
General machinery	10 373	13 390	12 411	2038	−979	0.7	−1.5
Ceramics/cement	9921	5406	4707	−5214	−699	−2.9	−2.7
Lumber, paper & furniture	8445	3807	3850	−4595	43	−3.1	0.2
Printing/publication	5954	7121	6630	676	−491	0.4	−1.4
Electrical machinery	5161	8355	9515	4354	1160	2.5	2.6
Instruments	3220	1787	1532	−1688	−255	−2.9	3.0
Other industries	4604	6722	6065	1461	−657	1.1	−2.0
TOTAL MANUFACTURING	129 604	87 478	81 508	−48 096	−5970	−1.8	−1.4

Source: Kitakyushu City, Economic Affairs Bureau, data for establishments with three or more employees.

Table 10.2 *Employment change in Kitakyushu and Fukuoka districts and Fukuoka prefecture, 1974–1987*

Area		Employment		Increase or decrease	
		1974 (1000s)	1987 (1000s)	1974–87 (1000s)	1974–87 (%)
Kitakyushu district	Kitakyushu City	295.3	271.1	−24.2	−8.2
	Yawata	116.7	97.8	−18.9	−16.2
	Kokura	104.2	108.4	4.2	4.0
	Moji	31.1	32.7	1.7	5.3
	Tobata	22.8	16.4	−6.4	−28.1
	Wakamatsu	20.5	15.7	−4.7	−23.1
	Yukuhashi	17.7	27.7	9.9	55.9
	Total district	313.0	298.7	−14.3	−4.6
Fukuoka district	Fukuoka City	324.4	400.8	76.4	23.6
	Total district	355.6	463.2	107.6	30.3
Fukuoka prefecture	Total prefecture	900.7	994.6	93.9	10.4

Source: Data are for workers under employment insurance, by public employment security office (from Shimodaira, Hiromi, 'Restructuring of Regional Labour Markets and Labour Demand–Supply Imbalance Since the Late 1970s in Japan' [paper presented at the International Symposium on Problems of Local Employment under Structural Adjustment], Tokyo, National Institute of Employment and Vocational Research, 12–14 September 1989).

situated about 50 kilometres to the south-west, has gained a greater share of the region's new jobs in light manufacturing industries, business services, and administration, and now easily surpasses Kitakyushu in population. Kitakyushu has developed some diversified general machinery, electrical machinery, and food processing industries, and has attracted a few high-technology electronics and robotics factories. New service-sector jobs have been added, too. But the city still largely depends on its traditional heavy industrial and materials base. As these heavy industries have undergone restructuring and reductions in the labour force, Kitakyushu's economic foundation and economic position have been weakened. Kitakyushu's largest employment declines have occurred in the old heavy industrial core districts of Yawata, Moji, Tobata and Wakamatsu (Table 10.2). In these older industrial districts, the population has also fallen, largely as workers and new school and college graduates have left to find jobs elsewhere. Between 1975 and 1990, population changes of −23 per cent were recorded in the eastern part of Yawata, −18 per cent in Tobata, and −14 per cent in Moji. Over the same period, Kitakyushu City as a whole saw its population drop by about five per cent.[7]

The Yawata Works: Growth and Decline

By far the largest industrial employer in Kitakyushu—and the source of the city's greatest job loss—is Nippon Steel. The company's Yawata works, comprised of the original Yawata plant, the newer and nearby Tobata plant, and accompanying processing, storage and dock facilities, dominates the centre of the city (Fig. 10.1).[8]

In 1934, the government merged the Yawata works with six other private companies to form the Japan Iron and Steel Company. The works was heavily bombed in the Second World War, but after the war it was quickly restored. In the Occupation Government's effort to break up the *zaibatsu* (large combines), the Japan Iron and Steel Company was dissolved in 1950 into four private companies—of which the two largest were Yawata Iron and Steel and Fuji Iron and Steel. In the 1950s and 1960s, both of these companies embarked upon large plant expansions. In 1957, Yawata Steel began construction of a new integrated steel works on a reclaimed coastal site in Tobata, six kilometres from the Yawata works and linked by private railway. The Yawata and Fuji companies merged into Nippon Steel in 1970, effectively recreating a private version of the old Japan Iron and Steel Company.

Production at the Yawata works grew steadily after 1945, reaching 9.2 million tons in 1967 (Fig. 10.2). In 1969, a master plan was drawn up to rationalise and modernise the old Yawata works and to expand production capacity at the combined Yawata and Tobata sites to 10 million tons.[9] At that time, there were nine blast furnaces and five steelmaking plants at the two sites. The plan concentrated raw materials handling, iron- and steelmaking, and mass-production of coil and sheet products at Tobata and high-grade steel rolling at Yawata. Six blast furnaces at the Yawata site were closed, along with associated sinter plants, converters and casters. By the mid-1970s, three smaller blast furnaces at Tobata had been replaced by two state-of-the-art large furnaces. However, as steel demand faltered in the mid-1970s, plans to build a third new blast furnace at Tobata were shelved, and the works capacity was reduced to 7.5 million tons. Actual production after 1976 never reached this level and by 1984, at the end of the fifteen-year master plan, production was just over 5.8 million tons. Nonetheless, the modernisation of the Yawata works resulted in energy savings and productivity improvements and allowed a large labour reduction. The regular workforce, which had peaked at 43 700 in 1963 and had stood at 30 000 at the start of the master plan, was reduced to 14 700 by 1984. In 1988, with steel production falling to 4.6 million tons, regular employment at the Yawata works decreased to about 12 300. By 1991, with production at 3.3 million tons, the plant's regular employment had further declined to 9800, of whom 7100 were directly engaged in steelmaking. Most of the other regular workers were on secondment to other Nippon Steel businesses and associated companies.

The changes in Yawata's regular workforce are only part of the picture of the employment structure—and employment reductions—associated with the works. The Yawata plant, as with other Japanese steel plants and most large manufacturers, has a complex structure of subcontractors. These subcontractors, organised hierarchically in a series of tiers, provide materials, equipment, specialised technologies and labour. The first tier of subcontractors are the most technologically sophisticated, supplying and installing equipment and/or providing workers to continuously operate or maintain equipment at the works. Regular first-tier workers are usually unionised, although not in the same union as regular Nippon Steel workers since most private unions in Japan are

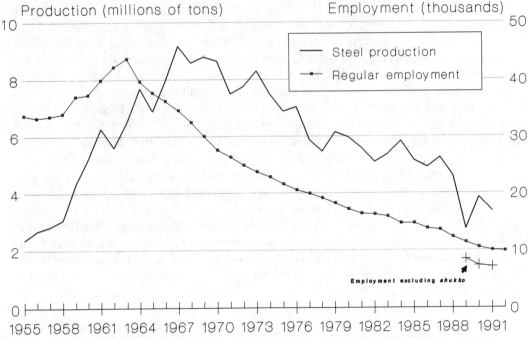

Fig. 10.2 Yawata Steel Works, production and employment, 1955–1992 (source: Nippon Steel)

enterprise-based. There are then further tiers of subcontractors, who are generally non-unionised, with lower wage levels than workers in the first tier of suppliers (who in turn have lower wages than regular Nippon Steel workers). Some lower-tier workers are regarded by their own companies as regular workers, some are temporary, and some are provided by other contractors. In many cases, subcontractors work inside the Yawata works, alongside regular Nippon Steel workers, sometimes taking responsibility for complete sections of the production process.[10]

Nippon Steel provides a large proportion of first-tier contractors' business and is able to limit the technologies they can sell to competing steelmakers. At the same time, this gives Nippon Steel an interest in ensuring these subcontractors continue to develop technologically. Transfers of personnel often take place, with former Nippon Steel executives assuming management positions in this tier of subcontract firms. In some cases, first-tier subcontractors have been aligned with Nippon Steel and the Yawata works for more than 70 years, developing very close relationships even though there are no legal or ownership ties. In a few cases, Nippon Steel has an ownership stake in close subcontractors. For lower tiers of contractors, Nippon Steel takes less of a direct interest.

Subcontracting is not unique to Japan. However, the subcontracting infrastructure associated with Yawata is more extensive and systematic than typically found in the USA and Western Europe. In the 1960s, when regular employment at the Yawata works exceeded 40 000 workers, there were approximately as many other workers employed in associated subcontractors. In 1988, with about 12 300 regular workers at Yawata, the subcontracting workforce to the plant was estimated at around 12 000.[11] By 1991, as Yawata's direct steelmaking employment fell to 7100, employment among plant subcontractors had declined to around 7000, of whom 5000 were employed in operational subcontracting firms and 2000 in repair subcontractors.[12] In the Japanese steel industry as a whole, there were 116 000 subcontract workers in 1987, compared with 118 100 regular workers—a subcontracting ratio of 49.6 per cent. In 1979, the subcontracting ratio was slightly lower, at 46.5 per cent, with 156 300 regular workers and 135 700 subcontract workers.[13] Thus, both at Yawata and elsewhere, the subcontracting workforce in steel has declined in parallel with the reduction in the regular workforce. While steel companies do use subcontractors as a reducible 'buffer' to save the jobs of regular workers (shifting work from subcontractors to regular workers) or to 'outsource' regular work at lower cost (shifting work from regular workers to subcontractors), they do not seem to have employed these strategies disproportionately.

Nippon Steel's Restructuring Strategies

In the mid-1980s, facing a slump in domestic demand, increased competition from newly industrialised economies, growing trade barriers, and a rising yen, Nippon Steel began developing a major corporate restructuring strategy. Announced in 1987, the strategy involved three major elements: the rationalisation of the basic steel business, the reduction of the steelmaking labour force, and diversification into new manufacturing and service businesses. The company planned to reduce its output to 24 million tons by 1990 yet to maintain close to a 100 per cent utilisation rate 'so as to maintain competitiveness with Korea'.[14] A capacity cutback of nearly one-third (10 million tons) was sought, with the closure of five blast furnaces, at Yawata, Muroran, Kamiashi, Hirohata and Sakai. It was anticipated that the shutdown of these blast furnaces and associated facilities would cause the loss of 19 000 steelmaking jobs by 1993, giving Nippon Steel a direct steelmaking workforce of 27 000—compared with 46 000 in 1986.[15] The planned workforce reductions would be made through a combination of normal retirement, transfer of workers to new businesses, and secondment to associated companies and suppliers. The company planned to concentrate production at four works which would continue to have blast furnaces (BFs), at Yawata (one BF), Nagoya (one BF), Kimitsu (three, including one shuttered blast furnace that was to be reopened), and Oita (two BFs) (Fig. 10.3).

After the initial publication of the company's restructuring strategy, Japanese industry did better in overcoming the effects of *endaka* than originally expected. Exports of steel-using products recovered and the government expanded domestic demand. After falling to 98 million tons in 1986, steel production recouped to 108 million tons in both 1989 and 1990, rather than the 90 million tons which had been expected a few years earlier. Nippon Steel implemented its plan to close blast furnaces at Yawata, Kamaishi and Sakai, but postponed the closure decision at Hirohata and reorganised the Muroran

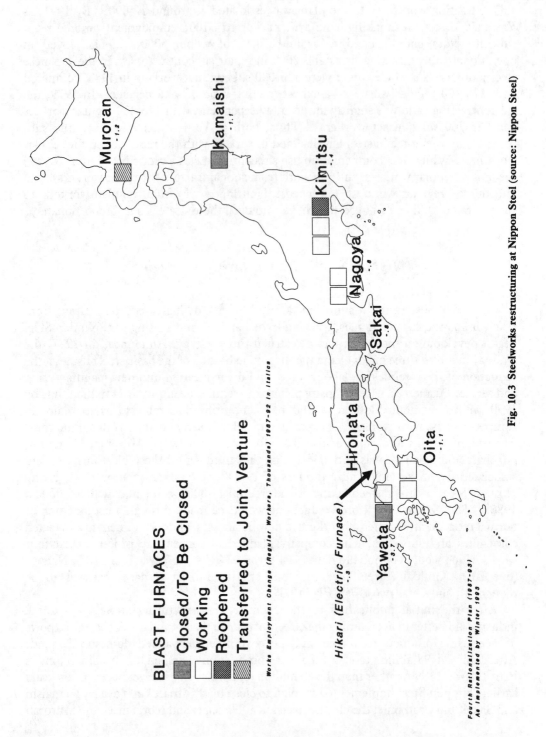

Fig. 10.3 Steelworks restructuring at Nippon Steel (source: Nippon Steel)

blast furnace into a new joint venture with Mitsubishi Steel. With capacity and employment slimmed down, Nippon Steel's plant utilisation rate and productivity surged, and ordinary profits swelled from a loss of 13 billion Yen in 1986 to a positive 202 billion Yen in 1990.[16]

However, with the collapse of the bubble economy towards the end of 1991, Japan entered an economic recession which has continued through to 1994. There has been a loss of steel demand in construction, car production and industrial machinery. Nippon Steel's production of crude steel fell from 29.0 million tons in 1990 to 27.7 million tons in 1991 and about 26 million tons in 1992, with company profits dropping to 100 billion Yen in 1991 and around 30 billion Yen for 1992. With the deterioration of the Japanese economy, a new medium-term management plan was prepared in 1991, setting a revised goal for the company of 24 650 steelworkers by the end of 1993 out of a total workforce of some 53 000, with a production target of 27 million tons. In March 1992, Nippon Steel's direct steelmaking workforce stood at about 29 000 (Fig. 10.4)—a decline of 17 000 workers compared with 1987. To further rationalise the workforce, the closure of the Hirohata blast furnace was re-set for mid-1993, and all works were required to make additional employment cuts. To maximise output from its reduced workforce, the company is centralising its integrated production at four works. At the same time, Nippon Steel has committed itself to additional capital equipment investment at its core facilities, to reduce bottlenecks, improve technology and quality, and produce high value-added products.[17] A new Research and Engineer Centre has been opened at Futtsu, Chiba, near Tokyo; major new or modernised steelmaking facilities have been put into operation or scheduled at Yawata, Nagoya, and Kimitsu; and new added-value or speciality steel products have been introduced. Nippon Steel's strategy of reducing employment, concentrating production, and upgrading its remaining plant will give it a highly productive steelmaking base. The company will be able to produce almost as much steel in the 1990s as it did in the 1980s (27–30 million tons) but with half the regular workforce.[18]

As part of its restructuring strategy, Nippon Steel instituted an ambitious long-term diversification programme. For many years, the company has operated chemical and engineering machinery and services divisions, based on by-products and skills derived from its basic steel business. In its 1987 corporate restructuring plan, Nippon Steel said it would adopt a new 'multiple-business' strategy, to build a range of other new businesses developed from its steelmaking, materials processing and technical expertise. As an extensive user of computer technologies, with over three thousand electronics engineers and software developers already on staff, Nippon Steel stated that it would capitalise on this skills base by developing new hardware and software businesses in electronics and information technologies. Similarly, the company planned to use its chemical and materials skills in producing new metallic and non-metallic advanced materials including fine ceramics, superconducting ceramics, and carbon fibres. Nippon Steel also established a biotechnology division, building on its expertise in chemicals and process control. Finally, the company sought to shift into urban development and community services, constructing new apartment buildings, developing large leisure and sports facilities, providing 'silver home' dwellings and medical services for the

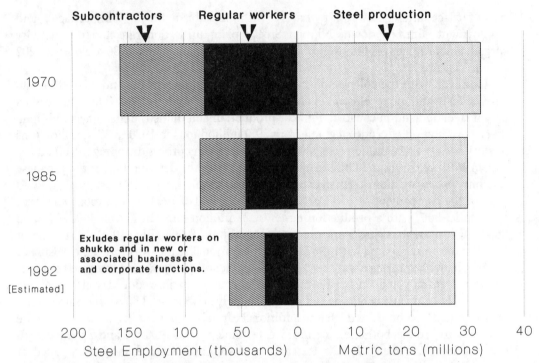

Fig. 10.4 Nippon Steel, steelmaking employment and production, 1970–1992 (source: Nippon Steel)

elderly, and offering training courses and conference management services. Again, Nippon Steel believed that its expertise in building and operating huge industrial plants, worker training, and managing worker housing and welfare was transferable to new development and service businesses.

These diversification plans were driven by Nippon Steel's desire to develop new technologies and businesses beyond steel, which could form a new basis for the company's activities in the 1990s and through to the twenty-first century. It was a strategy which envisaged a fundamental transformation of the company. In 1987, about 80 per cent of Nippon Steel's sales were from steel, with the other 20 per cent from engineering and chemicals. By 1995, Nippon Steel projected that steel would generate less than 50 per cent of sales. Electronics and information technologies were expected to contribute 20 per cent, urban development and community services 10 per cent, chemicals and advanced materials 10 per cent, engineering services 10 per cent, and biotechnology under one per cent.

However, achieving diversification at this scale and pace has turned out to be a difficult challenge for Nippon Steel. The company's search for diversification has led it into many new business areas, some of which are only tenuously linked to existing expertise. For instance, Nippon Steel has sponsored businesses to grow mushrooms at the axed Kamaishi Steel Works and flowers at Yawata—arguing that such products require temperature and process control, just like steel. Nippon Steel has also established several restaurants. In several cases, the company has failed in, or pulled back from, new businesses, including a mail order operation and ventures in training and conference management. An effort to employ displaced steelworkers to sew uniforms at the Muroran plant was closed down, facing severe cost competition from foreign manufacturers. Whether Nippon Steel ever really expected such largely non-technological ventures to continue into the long term is arguable. Their main function may well have been to provide employment opportunities for displaced workers near to retirement and to assure local communities fearing economic and social crisis that the company was making an effort to generate new jobs. More seriously, the company has had problems in new technological businesses designated by the company as critical to its future. In its electronics and information systems division, an effort to make and sell notebook computers was unsuccessful. The biotechnology business division was merged into the central corporate research and development programme, as the company realised it would take longer and require more research resources than originally anticipated to commercialise products. Moreover, while other Nippon Steel new information, software and electronics businesses have experienced growth, their contribution to total corporate revenue remains small (especially when sales to other parts of Nippon Steel are excluded). Recognising this, the company's 1991 revised medium-term plan established new targets, scaling back the planned contribution of other non-steel businesses to Nippon Steel's sales to 36 per cent by FY 1993, with engineering and chemicals comprising 25 per cent, and electronics, information, communications, and services 11 per cent. With the post-bubble economy slowdown, which has hurt electronics, information services and real estate development more than basic manufacturing industries, Nippon Steel now realises that even these revised targets will take some years after 1993 to achieve.

Nippon Steel's great strength in pursuing these new, albeit slimmed down, diversification targets is the strength of its core steelmaking business, where the company's continuous upgrading programmes provide it with a good technological and financial base. Nippon Steel is supplementing this with foreign joint ventures and acquisitions.[19] Still, the company is likely to face considerable difficulties as it moves outside its core steel business. Nippon Steel has to transform its traditional heavy industry management structure to one that can manage different and rapidly evolving technologies and markets. Moreover, while Nippon Steel could easily bankroll its fledgling new enterprises in the booming late 1980s, Japan's economic downturn of the early 1990s has already caused the company to pull back and rethink in some diversified areas. A continuation or deepening of this recession might further curtail Nippon Steel's ability to support unprofitable diversification efforts. Equally important, Japan's other major steelmakers are following similar diversification strategies. NKK, Sumitomo Metals and Kawasaki Steel are also diversifying into electronics, software, advanced materials (especially ceramics), biotechnology, urban development, and leisure.[20] There has been something of a 'follow-my-leader' approach, based in part on encouragement by the Ministry of International Trade and Industry (MITI). With numerous companies trying to squeeze into the same areas of new technology at a time of limited growth, the likelihood of failure for some is high.

Workforce and Supplier Adjustment

A major element of Nippon Steel's restructuring strategy is to reduce its steelmaking labour force. Here, Nippon Steel has to take account of the distinctive employment practices which structure labour relations in large Japanese companies. First, blue-collar workers in large Japanese firms are treated more like salaried employees in the USA or Europe. Male regular blue- and white-collar workers in Japan usually stay with a single company throughout their career and, in return, the company makes a commitment to job security. Second, there is a seniority-wage system, where a worker's basic wage rises each year, reinforcing the worker's commitment to the company. (There are also twice-yearly bonuses based on company performance and evaluations.) Third, large companies provide an array of non-wage benefits such as housing, health insurance, and leisure facilities. These non-wage benefits further strengthen ties between workers and the company. Finally, the union (which usually organises both white- and blue-collar workers) operates on an enterprise basis. This encourages the union to identify with the company and seek long-term company stability.[21]

These employment practices were largely established in the 1950s as the result of management strategies to stabilise labour relations and productivity and union efforts to improve working conditions and worker status.[22] One effect has been to make it hard directly to lay off regular workers in large firms. Although unions are enterprise-based, this does not mean they are unassertive. For the union, maintaining employment security is an absolute bottom line. However, for both the company and the union, this does not mean maintaining employment in the same job. Workers can be shifted between jobs, locations, division and companies. For example, as employees approach retirement age in large companies, they may go on *shukko*—or secondment—to smaller suppliers or even unrelated companies. The *shukko* worker receives seniority wages and benefits as if still employed at the parent company, but as the rate for the job in the out placement company is usually lower (since the out placement company will be smaller and the worker will have no seniority there), the parent company makes up the difference. By increasing the number of workers on *shukko*, a manager at a large company can decrease the direct workforce. Similarly, workers not near the age of retirement but in a business which needs to be cut back can be transferred to other divisions in the company which are doing well or, indeed, to a separate company.

At Nippon Steel, the company planned in 1987 for about 11 000 regular workers to leave the company by 1993 as a result of normal reductions—about one-quarter of the workforce at that time. Just a small share of this reduction was to be through normal worker turnover, as only about 200–300 workers a year leave the company voluntarily. Most (about 10 750) of the reduction was to come from workers retiring at the age of retirement (which is now 59 years old). As a result of hiring increases in the 1950s and 1960s, the company now has many older workers reaching the age of retirement. The company has offered additional financial incentives for early retirement for workers aged over 50 years. But few workers accept this since it is more beneficial (given seniority wages) for workers over 50 to stay with the company. Hence, the company operates a system of temporary suspension, for workers who have one year to go to retirement (at age 58). These workers take training and educational courses designed to help them get other jobs when they leave the company. This programme has reduced the workforce by an additional 2000. Nippon Steel has also absorbed more than 6000 steelworkers through *shukko* in other parts of existing businesses, new company non-steel businesses, suppliers, and transfers outside Nippon Steel. This is at some cost to the company, which in early 1992 had a total of 15 900 workers on various forms of *shukko* or transfer. In certain cases, for example, where Nippon Steel transfers workers to non-Nippon Steel businesses in designated employment development areas, the company can get a partial government subsidy for *shukko* costs, although most company *shukko* workers are not subsidised. Generally, *shukko* workers are trained on the job in their new workplace. The company has retrained a handful of production workers to become computer programmers in its new information businesses, but most of the workers shifted to new high technology businesses have been white-collar workers. By early 1992, Nippon Steel was not only on track to meeting its workforce rationalisation targets, but as noted earlier, was planning further reductions.

In addition to cutting its direct steelmaking workforce, Nippon Steel has slimmed its subcontracting labour. In 1987, Nippon Steel had a workforce of 20 000 contractors. By 1993, the company expected to halve its subcontract workforce, and in 1992, was well on the way to reaching this goal (Fig. 10.4). Some of the larger first-tier suppliers are unionised and try to avoid lay-offs of regular workers. These larger suppliers typically develop their own diversification strategies to reduce their dependence on Nippon Steel and develop new lines of business to re-employ regular workers. But temporary workers at suppliers and smaller labour contractors have no employment security. For example, in 1980, Kurosaki Refractories, a Yawata-based affiliate of Nippon Steel and manufac-turer of ceramic refractory bricks, employed 2800 regular workers and 1500 subcontract workers (who worked at Kurosaki).[23] Today, the company has 1750 regular workers and 1000 subcontract workers. A number of the regular workers retired at the age of retirement; others volunteered for early retirement and were helped to find other jobs. About one-third of the regular reductions were transferred to affiliates and suppliers of Kurosaki. The subcontract workers were let go at the end of their contracts.[24]

Employment and Community Impacts of Steel Restructuring in Kitakyushu

At the Yawata works, the cumulative effects of Nippon Steel's restructuring strategies have been severe. Although Yawata is one of the four works to survive Nippon Steel's restructuring strategy, its role has been downgraded. Yawata was once the most important and most advanced plant in the company. But this role has now been assumed by the Kimitsu works, which is not only newer but close to Tokyo. About 2500 regular jobs were lost at the plant between 1984 and 1988. Then, under Nippon Steel's restructuring strategy, another 650 regular jobs were cut when one of the two remaining blast furnaces at Yawata closed in December 1988. Yawata's research and development facility, employing 500 researchers, has been moved to the new Nippon Steel R and D centre close to Kimitsu. The Yawata works now has many vacant buildings and much unused land.

The Yawata works union branch, an affiliate of the national Nippon Steel Workers Union, has cooperated fully in the restructuring of the works. In February 1987, the national union was informed of the company's restructuring plans.[25] The union was concerned to maintain employment and develop procedures for worker adjustment. From February to May, there were 17 meetings between the company and the national union, after which an agreement was reached. At Yawata, the first decisions were not implemented until September 1987, while the blast furnace did not close until December 1988. Thus, the union felt there was a satisfactory period of notice. There have been no direct lay-offs of regular workers at Yawata. Workers have been transferred elsewhere in Nippon Steel (especially to Kimitsu, where a third blast furnace was re-opened), sent to new Nippon Steel enterprises, sent to work at supplier or customer plants, or retired one year early (on temporary suspension). Unlike some large closures or lay-offs in the United States or Europe, there were no local protests at Yawata, nor was any anti-closure labour-community coalition formed.[26] Although Japanese steel union officials naturally do not like plants to close, the commitment to employment security and the enterprise focus of the union minimises the possibility of local coalitions between community interests and the local union.

For the city of Kitakyushu, the restructuring of the Yawata works poses difficult economic challenges. The city is known as a 'castle town' for industries related to steel. City officials estimate that between 700 and 800 firms in the area are related to the Yawata plant. As employment and production at the Yawata works have declined, work for subcontractors and suppliers has fallen too, leading to increased unemployment. Immediately after *endaka*, in 1986, there were 4.3 workers seeking work for each job available in Kitakyushu, compared with 1.6 job seekers per available job for Japan as a whole. During Japan's period of strong economic growth from 1988 to 1991, there was an acute labour shortage for the country as a whole. But, even though the city's economy improved over these years, Kitakyushu consistently had more job seekers than available jobs. By 1992, the city still had 1.4 job seekers for each job, compared with one job available for every 0.9 job seekers for all of Japan.[27] Yet, while joblessness is higher in Kitakyushu than the national average, the city has not suffered the wholesale lay-offs and massive destruction of communities seen in US steelmaking areas such as Pittsburgh or in Sheffield and other parts of Northern Britain.[28]

Kitakyushu has seen an expansion in tertiary services employment since the 1970s, but at a slower rate than the national average.[29] Employment in the city's tertiary sector stood at 306 500 in 1990, a small increase of 15 000 over the 1980 level, or 4.4 per cent. Over the same period, Japan's employment in the tertiary sector grew by 18 per cent (Table 10.3). Between 1981 and 1986, tertiary employment actually fell in Kitakyushu by over 1900 jobs—a drop of 0.5 per cent, compared with a national increase of 9.4 per cent.[30] Tertiary jobs recovered somewhat in the late 1980s, but over the 1980–90 period, the city had employment declines in transportation, government services, and utilities, with zero growth in trade, eating and drinking establishment jobs. These tertiary industry declines reflected the general reduction in the city's core manufacturing base, which fell by 10 per cent over the 1980–90 period. Where tertiary industry jobs increased, the growth rates were much lower than for the country as a whole. Overall, tertiary employment growth in Kitakyushu in the 1980s has been weak.

Economic Regeneration Strategies

Although joblessness is higher in Kitakyushu than for the country as a whole, the most fundamental challenge facing the city is not so much one of dealing with immediate unemployment, but rather the longer-term one of creating new sources of economic activity and employment to replace the city's declining steel and heavy manufacturing base. Kitakyushu City has to define and develop a new economic future and rationale. Within the city government, as well as at the prefectural and national governmental levels, this problem is well recognised. Indeed, other Japanese heavy industrial cities, particularly those outside the Tokyo-Osaka core, confront similar problems.

At the national level, the Japanese government has long pursued policies to reduce Japan's chronic over-centralisation in large central cities (especially Tokyo) and promote balanced regional development. Comprehensive National Development Plans with such aims have been issued in 1962, 1969, 1977 and 1987 by the National Land Agency.[31] Over the years, a number of regional assistance measures have also been introduced by MITI and other agencies. Among the measures of this kind introduced in the 1980s are MITI's 'Brains-of-Industry Location Policy' (1988) to shift research and advanced technological facilities to outlying regions, and the well-known Technopolis programme (1983) to develop greenfield, regional high-technology centres.[32] MITI also administers the Law on Temporary Measures to Facilitate Industrial Structural Adjustment, which designates economically-depressed areas and provides funding, through the Facilitation Fund for Industrial Structural Adjustment, to promote the adjustment of troubled industries and support new businesses. The Ministry of Labour has special measures under the Employment Security in Designated Industries Law (1983) and the Law Concerning the Promotion of Local Economic Development (1987) to provide wage subsidies, job training, local economic development planning, and regional employment subsidies. Under another law, the Private Participation Promotional Law (1986), MITI supports the construction of research complexes, training centres, and technology and business incubator facilities by 'third sector' public and private entities in central cities. Other Japanese central ministries support a range of technology-based infrastructure programmes aimed broadly at regional development and industrial modernisation.[33]

Kitakyushu City has used several of the regional and economic development measures offered by central government in developing its own strategy for economic revitalisation. The city has initiated efforts to develop a new long-term vision of Kitakyushu, improve its image, develop new economic development organisations, and generate new employment through high technology, small enterprises, infrastructure

Table 10.3 *Kitakyushu City and Japan, employment change by sector, 1970–1990*

Sector	Employment by sector Kitakyushu (1000s)			Per cent employment change			
				Kitakyushu		Japan	
	1970	1980	1990	1970–80 (%)	1980–90 (%)	1970–80 (%)	1980–90 (%)
Agriculture forestry	9.9	6.0	4.5	−39.4	−25.5	−41.3	−28.6
Fishing	2.0	1.7	1.1	−16.4	−38.4	−14.5	−20.8
Mining	1.8	0.7	0.5	−60.7	−33.2	−50.0	−41.3
Construction	45.8	54.1	51.4	18.1	−5.1	35.8	8.5
Manufacturing	126.4	97.6	87.8	−22.8	−10.0	−3.4	10.5
Tertiary sector	270.2	293.5	306.5	8.6	4.4	26.1	17.8
Utilities	3.4	3.0	3.0	−9.5	−1.0	20.1	−4.3
Transportation	52.9	45.8	39.4	−13.5	−14.0	8.3	4.9
Retail, wholesale, eating & drinking	108.1	121.9	121.9	12.8	0.0	25.6	8.4
Finance, insurance, real estate	13.0	16.5	19.9	27.6	20.6	42.8	32.9
Business and personal services	77.4	92.3	108.9	19.3	17.9	33.7	34.9
Government	15.5	13.9	13.4	−10.6	−3.1	16.3	1.8
TOTAL EMPLOYMENT (includes unclassified)	456.6	454.5	453.7	−0.5	−0.2	6.1	10.5

	Indices of employment change (1970=100)					
	Kitakyushu			Japan		
	1970	1980	1990	1970	1980	1990
Primary sector	100	65	46	100	60	43
Secondary sector	100	88	80	100	105	115
Tertiary sector	100	109	113	100	126	149

Source: National Census, Management and Coordination Agency of Japan, various years.
Note: Primary sector = agriculture, forestry and fishing.
  Secondary sector = mining, construction and manufacturing.
  Tertiary sector = utilities, transportation services, retail and wholesale trade, eating and drinking establishments, business and personal services and government.

improvement, and tourism and services. The City's Economic Affairs Bureau, under the control of the mayor, is the main city economic development agency.[34] Bureau staff work with other city agencies, such as the Planning Bureau, with private and non-profit economic development groups, and with the Prefectural Government and MITI's Kyushu Bureau in nearby Fukuoka in developing and approving specific projects. The main elements and projects of Kitakyushu's regeneration strategy are described below.

STRATEGIC PLANNING

In 1987, Kitakyushu City established a 'City Basic Concept Study Council' to chart a new long-term strategy for Kitakyushu. The Council consists of elected officials, leaders from citizens' groups and business, academics, and other experts. To guide Kitakyushu through to the twenty-first century, the Council developed as its main theme: 'Towards an international technology-intensive waterfront city with greenery and heart-to-heart communication'. Five specific objectives were also defined: a comfortable residential city; a welfare-minded cultural city; an international technology-intensive, information city; a city of lively exchange with the world; and a science and research city of Asia. This initiative seems largely gauged to help Kitakyushu develop a new, modern image, but more specific work is under way to draft plans which will give more direction to the Council's concepts.

GROWTH COALITIONS AND PUBLIC-PRIVATE PARTNERSHIPS

Like other American and European cities struggling with industrial restructuring, Kitakyushu has developed new 'growth coalitions' aimed at mobilising resources, forging consensus, and speeding regeneration.[35] A particular case is the Kitakyushu Prosperity Enrichment Council (KPEC), a city-wide economic development organisation formed in 1988 with a membership of about one thousand individuals and companies. The KPEC explicitly models itself after the Allegheny Conference on Community Development in Pittsburgh, USA.[36] The KPEC has provided a forum for local leaders in the public and private sectors to discuss problems and coordinate strategies and projects.[37] Other organisations, such as the Kitakyushu Chamber of Commerce and Industry, the Kyushu Economic Research Centre, and the Kyushu-Yamaguchi Economic Federation, have also been involved in researching, developing, and supporting economic revitalisation in the city. To implement specific economic regeneration projects, Kitakyushu has seen the development of a number of public-private partnerships (also known as third-sector projects).[38] These usually involve city and prefectural agencies, MITI or another agency of central government, and private groups. Public-private partnerships become highly favoured vehicles to launch development projects in Kitakyushu (as elsewhere in Japan), through their ability to leverage public resources and engage private organisations and finance. Some of these projects are described in the following sections.

INTERNATIONALISATION

Internationalisation is a major theme of Kitakyushu's revitalisation strategy. City planners hope to change the city's industrial smokestack image and develop new business opportunities abroad, especially in East Asia. An International Centre has been built in Yahata Higashi ward to host academic, training and cultural exchanges. The city has developed sister-city ties with several Asian cities, including Inchon, South Korea.[39] International events, such as the Kyushu International Techno-Business Forum and Kyushu Asia Techno Fair (both in 1990) have been sponsored in cooperation with MITI and other regional and local economic organisations to advance technological exchange and business linkages between the city and economies such as Korea and Singapore. Kitakyushu City is also a partner in MITI's 'Internationalisation Model City' programme, designed to promote investment in internationally-oriented facilities (e.g. transport, communications), international exchange, and international awareness and education. The city has designated an International Convention Zone in downtown Kokura. Additionally, the city and central government have established an International Centre for the Study of East Asian Development in Kitakyushu (headed by a former Nippon Steel economist).

HIGH-TECHNOLOGY DEVELOPMENT

A major goal of the city is to develop new high-technology small firms. Financial incentives and technical assistance are offered for R and D, training and equipment. A city-sponsored group, Technomix Kitakyushu, has been organised among small and mid-sized companies in a variety of industries to provide opportunities to research and disseminate advanced technologies. By the end of 1992, sixteen companies had joined Technomix, participating in meetings, personnel interchange, networking, study tours (including visits overseas), and interactions with academic, governmental and industrial organisations. Additionally, an embryonic computer network called 'Kitten' is being sponsored to help information exchange among member small and mid-size firms. The city is also developing a Techno Centre park for innovative small firms. This 11 hectare facility will provide shared manufacturing research and development, and software facilities. It is being developed under MITI's 'Brains-of-Industry Location Policy' to decentralise research facilities in Japan in a public-private partnership, with funding from the Japan Regional Development Corporation, Fukuoka prefecture, Kitakyushu City and private business and financial organisations. The Techno Centre's main building opened in 1993, with 20 member companies, including four new 'incubator' enterprises.

The city is also promoting a new policy for the 'Multi-Media Town of Kitakyushu'. This project has the goal of promoting a visual information and multi-media industry in Kitakyushu, targeting technologies such as computer graphics, computer-aided design, and high-definition television for industrial uses. A software centre, an educational centre, and a 'soft park' to locate software companies are proposed. To guide the project, an Advisory Council has been established, which in late 1992 had a membership of 81 people, including representatives from 45 corporations.

TECHNOLOGY DEPLOYMENT AND ENTERPRISE ASSISTANCE

Several organisations exist in Kitakyushu City to help existing small and mid-size (i.e. with less than 300 employees) industrial firms modernise their technology, upgrade worker training, and develop new products and markets. These organisations include the Fukuoka Industrial Technology Centre, which provides research, technical assistance, access to new technology machines, training, and expert consultation to local industrial companies.[40] The centre is supported by the prefecture and city, with a small amount of additional assistance from MITI. Similar services are provided by the Kitakyushu Machine Industry Development Association, a member-sponsored organisation of local machining firms (although also with some MITI assistance too).[41] The city's Economic Affairs Bureau provides loans and grants to help smaller firms modernise. These organisations have assumed a renewed importance in the city as Nippon Steel and other larger companies have declined, and small local firms have to seek new technologies, products and markets to survive.

INDUSTRIAL SITES AND INDUSTRIAL ATTRACTION

The city plans to upgrade transport and port facilities in some of the coastal heavy industrial areas and is reclaiming and developing the 579 hectare Hibikinada Tobu Industrial Park. This industrial park will offer in-coming establishments a central government regional employment promotion subsidy and loans from the Japan Development Bank and the Japan Regional Development Corporation.

A handful of new companies have announced that they will locate new facilities in Kitakyushu. These include Yoshino Sekko, a plasterboard manufacturer which plans to open a factory with 100 employees in October 1993, and Nihon Denso, which expects to open a new automotive air-conditioner manufacturing plant with 350 jobs, also in 1993.

SPACE WORLD

Nippon Steel has located branches of some new businesses at Yawata, but its biggest diversification project at the works is Space World—a 20 hectare theme park modelled on a similar space theme park in Huntsville, Alabama. Opened in April 1990, Space World contains a large-scale amusement park with a space theme and an overnight-stay space camp for children.[42] Nippon Steel is the primary sponsor of the 30 000 million yen ($214 million) project, with minority participation by Kitakyushu City, Fukuoka prefecture, and the Facilitation Fund for Industrial Structural Adjustment of the Ministry of International Trade and Industry. A series of public infrastructure improvements have been made, including new roads, with the realignment of a major railway planned.[43]

INFRASTRUCTURE AND URBAN REDEVELOPMENT

Kitakyushu is linked by Shinkansen high-speed train to Tokyo, but it lacks the airport capacity to accept large domestic and international jet planes. The city has begun construction of a new 2500 metre runway on reclaimed land in the sea to the east of the city. About two-fifths of the land has already been reclaimed and city planners anticipate completion by 2005.[44] The city is also sponsoring several other major construction and redevelopment projects. These include the Magari District Redevelopment Project, to the west of the city, where Mitsubishi Chemicals and the Prince Hotel Chain are developing hotel and large-scale urban leisure facilities on the site of former Mitsubishi company housing. The city is working with Japan Railways to redevelop areas to the east and west of Kokura Station, and has also formulated a redevelopment plan for the Yawata Station area. Several other parts of the city have been designated as special development, industrial, resort, and residential zones, with improvements in transportation and other facilities planned. In particular, the city is promoting an urban development concept plan for 'Interface City Kokuraeki-Kitaguchi'. This plan, for a large zone between the waterfront and the northern entrance to Kokura Station, includes waterfront redevelopment and the building of business and commercial facilities, residential and hotel accommodation, amusement and recreation areas, exhibition and convention centres, and a trade mart. The proposed redevelopment is designed to form a 'twenty-first century' core district 'with creative space for exchange, gathering, and the development of a variety of urban activities'.[45]

Assessing Kitakyushu's Initiatives

Kitakyushu's economic development strategies are similar to those adopted elsewhere in Japan—and in comparable cities in the USA and Europe. The main thrust is to achieve economic diversification through a combination of image building, organisational development, technology, infrastructure improvement, small business, and tourism. How likely is it that these initiatives will succeed in Kitakyushu?

The biggest project to date in Kitakyushu is Space World. Many of the city's hopes for tourism, image improvement, and regeneration of the old Yawata works hinge on this venture. Yet the early signs are not promising. Space World was expected to attract two million visitors a year after opening, and then see increased attendance beyond that, but actual visitor attendance has not reached the planned levels. In 1990, Space World attracted 1.85 million visitors; in 1991, 1.65 million. The park employs 250 full-time and 500 part-time workers. About a half of the full-time workers are regular or permanent employees, with the other half on one-year temporary contracts. Of the part-time workers, three-fifths are women. Only about 80 former Nippon Steel employees work at Space World, mainly in maintenance. Most of the other park employees are new hires, generally in their early twenties. Average wages for these workers are about 550 Yen/hour—just below the level of the local Japanese McDonalds fast-food chain.[46] In short, Space World has yet to attract significant numbers of visitors and has generated few well-paid regular jobs.

Space World is one of numerous theme parks and leisure resorts now being developed in Japan. In addition to the Yawata project, Nippon Steel is developing a leisure park in conjunction with MCA of America at its Sakai plant. Other large industrial companies are developing similar projects—many at rundown shipyards, ironworks, coalmines, and similar disused industrial facilities.[47] MITI, through the 1987 General Recreational Resort Development Law, has been encouraging companies to initiate such projects. It provides financial incentives for leisure developments in areas of industrial depression and encourages industrial cities to become partners in these 'third sector' projects. But it does not appear to conduct any regional planning or comprehensive evaluation of proposed projects (in part because turning down a project would create political problems).[48] The Ministry has designated resort development and theme park sites in 35 of Japan's 47 prefectures (other theme parks have also been developed at non-designated sites). Japan's increased prosperity, the popularity of 'organised leisure', and the shortage of land for recreational purposes provide the basis for hopes that visitors will be attracted to theme parks and leisure projects in what are sometimes dirty and depressed industrial areas. Again, however, there seems to be a 'follow-my-leader' syndrome at work and it is not clear that all of the planned parks will succeed. Indeed, after the collapse of the 'bubble-economy' in late 1991, many resort development and theme park projects have run into difficulty, and have either been reduced in scale or partially cancelled.[49]

The lack of critical evaluation of large development projects extends to local government. Although Kitakyushu City is a financial contributor to Space World, the city government did not carry out any independent evaluation of the Space World project. The city was simply notified by Nippon Steel and asked to participate. The city did not do its own cost-benefit analyses or explore alternative uses for the site which— given the shortage of land in the city and the small number of new jobs that Space World will create—would seem to have been an important step. Rather, the city followed Nippon Steel's lead. Officials took the view that if the company was willing to risk its money, so was the city. But whether two million visitors will come to the park each year seems questionable. The works, located in an old industrial area, has no adjacent tourist-related facilities (such as hotels, shops or restaurants), there are few other visitor attractions in the city, and the present transportation infrastructure is limited.

Kitakyushu's efforts to attract high-technology industry are also likely to prove difficult. The city is not especially favoured as a high-tech site. Kitakyushu was developed by the Japanese government for the single purpose of making steel. Other aspects of the local economy have been traditionally under-developed. For example, the city is dominated by a few large heavy industrial plants, leading, according to local analysts, to an unfavourable 'smokestack' image and a dependent branch plant industrial culture. Factories with over 1000 workers engage 61 per cent of Kitakyushu's manufacturing workforce, compared with the national average of 13 per cent. Conversely, the city has a much lower than average share of small, innovative companies and plants, especially in high-technology industries. The island of Kyushu has attracted a large share of Japan's semiconductor plants, but few of these are in Kitakyushu. The city lacks a major technological university. Moreover, there is competition from other locations in Kyushu, especially through MITI's own programme of new technopolis centres designed to attract high-technology industries to peripheral sites. There are six new technopolises in Kyushu but, in order to create a spacious, greenfield environment, these centres have been deliberately placed outside older industrial areas.

Moreover, while the Japanese central government maintains industrial and regional policies to decentralise technology-intensive activities to peripheral regions such as Kitakyushu, in practice it is very difficult to overcome the pull of the major metropolitan areas in the Tokyo-Osaka belt. Corporate head offices, financial institutions, information resources, research and development centres, and political power cluster in this central belt, attracting most new high-technology activities too. Nippon Steel's decision to shift its research and development centre from Yawata to Kimitsu, close to Tokyo, and to put its most modern technology in the Kimitsu plant, reflects this. Additionally, while MITI does support regional development, the agency is also pursuing strategies to develop Tokyo as an international city to rival London and New York (which means increasing Tokyo's power over finance, technology and information). The view in both Kitakyushu and at MITI was that the strategy of making Tokyo a global city was much more important than decentralising some of Tokyo's functions to the regions.[50]

Kitakyushu's efforts to strengthen its existing small and medium-sized enterprises, to improve their technology and to help them develop new markets, especially in Asia, may be more promising. Many hundreds of smaller industrial firms in Kitakyushu have been helped by city industrial technology centres to modernise their manufacturing processes, learn about new research and products, and improve workforce training.[51] This activity is seen as relatively mundane by city officials, lacking the glamour of Space World and other mega-development projects. But, ultimately, the recasting and upgrading of the city's small-firm industrial base may prove one of the most fruitful and enduring ways of strengthening economic activity in Kitakyushu.

Concluding Comments

The experience of industrial restructuring at Kitakyushu provides several contrasts with experience in the United States and Europe. Perhaps one of the most striking differences is the way in which employment adjustment has been carried out. In Japan, the steel workforce at Nippon Steel has declined, but the employment practices and adjustment strategies used in the industry have avoided the massive displacement of regular workers. These practices and strategies include the commitment to employment security, temporary suspension (with pay) for workers close to retirement, and the use of buffer strategies, such as *shukko*, to transfer workers to suppliers and new diversified businesses. Nippon Steel's diversification efforts are based, in part, on the need to develop alternative sources of employment for redundant workers, as well as to develop new business and technological areas.

In important ways, Nippon Steel, as with other large Japanese companies, has taken on many of the functions of employment adjustment (e.g. job development and income maintenance) associated with the public sector in the USA and Europe. Workers in suppliers and subcontractors have received much less protection and have experienced unemployment. Nonetheless, taken as a whole, Nippon Steel has achieved a remarkably consistent and controlled decline in its total workforce in Kitakyushu, avoiding peaks of displacement (despite recessions).

However, while the worker adjustment process is different in Japan compared with the United States or Europe, the ultimate regional and economic development consequences have similarities. Although the worst excesses of massive displacement appear to have been avoided, Japanese communities like Kitakyushu which lose their heavy industries also lose the mainstay of their economic structure, and also have to develop new economic futures. Moreover, the decline of the steel industry (along with the decline of other heavy industries) has intensified regional disparities in Japan. As older heavy industries have waned in peripheral regions such as Kitakyushu and Nagasaki in Kyushu, Kamaishi in northern Honshu, and Hakodate and Muroran in Hokkaido, growth in new technology industries, research and development, and producer services has been concentrated in central Japan (in the Tokyo-Osaka belt), reinforcing core-periphery differences. Despite central government regional policies to decentralise technology and new industries, Tokyo has consolidated its position as the centre of Japanese political, financial and corporate power.

The restructuring of steel illustrates how the overall policy roles of Japanese government—at both central and local levels—appear to be changing. In the 1950s and 1960s, MITI played a critical role in rebuilding and expanding the Japanese steel industry, although often under the influence of the industry itself (MITI was known then as the 'Tokyo office of Yawata Steel').[52] Today, the links between MITI and the steel industry are still close and much formal and informal exchange goes on between the industry and the Ministry. But the role of MITI in guiding the recent restructuring of the steel industry does not seem to have been a large or conclusive one. Instead—and perhaps in search of a new role—MITI has focused its efforts on assisting smaller firms, policies to aid development of new technology industries and services (such as leisure parks), and regional development.

Local government, as in the case of Kitakyushu, has also been forced into a new role—one of devising economic development strategies to replace declining industries. This is an unfamiliar role for most Japanese cities, which now have to take leadership where it was once assumed by central government or large corporations. Older industrial cities in the USA and Europe have not found it easy to develop good jobs to replace those lost in declining heavy industries, and now increasingly suffer labour market polarisation. In Japan, despite much new enthusiasm for local economic development, it seems that heavy industrial cities like Kitakyushu will find it equally difficult to develop good new sources of employment to replace manufacturing jobs lost in the process of industrial structural change. The city's traditional industrial base is in decline and it has yet to find satisfactory alternatives. Efforts to develop high-technology industries and service industries (especially tourism) are under way, but face many difficulties. Central government policies conflict, working simultaneously to assist development but also to hinder it. The city government has been thrust into a new development role, but this role is often subsidiary to large and powerful private interests (such as Nippon Steel). The restructuring of industry and the pattern of regional development in Japan has shifted Kitakyushu City from its place as a centre of Japanese industrial development to a peripheral location with an uncertain future. Over the longer term, despite the city's ambitious revitalisation strategies, Kitakyushu's future may be one of declining population and employment and slower income growth.

NOTES AND REFERENCES

1 See, for example, Harrison, B. and Bluestone, B., *The Deindustrialization of America*, New York, Basic Books, 1982; and Wadley, D., *Restructuring the Regions*, Paris, Organisation for Economic Cooperation and Development, 1986.

2 Staudohar, P. and Brown, H. (eds.), *Deindustrialization and Plant Closure*, Lexington, MA, D. C. Heath, 1987; Rodwin, L. and Sazanami (eds.), *Deindustrialization and Regional Economic Transformation: The Experience of the United States*, Boston, MA, Unwin Hyman, 1989; and Hudson, R., *Wrecking a Region: State Policies, Party Politics, and Regional Change in North East England*, London, Pion, 1989.

3 Hein, L., *Fueling Growth: The Energy Revolution and Economic Policy in Postwar Japan*, Cambridge, MA, Harvard University Press, 1990. See also Vogel, E., *Comeback*, New York, Simon and Schuster, 1985 (esp. Chapter 4, 'Kyushu Without Coalmining: Managing Decline and Regional Renaissance').

4 Dore, R. P., *Structural Adjustment in Japan, 1970–82*, Geneva, International Labour Office, 1986.

5 Saxonhouse, Gary R., 'Industrial Restructuring in Japan', *Journal of Japan Studies*, 5 (2) Summer 1979, pp. 273–320.

6 Borrus, A. and Gross, N., 'Can Japan Keep its Economy from Hollowing Out?', *Business Week*, 13 July 1987.

7 National Census data, reported in the *Japan Statistical Yearbook*, Tokyo, Management and Coordination Agency of Japan, various years.

8 Information in this section is based on interviews at the Yawata plant in July 1989 and July 1990, and at Nippon Steel's Tokyo Office in July 1989, July 1990, and January 1993.

9 Kimura, T., *The Total Restructuring of Nippon Steel's Yawata Works*, Kitakyushu, Nippon Steel, mimeo, n.d.

10 The structure of subcontracting and employment at Yawata is similar to that described by Chalmers in her analysis of labour market segmentation and peripheral workers in Japan. See Chalmers, Norma, *Industrial Relations in Japan: The Peripheral Workforce*, London and New York, Routledge, 1989. Also Nakamura, Takafusa, *The Postwar Japanese Economy: Its Development and Structure*, Tokyo, University of Tokyo Press, 1981 (Chapter 5 on development of dual employment structure).

11 This estimate was provided by Professor Sadayuki Saito of the Kitakyushu Institute of Regional Studies in an interview at Kitakyushu University, 13 July 1989.

12 Information provided by Nippon Steel, Corporate Planning Division, 12 November 1992.

13 Data provided by Takuo Ishizuka of the Policy Department of the Japan Federation of Steel Workers' Unions (Tekko Roren), interview in Tokyo, 2 August 1989.

14 Discussion of Nippon Steel's restructuring assumptions and strategy is based on an interview with Shigeki Sugita, Senior Manager, Corporate Planning Division, Nippon Steel, Tokyo, 1 August 1989 and on company documents. See also Kashiwagi, Y., 'Steelyard Blues No More', *Look Japan*, August 1989.

15 Nippon Steel's total workforce in all lines of business totalled 65 100 in 1986, which included steelworks, engineering services, head office functions, and workers allocated to new businesses and associated companies (source: Nippon Steel, Corporate Planning Division, Tokyo, 12 November 1992).

16 Nippon Steel Corporation, Reference Data, supplied by Corporate Planning Division, Tokyo, January 1993.

17 Nippon Steel's capital investment was set at $600 billion Yen for 1991–93 in the company's 1991 medium-term plan. Actual investment totalled $200 billion Yen in 1991, the company's largest annual investment since 1983. Spending of $200 billion Yen is planned

for 1992 (Nippon Steel Corporation, *Basic Facts About Nippon Steel*, Tokyo, Nippon Steel Corporation, 1992; and Nippon Steel, *Annual Report*, Tokyo, Nippon Steel, September 1992).

18 If achieved, this will be equivalent to a 3.9 per cent average annual growth in regular steel workforce productivity between 1985 and 1993. While remarkable, this seems possible given that Nippon Steel attained a 3.4 per cent average annual growth in regular steel workforce productivity between 1970 and 1985.

19 Nippon Steel has signed joint ventures with Concurrent Computer Corporation (USA) to build supermini computers, GTX Corporation (USA) to develop CAD systems, Calgene (USA) to produce genetically engineered agricultural plants, and Philips (Netherlands) to create fundamental ceramics. Nippon Steel has also bought equity positions in small electronics industry start-ups, such as Soliton (ASIC') and Tau Engineering (data transmission and LSI design), developed a value-added agreement to use Nippon Steel applications software with SUN Microsystems workstations, and headhunted high-level biotechnology researchers from other corporated laboratories.

20 Isojima, Takeshi, 'Iron and Steel', *Japan Economic Almanac*, 1989.

21 Gordon, Andrew, *The Evolution of Labor Relations in Japan: Heavy Industry, 1853–1955*, Cambridge, MA, Harvard University Press, 1985.

22 Ibid.

23 Interview with Tateki Watanabe and Teruhisa Shiraishi, Kurosaki Refractories Co. Ltd, Kitakyushu, 20 July 1989.

24 Unfortunately, no specific statistics seem to be collected on what happens to subcontract workers, what levels of unemployment they suffer, and how many subcontract companies go bankrupt.

25 Interview with Kiyohara Matsuura, Assistant General Secretary, Nippon Steel Yawata Workers Union, Kitakyushu, 11 July 1989.

26 For US steel industry comparisons, see, for example, Lynd, Staughton, *The Fight Against Shutdowns*, San Pedro, CA, Singlejack Books, 1982; Bensman, David and Lynch, Roberta, *Rusted Dreams: Hard Times in a Steel Community*, New York, McGraw Hill, 1987.

27 Interview with Ryosuke Sonada, Manager, Yahata Public Employment Security Office, 18 July 1989, supplemented by employment security data from the Kitakyushu City Bureau of Economics, 1 December 1992. Figures for 1992 calculated from data for first nine months.

28 Hoerr, John P., *And the Wolf Finally Came: The Decline of the American Steel Industry*, Pittsburgh, University of Pittsburgh Press, 1988.

29 The tertiary sector covers employment in wholesale and retail trade, eating and drinking establishments, business and consumer services, transportation and communication, finance and insurance, real estate, utilities, and government not elsewhere counted.

30 *Annual Report on Labour Force Survey*, Tokyo, Statistics Bureau, Management and Coordination Agency; and Kitakyushu City, Economic Affairs Bureau data, various years.

31 National Land Agency, *The Fourth Comprehensive National Development Plan*, Tokyo, NLA, 1987. See also Alden, J. D., 'Metropolitan Planning in Japan', *Town Planning Review*, 55 (1) 1984.

32 Ministry of International Trade and Industry, *Regional Economic Policies in Japan*, Tokyo, Industrial Location and Environmental Protection Bureau, MITI, May 1989; Masser, I., 'Technology and Regional Development Policy: A Review of Japan's Technopolis Programme', *Regional Studies*, 24 (1) 1989.

33 See Edgington's chapter in this volume.

34 Interviews were conducted with officials from the Kitakyushu Economic Affairs Bureau on 12 July 1989 and 9 July 1990.

35 See Judd, D. and Parkinson, M. (eds.), *Leadership and Urban Regeneration: Cities in*

North America and Europe (Urban Affairs Annual Reviews, Vol. 37), Newbury Park, CA, Sage, 1990.

36 In 1987, sixty people from Kitakyushu, including the Mayor, went to visit Pittsburgh to examine the city's revitalisation efforts after the collapse of Pittsburgh's steel industry in the early 1980s. The group met with Pittsburgh officials and personnel from the Allegheny Conference on Community Development.

37 Interview with Tamotsu Takahashi, Chairman, Kitakyushu Prosperity Enrichment Council, Kitakyushu, 18 July 1989.

38 Yamazaki, H., *Japan's Regional Development Through Third Sector Projects: The Cases of Kitakyushu and Omuta* (Research Paper 9011), Morgantown, WV, Regional Research Institute, West Virginia University, 1990.

39 Japan Economic Newswire, 'Kitakyushu agrees sister-city ties with Inchon', 20 December 1988.

40 Interview with Mr Akaboshi and staff at the Fukuoka Industrial Technology Institute, Kitakyushu, 10 July 1990.

41 Interview with Noboru Kobayashi, Kitakyushu Machine Industry Development Association, Kitakyushu, 11 July 1990.

42 See Klamann, Edmunds, 'Can Mouse Ears Fit Steel Hats?', *Japan Economic Journal*, 28 April 1990.

43 Interview with Hiroshige Kobayashi, Spaceworld Inc., 9 July 1990.

44 The City of Kitakyushu's efforts to develop a new airport illustrate the long time gap that can occur between plan and implementation of major public development projects in Japan—if they are implemented at all. The city began planning the airport in 1971, with an initial request to the Ministry of Transport. The Ministry authorised the airport in the 1981 Comprehensive National Transport Plan. However, even though the city is reclaiming land, the central government has not finally approved the construction of the airport. Up to 1992, the Ministry of Transport had only designated funds (100 million Yen) for the airport design. But these funds are being held up by the Finance Ministry, pending agreements with the Defence Administration Facilities Agency and for compensation of fishermen. Another issue is duplication of new facilities completed at Fukuoka's Hakata Airport. Kitakyushu City, which in 1989 had projected completion by the year 2000, now hopes for completion by 2005.

45 City of Kitakyushu, *Overall District Development Plan: Interface City Kokuraeki-Kitaguchi*, provided by Bureau of Economic Affairs, December 1992.

46 Interview with Hiroshige Kobayashi, op. cit.

47 Other theme park projects are being developed by Sumitomo Heavy Industries (Kawana Marina at Oihama Shipyard, south west of Tokyo), Mitsui Mining (Coal-Geo-thermal-Bio-Park at Miike Mine, Omuta), Marubeni (Tanabe Bay Resort, Wakayama-ken), Matsushita (theme park at Yubari coal mine, Hokkaido), Nissan (a Mobility Park 'where people enjoy nature by car', Shizuoka-ken), and Honda (a mammoth 700 hectare Mobility World Motegi, Tochigi-ken). See 'Giant Resort-Leisure Land Development Projects in Japan', *Diamond Industria*, Japan Economic Journal, **19** (7) July 1989. This article lists many other theme park and leisure projects in addition to those described in the text.

48 Besides problems of over-supply, the demand for new leisure facilities—while growing in Japan—may be constrained by the fact that Japanese workers still work the highest number of hours a year of any industrialised country, taking few holidays. There has been a notable lack of success in reducing time spent at work.

49 One report indicates that two-thirds of designated resorts and theme parks have now been cut back (Murakami, Morio, 'After-Effects of the Bubble Economy', *Journal of Japanese Trade and Industry*, **4**, 1992).

50 Interview with Tetsuaki Nonaka and Yashuhide Yamada, Industrial Location and Environmental Protection Bureau, Ministry of

International Trade and Industry, Tokyo, 31 July 1989; interviews with officials from Kitakyushu City, July 1989 and 1990.

51 Shapira, P., 'Modernizing Small Manufacturers in Japan: The Role of Local Public Technology Centers', *Journal of Technology Transfer*, 17 (1) Winter 1992, pp. 40–57.

52 Johnson, Chalmers, *MITI and the Japanese Miracle*, Stanford, CA, Stanford University Press, 1982.

ACKNOWLEDGEMENTS

The author acknowledges the valuable assistance of Hiroe Yamazaki and Shuichi Hashiya in conducting the research on which this chapter is based. Further assistance was provided by Masao Maeoka. Initial support for the research was provided by West Virginia University. Additional support was provided by the School of Public Policy at Georgia Institute of Technology, the Georgia Tech Foundation, and the Japan Institute of Labour.

Chronology of Major Urban and Regional Planning Legislation in Japan

DAVID W. EDGINGTON

This appendix provides a chronological listing of major urban and regional planning legislation in Japan. The Ministry or agency responsible for administering the specific legislation is shown in brackets, using the following key:

CRDC	Chubu Regional Development Committee
EA	Environment Agency
EPA	Economic Planning Agency
HUDC	Housing and Urban Development Corporation
KRDC	Kinki Regional Development Committee
MAFF	Ministry of Agriculture, Forests and Fisheries
MITI	Ministry of International Trade and Industry
MOC	Ministry of Construction
MOE	Ministry of Education
MOF	Ministry of Finance
MOW	Ministry of Welfare
NCRDC	National Capital Regional Development Committee
NLA	National Land Agency

Chronology

The Tokyo Urban Improvement Ordinance, 1888
The start of Japanese modern town planning. This Act facilitated the construction of urban infrastructure in Japan's national capital (e.g. construction of new streets, bridges, water supply systems and parks).

'Old' City Planning Act, 1919
This provided the first national legal framework for land use controls and urban zoning systems in Japan's major cities, as well as the provision of major roads and other infrastructure and urban land readjustment. It was superseded by the City Planning Act, 1968.

Urban Building Act, 1919
Japan's first national building control legislation.

Outdoor Advertisement Act, 1949
In order to maintain the attractiveness of the cities, regulations may be framed to control the methods of display, form, colour, design and place of exhibition (MOC).

Building Standards Act, 1950
This Act revised the 1919 legislation. It set the basic standards of building construction and regulation of building activities necessary to redevelop cities after the war, in accordance with the zoning plans, and so encouraged orderly city planning (MOC).

Protection of Cultural Properties Act, 1950
Established zones for the preservation of a group of traditional structures to ensure an environment which promotes the value of groups of traditional buildings (MOE).

Housing Loan Corporation Act, 1950
Established a system of lending low-interest funds for the construction of houses for ownership on long term. Funds were extended by the national government through the Housing Loan Corporation due to the unwillingness of the general banking system to enter this market (MOF/MOC).

Comprehensive National Development Act, 1951
Authorised the Comprehensive National Development Plan which provides the basic guidelines for national development. The first Comprehensive National Development Plan was formulated in 1962, the New Comprehensive National Development Plan in 1966, and the Third Comprehensive National Development Plan in 1977. The Fourth and present Comprehensive National Development Plan was published in 1987 (NLA, formerly EPA).

Public Housing Act, 1951
Set up to supply low-rent public housing constructed by local government with subsidies from central government. The Ministry of Construction is empowered to set standards for public housing and lay out five-year construction plans under the Housing Construction Plan Act of 1966 (MOC).

Roads Act, 1952
The basic piece of legislation relating to roads. The law stipulates the procedures for classification, designation, definition etc. of roads. Furthermore, it establishes standards for road design and construction to encourage orderly city planning (MOC).

Land Readjustment Act, 1954
Set up to facilitate preemptive urban development by land consolidation in specific areas in authorised city plans. The method is to select a particular area and readjust housing land by means of land area reduction and land substituting, and to improve public facilities such as roads and parks (MOC).

Japan Housing Corporation Act, 1955
Founded the Japan Housing Corporation to procure land and construct apartment dwellings in large numbers, usually in suburban areas of large cities (MOC).

City Parks Act, 1956
Sets standards for city parks and green belts (MOC).

National Capital Region Basic Development Plan, 1956
Sets out a comprehensive plan to encourage decentralisation of economic activity away from the metropolitan core districts. The first plan of 1958 emphasised a strict green belt, while the current 1976 plan stresses suburban development areas and a number of long-term projects, such as expressways, new towns and the preservation of selected green areas (NLA, formerly NCRDC).

Natural Parks Act, 1957
Designates areas as National or Quasi-National Parks (MOW).

Industrial Location Control in the National Capital Region Act, 1959
Intended to constrain the further concentration of population and industry in the capital region by restricting the building and expansion of new factories, schools and universities in designated built-up areas (NLA, formerly NCRDC).

First Comprehensive National Development Plan, 1962
This Plan was formulated in line with the National Income Doubling Programme worked out in 1960. It aimed at balanced development to prevent excessive urban growth and to reduce income differentials between Japan's regions. To solve these problems, attempts were made to disperse industry and population from major cities to local communities. Certain local cities were designated as 'New Industrial Cities' and 'Special Areas for Industrial Consolidation'. These 'growth poles' comprised heavy-chemical and steel complexes ('kombinats') mainly in coastal regions (EPA).

The Development of the New Industrial Cities Act, 1962
From 1964 to 1966, fifteen (mainly coastal) areas throughout Japan were designated for special financial grants and other measures. Together they accounted for about 7.5 per cent of the national land and about 11 per cent of the total population (MITI and others).

Kinki Region Basic Development Act, 1963
This act contains provisions for the curtailment of over-concentration similar to those of the Act for the National Capital Region Development discussed above. The current plan of 1978 encourages the dispersal of population and industry from the built-up areas, to the suburban areas reflecting the rich historical and cultural background of this region and the need to revitalise the regional economy (NLA, formerly KRDC).

New Residential District Development Act, 1963
This legislation provides the legal basis for the compulsory acquisition of large parcels of land by local authorities or other development agencies, such as the HUDC (MOC).

Industrial Location Control in the Kinki Region Act, 1964
Intended to constrain the further concentration of population and industry in the capital region by restricting the building and expansion of new factories, government offices, schools and universities (NLA, formerly KRDC).

Development of the Special Areas for Industrial Consolidation Act, 1964
Similar to the Industrial Cities legislation, six areas in the Pacific belt were so designated, amounting to about two per cent of the national land and about 3.5 per cent of the population (MITI and others).

The Chubu Region Development Act, 1966
This region (centred on Aichi and surrounding prefectures in central Japan) is the third largest industrial and economic centre of Japan. This Act aims at promoting balanced development in the Chubu Region and contains provision similar to those of the National Capital Area and Kinki Development Acts (NLA, formerly CRDC).

Special Measures for the Preservation of Historic Landscape in Ancient Capitals Act, 1966
Allows special zones for preservation of landscape areas for cities with historical status as the political and cultural centres of previous eras in Japan, such as Kyoto, Nara and Kamakura (MOC).

Basic Law for Pollution Control, 1967
The first national measure in which the government recognised its duty to protect citizens from environmental harm. This legislation was strengthened in 1970, by giving local authorities power to regulate air and water pollution, and by providing relief for pollution victims (EA, formerly MOW).

City Planning Act, 1968
This extended the 'old' city planning legislation to allow for a system of development control and more concrete zoning provisions in order to control rapid urban sprawl. The control of city planning was delegated in principle to prefectural and municipal governments, and city planning areas of major cities were divided into urbanisation promotion areas and urbanisation control areas. This Act (together with the Building Standard Act) was amended in 1980 to introduce selective district planning, i.e. on a detailed block-by-block basis (MOC).

Urban Redevelopment Act, 1969
Set up to facilitate urban renewal, particularly in large cities. The method is to redevelop urban areas by pooling property rights (often by a 'vertical' exchange of property rights) and by developing public facilities together with buildings (MOC).

New Comprehensive National Development Plan (Shinzenso), 1969
Under this new plan, networks of Shinkansen rail and express road transport were advocated on a national scale, together with further large-scale industrial 'kombinat' projects (EPA).

Land Price Publication Act, 1969
Introduced measures to cope with land price inflation. Specifically, it provided a reliable pricing guide to land in order to formulate rational land prices (NLA, formerly MOC).

Introduction of Industry into Rural Areas Act, 1971
This encouraged the induction of industry, wholesalers and transportation activities into rural areas in a more systematic manner, with loans and special grants (MITI/MAFF).

Promotion of Industrial Relocation Act, 1972
Has the purpose of promoting the relocation of factories from overcrowded areas of the national capital region, the Kinki region and other metropolitan regions (relocation promotion areas), to peripheral areas (inducement areas), by means of subsidies and loans from the Japan Regional Development Corporation (MITI).

Nature Conservation Act, 1972
Set up an administration framework for nature conservation, including surveys of the natural environment and the establishment of wilderness and nature conservation areas (EA).

Urban Green Conservation Act, 1973
Allowed local governments to fix green space conservation districts as open spaces which have meritorious natural environment within city planning areas (MOC).

National Land Use Planning Act, 1974
This Act provided for a fundamental legal designation of all national land for the whole country according to five basic categories (i.e. urban areas, agricultural areas, forests, natural parks and nature preservation areas). This designation was designed to enhance rational use of national land. The legislation also incorporates land transaction control measures in order to keep track of major land transactions for taxation purposes, and to have control over land prices (NLA).

New Town Development Public Corporation Act, 1975
This Corporation was established to supply large-scale housing land in the suburban areas in large metropolitan regions where there was an acute shortage of housing. This body was amalgamated with the Housing Corporation in 1982 to form the Housing and Urban Development Corporation (MOC).

Third Comprehensive National Development Plan (Sanzenso), 1977
Under the third plan, priority was given to a system of 'settled habitation areas' where balanced development would occur through natural increase rather than immigration. Moreover, for the first time, conservation of the environment was addressed, together with the provision of urban social and welfare facilities in local communities, rather than merely industry (NLA).

Acceleration of Regional Development Based upon High-Technology Industrial Complexes Act (Technopolis Law), 1983
Set up to facilitate the Technopolis Development Plan by establishing a process for the designation of 'technopolis' zones. By 1989, 26 technopolis zones had been designated across the nation (MITI and others).

Promotion of the Construction of Special Facilities through the Participation of Private Enterprises Act (Private Participation Promotional Law), 1986
This legislation allows private-sector enterprises to participate in local development plans (e.g. for new research complexes) through contributing to the technology and expenses of public infrastructure (roads, interchanges etc.). It is hoped that the use of private technical and financial resources in public projects would keep public funding to a minimum and allow new projects to be profitable (MITI and others).

Fourth Comprehensive National Development Plan (Yonzenso), 1987
Intended to set the nation's development plan to the year 2000. It recognises the strong trends towards internationalisation, ageing, informationisation, and attempts the transformation of the uni-polar national structure focused on Tokyo to a multi-core structure, in which each area shares urban functions and supports the others (NLA).

Promotion of Group-Siting of Designated Types of Businesses' Contribution to More Sophisticated Local Industrial Structures Act (Key Facilities Siting Law), 1988
Provides for the Japan Regional Development Corporation to develop business parks, and other incentives, to encourage group-siting of 'brains of industry' functions (e.g. R and D laboratories, design and information services). These are located in designated peripheral areas in order to promote the decentralisation of industry (MITI).

Formation of a Multi-Polar Pattern of National Land Use Act, 1988
Provides for special measures (grants, subsidies etc.) to implement the objectives of *Yonzenso* (NLA).

Development of Local Growth-Pole Cities and Promotion of Relocation of Industry and Business Act, 1992
Provides for special measures to implement urban infrastructure in major regional centres (MOC and others).

Relocation of the National Diet Act, 1992
Legislation introduced by Japan's parliament (*Diet*) authorising the government to consider strategies for relocating parliament and government offices outside the metropolitan area (NLA).

ACKNOWLEDGEMENTS

A number of sources were used in compiling this list, including Japan International Cooperation Agency and City Bureau, Ministry of Construction, *City Planning in Japan*, Tokyo, JICA, 1990 (mimeo); Industrial Location and Environmental Protection Bureau, MITI, *Regional Economic Policies in Japan*, Tokyo, MITI, 1990 (mimeo); and personal communication with Makoto Taketoshi, Ministry of Construction, March 1993.

Appendix II

Selected Literature on Japanese Urban and Regional Planning

PHILIP SHAPIRA, CHET ASKEY and DAVID W. EDGINGTON

This appendix provides a selective listing of English-language literature on Japanese urban and regional planning, including books, government reports, articles and book chapters. The list does not claim to be exhaustive, but it should provide sources for further reading on topics discussed in the chapters of this book. General references on Japan and its history, politics and economy are not included, as this literature may be readily found elsewhere. However, on the interrelationship between national policies and development in Japan, which provides an important context for understanding urban and regional planning, see ALLEN, G. C., *The Japanese Economy*, London, Weidenfeld and Nicolson, 1980; JOHNSON, C., *MITI and the Japanese Miracle*, Stanford, CA, Stanford University Press, 1982; and OKIMOTO, D., *Between MITI and the Market: Japanese Industrial Policy for High Technology*, Stanford, CA, Stanford University Press, 1989. A contrary view, downplaying the effects of government intervention, is offered by FRIEDMAN, D., *The Misunderstood Miracle: Industrial Development and Political Change in Japan*, Ithaca, NY, Cornell University Press, 1988—also of interest due to his case study of small firm regional industrialism in Sakai, Nagano prefecture. For analyses of community organisation and ethnography—another important context for understanding urban and regional planning in Japan—see the classic study by DORE, R., *City Life in Japan*, Berkeley, CA, University of California Press, 1958; and more recent studies by BESTOR, T., *Neighborhood Tokyo*, Stanford, CA, Stanford University Press, 1989, and ROBERTSON, J., *Native and Newcomer: Making and Remaking a Japanese City*, Berkeley, CA, University of California Press, 1991. For a well-referenced perspective on contemporary rural life in Japan, see KELLY, W. W., 'Regional Japan: The Price of Prosperity and the Benefits of Dependency', *Daedalus*, **119** (3) Summer 1990, pp. 209–27.

Books and Reports

ASSOCIATION OF JAPANESE GEOGRAPHERS (ed.), *Geography of Japan*, Tokyo, The Teikoku-Shoin Co., 1980. A good introduction to the geography and regions of Japan. Includes an appendix of source materials and a glossary of Japanese terms.

Another concise book on Japan's regional and economic geography is NOH, T. and KIMURA, J. C. (eds.), *Japan: A Regional Geography of an Island Nation* (second edition), Tokyo, Teikoku-Shoin Co., 1989. A useful accompanying atlas is TEIKOKU-SHOIN CO., *Teikoku's Complete Atlas of Japan* (ninth edition), Tokyo, Teikoku-Shoin Co., 1987. Another standard, but now economically outdated, book on Japanese regional geography is TREWARTHA, G., *Japan: A Geography*, Madison, WI, University of Wisconsin Press, 1965.

BARRETT, B. and THERIVEL, R., *Environmental Policy and Impact Assessment in Japan*, London, Routledge, 1991. Reviews national and local policies towards the environment in Japan, including the role of citizen groups, and discusses how environmental assessment tools are used. Included are case studies of environmental planning and assessment for several large Japanese development and infrastructure projects.

CYBRIWSKY, R., *Tokyo: The Changing Profile of an Urban Giant*, London, Pinter, 1991. Discusses Tokyo's varied districts and neighbourhoods in the context of the city's development and planning (or, at times, lack of planning). The effects of geographical, historical, and natural events are also examined. Cybriwsky discusses the planning activity of present-day Tokyo, including the *My Town Tokyo* projects developed by the Tokyo Metropolitan Government and waterfront development projects along Tokyo Bay, and looks at planning efforts in prefectures adjacent to Tokyo. There is a bibliography of English-language materials on Tokyo.

EYRE, J. D., *Nagoya, the Changing Geography of a Japanese Regional Metropolis*, Chapel Hill, NC, Department of Geography, University of North Carolina at Chapel Hill, 1982. This monographic study of Nagoya and its metropolitan area is based on extensive field work and repeated visits over more than twenty years. Among the topics covered are the city's history, the development of industry during the twentieth century, the massive in-migration to the city after the Second World War, and the more recent out-migration from the city to the suburbs. Other chapters discuss the construction of housing, the development of modern transportation systems, and the economy of the wider metropolitan (Chukyo) region.

FUJITA, K. and HILL, R. C. (eds.), *Japanese Cities in the World Economy*, Philadelphia, PA, Temple University Press, 1993. A collection of essays on Japanese cities which emphasises the interaction between economic organisation, industrial restructuring, and government policy with urban development. The places examined include the large metropolises of Tokyo, Osaka and Nagoya, the industrial cities of Kamaishi, Kitakyushu and Toyota, the high-tech centre of Kanagawa, and the small-firm industrial district of Tsubame in Niigata prefecture. There are also contributions on urban growth in pre-war Japan, the current role of Japanese cities in the world economy, and the export of Japanese city planning ideas.

GLICKMAN, N. J., *The Growth and Management of the Japanese Urban System*, New York, Academic Press, 1979. A now classic regional science analysis of Japanese urban growth from the end of the Second World War until the 1970s. Core cities and surrounding areas in Japan are analysed as Regional Economic Clusters, with comparisons made with trends in both developed and less developed countries during the 1950s and 1960s. Glickman studies the relationships between population migration and employment growth in Japan, as well as the distributional effectiveness of Japanese regional planning, concluding that Japanese urbanisation is shifting from centralisation to deconcentration.

HANAYAMA, Y., *Land Markets and Land Policy in a Metropolitan Area*, Boston, Oelgeschlager, Gunn and Hain, 1986. This study of Tokyo's land problems aims to demystify issues related to the shortage of land for housing, the continuous increase in land prices, and the apparent futility of land policies. It provides a historical sketch of Tokyo's development and various government land tax policies, followed by an in-depth analysis of the structure of the land market in the 1960s and 1970s. Several policy options for controlling land price increases and promoting the more rational use and development of land are proposed. The author argues that only a full integration of policy instruments among the many Ministries responsible for housing and land will effectively address this important policy issue.

HEBBERT, M. and NAKAI, N., *How Tokyo Grows: Land Development and Planning on the Metropolitan Fringe*, London, Suntory-Toyota International Centre for Economics and Related Disciplines, London School of Economics, 1988. After reviewing contemporary urbanisation and suburbanisation in Japan, the authors provide a detailed examination of the mechanisms of land development and planning. There are discussions of stakeholders in the land development system, government policies and planning measures, and land use promotion and control tools. A case study is presented of planning and land development in Chiba prefecture, on Tokyo's outer metropolitan edge, which shows how politics, planning, and land interests interact to produce high-priced yet low-intensity development.

KORNHAUSER, D., *Japan: Geographical Background to Urban-Industrial Development* (second edition), London and New York, Longman, 1982. A concise reference to the geography, urban and regional development, and industrialisation of Japan. Kornhauser discusses phases of urbanisation in Japan before and after the 1868 Meiji restoration through to the post Second World War period and considers Japan's approach to urban and regional planning. A good bibliography is provided. The second edition supplies an update through to Japan's economic maturation and the energy crises of the 1970s. Earlier works by the same author which are also of interest include KORNHAUSER, D., *Urban Japan: Its Foundations and Growth*, London and New York, Longman, 1976; and KORNHAUSER, D., *Studies of Japan in Western Languages of Special Interest to Geographers*, Tokyo, Kokon-Shoin, 1984.

MINERBI, L., NAKAMURA, P., NITZ, K. and YANAI, J. (eds.), *Land Readjustment: the Japanese System*, Boston, Oelgeschager, Gunn and Hain, 1986. A collection of essays which reviews the role of land readjustment in shaping urban development in

Japan. It introduces differing views on the merits of this management tool and identifies its possible future applications in other countries, such as Hawaii.

MINISTRY OF CONSTRUCTION, *White Paper on Construction in Japan, 1992*, Tokyo, Research Institute of Construction and Economy, 1993. An English summary of the Ministry of Construction's annual White Paper. In this synopsis of the 1992 edition, the Ministry focuses on the issue of regional revitalisation in Japan. Demographic trends (including out- and in-migration) in provincial regions are discussed, along with measures to extend development in provincial regions by strengthening core local cities. The White Paper also discusses strategies to improve infrastructure and development in Tokyo and other metropolitan cities.

MINISTRY OF INTERNATIONAL TRADE AND INDUSTRY, *Industrial Location Policies in Japan*, Tokyo, Industrial Location Policy Division, Industrial Location and Environmental Bureau, MITI, 1992. This mimeographed report provides a useful review of the MITI's industrial location and regional development policies. There is a history of Japan's industrial and regional development from the late 1940s through to the present, followed by information on several key MITI projects, including industrial location, technopolis, and brains-of-industry. A complementary reference is MINISTRY OF INTERNATIONAL TRADE AND INDUSTRY, *MITI Handbook*, Tokyo, Japan Trade and Industry Publicity, Inc., 1992, which contains comprehensive descriptions of the MITI's structure, policies, and related developmental organisations.

MURATA, K. (ed.), *An Industrial Geography of Japan*, New York, St Martin's Press, 1980. A collection of articles on the post-Second World War industrialisation of Japan. Three major industrial regions are studied, the Keihin, Chukyo-Tokai and Hanshin, in addition to the regions of Setouchi and Northern Kyushu and other industry towns. The development and distribution of the following manufacturing industries is also examined: textiles, energy, iron and steel, motor vehicles, and shipbuilding. Industrial location policy and environmental issues are discussed in the last two articles. The National Income Doubling Plan 1960, along with several other national and regional industrial development policies, are briefly described. There is also a short study of environmental issues generated by industrial development policy, the effects of air, land and water pollution, and the government's response to the problem.

NATIONAL LAND AGENCY, *Sanzenso: The Third Comprehensive National Development Plan*, Tokyo, National Land Agency, 1979. The full English translation of the Third Comprehensive National Development Plan, published by the Japanese government in 1977 to guide development for the next ten years, as stipulated in the Comprehensive National Land Development Act. The objective is to promote decentralisation of population and jobs away from the crowded Pacific Belt. The central thrust of the programme is the creation of employment opportunities for rural youth within commuting distance of their homes. The Plan goes beyond the provision of job opportunities and also stresses the importance of providing a total environment for living. It underlines the necessity of making local cities more attractive and envisages the establishment of a nationwide network of 200 to 300 integrated residence areas (*teijuken*), with each area suitably structured to offer local employment, education, cultural activities, medical services, and so forth.

NATIONAL LAND AGENCY, *The Fourth Comprehensive National Development Plan*, Tokyo, National Land Agency, 1987. The full English translation of the Japanese government's fourth and most recent comprehensive national development plan. This addresses the increasing concentration of international functions as well as national economic, cultural and political activities in Tokyo since the early 1980s. It attempts to achieve a more balanced distribution of activities by promoting a multi-nodal structure whereby Tokyo will share its function with Kansai metropolitan area and Nagoya metropolitan area. Analyses and development guidelines for rural and non-core regions are also presented.

OECD, *Salient Features of Regional Development Policy in Japan*, Paris, Organisation for Economic Cooperation and Development, 1971. Presents Japanese expositions on the country's regional development policies, including the relationship between geographical conditions and regional development, industrial location, legislation relating to regional development policy, and over-concentration and environmental protection. A retrospect of past policies up through 1965 is offered, as well as descriptions of measures for the promotion of regional development and industrial infrastructure.

OECD, *Environmental Policies in Japan*, Paris, Organisation for Economic Cooperation and Development, 1978. By the late 1960s, Japan's high industrial growth caused it to become one of the most polluted countries in the world. This led the Japanese government at both a national and local level to take a number of measures aimed at preventing further deterioration and at fostering the improvement of the environment. In 1976–77, the OECD Environmental Committee conducted a review of these new environmental policies in Japan. After discussing the causes and indicators of environmental degradation, four major policy themes are covered in this report: the setting of standards; compensation schemes; siting of development projects; and economic consequences of pollution control systems. The report concludes with an assessment of the Japanese experience up to the mid-1970s.

OECD, *Urban Policies in Japan*, Paris, Organisation for Economic Cooperation and Development, 1986. This review by the OECD took place in 1984–85. The report notes that urban Japan, following a period of rapid growth since the end of the war, is now in a transitional phase. In the coming decades it will be confronted not only with the need to cater for continuing urban growth, but with the considerable task of urban renewal and improving the quality of urban community life. Policy recommendations cover the rational use of urban land, housing and urban revitalisation, urban infrastructure and the urban environment. They relate mainly to developing and refining existing urban policies in Japan, rather than making radical departures. The stress is on raising quality, and improving targeting. It is argued that without an increase of resources, urban living conditions by the year 2000 are unlikely to show the degree of improvement necessary to meet the evolving needs of Japanese society.

SAMUELS, R. J., *The Politics of Regional Policy in Japan, Localities Incorporated?*, Princeton, NJ, Princeton University, 1983. This study of local government in Japan looks at how local public administration is embedded in broader political, social, economic and administrative environments. It traces the political history of regional policy in Japan, and provides in-depth coverage of the intricate inter-governmental linkages between central and local government in the implementation of public policy. Samuels concludes that the 'Japan Incorporated' concept is inappropriate for capturing the richness of political conflict which exists between the various levels of government. For further discussion of the complex roles of local government in Japan, see also REED, S. R., *Japanese Prefectures and Policymaking*, Pittsburgh, PA, University of Pittsburgh Press, 1986; and CALDER, K. E., *Crisis and Compensation: Public Policy and Political Stability in Japan, 1949–1986*, Princeton, NJ, Princeton University Press, 1989 (especially the discussion on political aspects of regional development and policy in Japan).

TATSUNO, S., *The Technopolis Strategy: Japan, High Technology, and Control of the Twenty-first Century*, New York, Simon and Schuster, 1986. Examines, in a popular fashion, Japanese strategies for promoting high-technology development in the face of competition from other Asian countries and the United States. Tatsuno gives great weight to the Ministry of Trade and Industry's regional Technopolis Programme. Tatsuno's subsequent book, *Created in Japan: From Imitators to World-Class Innovators*, New York, Harper Business, 1990, offers an updated view of the Technopolis initiative, along with a discussion of Research Core and other regional technology development measures (see Chapter 7).

TOKYO METROPOLIS LONG-TERM CONSULTATIVE COUNCIL, *Long-Term Plan for Tokyo Metropolis: 'My Town Tokyo' Heading into the 21st Century*, Tokyo, Tokyo Metropolitan Government, 1984. A review and implementation plan for the earlier study by the Tokyo Metropolitan Government *My Town Tokyo* (1982). Develops planning guidance for Tokyo's future development based on assumptions of an increasingly older population, slower growth, and tendencies towards an internationalised and information-based society

TOKYO METROPOLITAN GOVERNMENT, *The Third Long-Term Plan for Tokyo Metropolis: My Town Tokyo—For the Dawn of the 21st Century*, Tokyo, Metropolitan Government Municipal Library, 1991. The most recent of this series of metropolitan planning exercises. The plan's concerns include housing and recycling issues, welfare and the needs of the elderly, business innovation, over-concentration of administrative infrastructure in metropolitan Tokyo, and the restructuring of the city to increase its contribution to world development. Detailed plans are discussed, along with proposed urban changes and projects for eight different zones of Tokyo.

Articles and Book Chapters

ABE, H. and ALDEN, J. D., 'Regional Development Planning in Japan', *Regional Studies*, 22, October 1988, pp. 429–38. This article examines regional development planning in Japan in the context of trends in regional income inequalities. The legal framework and experience of regional development planning in Japan is reviewed.

AKIRA, T., 'Deconcentrating Tokyo, Reconfiguring Japan', *Japan Quarterly*, October–December 1987, pp. 378–83. Discusses the Fourth National Comprehensive Development Plan and its aim to create a multipolar, decentralised pattern of urban development by the year 2000. The deconcentration of economic activity out of Tokyo is a central element of the Plan, but Akira doubts whether this is feasible. He argues instead for a greater political decentralisation to local areas and regions.

ARISUE, T. and AOKI, E., 'The Development of the Railway Network in the Tokyo Region from the Viewpoint of Metropolitan Growth' in Kiuchi, S. et al. (eds.), *Japanese Cities: A Geographical Approach*, Tokyo, The Association of Japanese Geographers, 1970, pp. 191–200. The authors trace how the growth of Tokyo's extensive suburbs over the period 1895 to 1970 was greatly influenced by the development of railway systems radiating from the centre of the city. Four technological and organisational stages are discussed: steam power; electric power; the beginning of underground lines and government control; and the continuation of underground lines and further modernisation.

BROADBENT, J., 'The "Technopolis Strategy" vs. Deindustrialization: High-Tech Development Sites in Japan' in *Pacific Rim Cities in the World Economy* (Comparative Urban and Community Research, Vol. 2, New Brunswick, NJ, Transaction Publishers, 1989, pp. 231–53. Analyses the Japanese government's Technopolis programme aimed at stimulating new locations for advanced technology industries. Broadbent suggests that the Technopolis programme is moving against current tendencies of internationalisation and offshoring of domestic manufacturing capacity in Japan. Using the case of Oita Technopolis, the author determines that it is difficult for the Japanese government to counteract these trends. Nonetheless, through strong links with high technology companies, Oita has achieved a considerable degree of success.

CHEUNG, C., 'Regional Innovation Strategies and Information Society: A Review of Government Initiatives in Japan', *Asian Geographer*, 10 (1) 1991, pp. 39–61. Regional information development policies such as 'teletopia', 'greentopia', 'intelligent city', 'information-oriented and futuristic city' and other new media facilities are reviewed, together with their relationship with the Fourth Comprehensive National Development Plan and impacts on the national land system. These policies are not seen as regional imbalance correctors since they are only awarded to regions with innovative visions and implementation abilities, and not necessarily the backward ones. Nevertheless, success in these projects will help secure nodal points of information and communication for the emerging network society in Japan, and contribute to the formation of a multi-nuclear national land system.

DOUGLASS, M., 'The Transnationalization of Urbanization in Japan', *International Journal of Urban and Regional Research*, **12** (3) September 1988, pp. 425–54. New patterns of urban development, particularly population and economic reconcentration in Tokyo, have been stimulated by the transnationalisation of Japanese business in recent years. Corporate business functions have been favoured in Tokyo over housing, public services and urban amenities. Douglass argues that unless there is a significant reorientation of Japan's priorities and increased attention to social investment, new urban development concepts such as the Technopolis programme are unlikely to result in substantial improvements for households.

EDGINGTON, D. W., 'Managing Industrial Restructuring in the Kansai Region of Japan', *Geoforum*, **21** (1) 1990, pp. 1–22. An examination of industrial development of Osaka and the Kansai region and the problem of this area's long-term economic decline relative to Tokyo. Current planning strategies and large-scale infrastructure projects in the Kansai region are discussed. These are aimed at strengthening Kansai's international and technology functions to be complementary to those of Tokyo.

EDGINGTON, D. W., 'Economic Restructuring in Yokohama: From Gateway Port to International Core City', *Asian Geographer*, **10** (1) 1991, pp. 62–78. Many Japanese cities are discovering 'internationalisation' as a means of solving problems associated with economic restructuring. Yokohama, Japan's second largest city, owes its very existence to Japan's need to internationalise and open up to trade in the 1850s. In the past twenty-five years or so, the city has lost much of its pivotal importance as a gateway port, as new forms of contact with the world have eroded the preeminent role of ships and seaports in global trade. At the same time, the phenomenal growth of Tokyo has put Yokohama under the shadow of its giant neighbour less than 30 kilometres to the north. This article reports on the city's current planning strategies and major projects designed to develop an international city more independent of Tokyo: one which is oriented to information and technology-based industries.

EDGINGTON, D. W., 'Industrial Restructuring and New Transport Infrastructure in Chukyo, Japan', *Geography*, 77, 1992, pp. 268–70. The city of Nagoya is the focus of the large industrial region of Chukyo in central Japan. Since 1985, structural economic pressures have made the upgrading of Chukyo's economic infrastructure both a national and local priority. The article discusses plans to implement a range of large-scale transport projects to enhance the region's competitiveness into the next century. These proposals include the new Chubu International Airport, the second Shinkansen (bullet train) line, and the second Tomei Inter-City Expressway.

FUJII, N., 'Directions for Growth', *Japan Echo*, **14**, 1987, pp. 12–19. Examines business and population migration in and around the Tokyo metropolitan area and the role of government development policy. Population trends from 1920 to 1980 for the different wards and prefectures of the Tokyo Metropolis are discussed. The demand for office space is seen as the primary factor behind Tokyo's upward spiral of commercial land prices. Businesses are drawn to the city centre because of the close proximity of central government offices and the ease of contact with other businesses. Tokyo's emergence as an international financial centre also contributes to the influx of businesses into the city. Fujii warns of possible relocations of Japanese corporations' headquarters to other Asian cities if development restrictions coupled with additional rent increases prove too oppressive, and argues for a multi-centred metropolitan approach to development to provide more space for business functions.

FUJITA, K., 'The Technopolis: High Technology and Regional Development in Japan', *International Journal of Urban and Regional Research*, 12 (4) December 1988, pp. 566–94. Using a case study of the Kumamoto Technopolis, the Technopolis programme is discussed as an example of the growing role of local agencies in economic revitalisation in Japan. This is contrasted with the prevailing emphasis on the policies of central government in Japanese development. However, Fujita also points out the limitations of local action from global and feminist perspectives.

FUJITA, K. and HILL, R. C., 'Global Production and Regional "Hollowing Out" in Japan', *Pacific Rim Cities in the World Economy* (Comparative Urban and Community Research, Vol. 2), New Brunswick, NJ, Transaction Publishers, 1989, pp. 200–30. The effects on manufacturing, regions, and workers in Japan of increased internationalisation and the currency revaluation (*endaka*) of the mid-1980s are discussed. The authors consider government strategies to respond to possible problems of industrial and regional dislocation, using a case study of Toyota's operations in Aichi prefecture.

FUJITA, K., 'A World City and Flexible Specialisation: Restructuring of the Tokyo Metropolis', *International Journal of Urban and Regional Research*, 15, 1992, pp. 269–84. Discusses Tokyo's renewed concentration of domestic and global economic activities. Fujita examines the social and spatial dynamics of Tokyo's industrial sector over the past two decades, as well as the conflicts inherent in the city's contemporary role as a world city. She considers the plans of the Tokyo Metropolitan Government, referring to the Tokyo Teleport and financial centres, as well as the desperate need for decent housing. Finally, there is a discussion of unevenness between the development of Tokyo and the rest of Japan.

FUJITA, M. and KASHIWADANI, M., 'Testing the Efficiency of Urban Spatial Growth: A Case Study of Tokyo', *Journal of Urban Economics*, 25, March 1989, pp. 156–92. The long-run efficiency of land development in the Tokyo metropolitan area is examined, using a dynamic urban land use planning model. For the time period 1955–1980, the authors indicate that while Tokyo's actual growth is more spatially dispersed, it has similar efficiency characteristics to those suggested by their model. However, actual land prices for middle suburbs are much higher than the efficiency model predicts.

GLASMEIER, A. K., 'The Japanese Technopolis Programme: High-Tech Development Strategy or Industrial Policy in Disguise?', *International Journal of Urban and*

Regional Research, **12** (2) June 1988, pp. 268–84. Discusses Japan's Technopolis programme in the context of growth-pole and propulsive industry theories, drawing implications for technology and regional development policies for other advanced economies. Also examines conditions and constraints in Japan which affect the likelihood of success for Technopolises.

HALL, P., 'Tokyo' in Hall, P., *World Cities* (3rd edition), London, Weidenfield and Nicholson, 1984, Chapter 7, pp. 179–97. Traces Tokyo's history and the city's post-war growth experience. Compared with other world cities, Tokyo is seen as richest in paradoxes: despite its size and economic vigour, its public services are at over-capacity and its physical standards below those cities of equivalent stature. The various administrative boundaries of Tokyo are described, together with the evolution of regional policies for the national capital region. It is also noted that Tokyo has joined New York as a world city in terms of fiscal crisis.

HARRIS, C. D., 'The Urban and Industrial Transformation of Japan', *Geographical Review*, 72, 1982, pp. 50–89. Examines urbanisation and industrialisation in Japan from the 1920s to the post-war period. Attention is directed to the rapid growth in the urban population and the associated demographic transition, changes in industrial and occupational structure, and inter-prefectural migration patterns. Recent trends are given in the distribution of population, both among and within the major urban centres.

ISOMURA, E., 'The Capital City Development in Japan', *Ekistics*, 5 (7) January 1990, pp. 340–41. Considers historic, present, and future roles of the capital city in Japan, and examines proposals to relocate Japan's capital or transfer major functions from Tokyo.

ITO, K. and TAKEUCHI, K., 'Medium and Small Sized Cities in Japan', *Journal of Regional Policy*, 5, 1985, pp. 501–17. The growth of Japan's small and mid-sized cities is examined in the context of regional policies and plans, including the comprehensive national development plans of the 1960s and 1970s.

KANEYASU, I., 'A Note on the Strategic Planning Process for City Development: A Case of Shiroishi City, Miyagi Prefecture, Japan', *Science Reports of the Tohoku University* (seventh series [Geography]), **38** (1) 1988, pp. 62–70. Presents a case study of planning in a relatively small-sized city (42 000) in southern Miyagi prefecture. Kaneyasu outlines the strategic planning process involved in the preparation for the city's Third Comprehensive Plan in the period 1987–1988.

KAWASHIMA, T. and STOHR, W., 'Decentralized Technology Policy: The Case of Japan', *Environment and Planning C: Government and Policy*, 6, 1988, pp. 427–39. The tiers of Japanese technology policy are examined, including national initiatives, regional technopolises, and dispersed 'research cores' aimed at stimulating small high-technology companies. These programmes, aimed at promoting decentralisation and innovation, are contrasted with earlier, more centralised efforts.

KIRWAN, R. M., 'Fiscal Policy and the Price of Land and Housing in Japan', *Urban Studies*, 24, 1987, pp. 345–60. Examines factors underlying the increase of land and house prices in Japan in the 1980s, and the difficulties this presents for improvements in urban living conditions. Kirwan discusses ways in which Japan's high land prices are maintained by public policy and systems of land use, planning, and development finance.

LATZ, G., 'The Persistence of Agriculture in Urban Japan: An Analysis of the Tokyo Metropolitan Area' in Ginsburg, N., Koppel, B. and McGee, T. G. (eds.), *The Extended Metropolis*, Honolulu, University of Hawaii Press, 1991, Chapter 11. Examines the persistence of agricultural land uses in Tokyo, despite the continued urbanisation of the metropolis. Agricultural land use and labour are analysed for five regions of the Tokyo metropolis. One of these regions—Saitama prefecture—is the subject of a more detailed case study.

MACHIMURA, T., 'The Urban Restructuring Process in Tokyo in the 1980s: Transforming Tokyo into a World City', *International Journal of Urban and Regional Research*, **16**, 1992, pp. 114–28. Tokyo experienced drastic urban restructuring in the 1980s, as a result of a political coalition between various private companies, national and local governments. The city's spatial structure has been transformed in response to its new function as an economic centre of global Japanese capital. Growth in the number of foreign residents has been part of the contemporary Tokyo scene. There has also been an increased social and spatial imbalance in the city.

MASSER, I., 'Technology and Regional Development Policy: A Review of Japan's Technopolis Programme', *Regional Studies*, **24**, 1990, pp. 41–53. The main features of Japan's technopolis programme are described and the setting in which these have been developed is considered with reference to regional development strategies and technology policies. The experience of one of the more successful technopolis sites, Shinanaogawa/Nagaoka, is examined in some detail and evaluated in relation to some of the key conceptual and operational issues involved.

MATSUKAWA, I., 'Interregional Gross Migration and Structural Changes in Local Industries', *Environment and Planning A*, **23**, 1991, pp. 745–56. Examines the interrelationships between migration between regions and changes in local industrial employment in Japan for the period 1974–85.

MAY, V., 'Kashima Industrial Complex, Japan', *Geography*, **67**, 1982, pp. 153–55. Briefly describes the development, since the late 1950s until 1980, of Kashima, one of Japan's Special Areas for Industrial Concentration.

MISRA, B., 'Japanese Experience in Physical Development and Land Management. Transferability of Development Experience: Case Studies on Japan', *Regional Development Dialogue* (special issue), Nagoya, United Nations Centre for Regional Development, 1984, pp. 143–206. Examines the *Kukaku-Seiri* land readjustment method, which seeks to either create or improve public-use land (roads, parks, etc.) by changing existing land plots into more regular shapes. Project funding is provided through land betterment fees paid by the landowners of the land earmarked for development. The strengths and weaknesses of this technique are discussed, along with implications for developing countries.

NAGAMINE, H., 'New Town Development in Japan: An Experience of Muddling Through' in Phillips, D. R. (ed.), *New Towns in East and South East Asia—Planning and Development*, Hong Kong, Oxford University Press, 1987, pp. 170–201. The types of large-scale residential developments commonly referred to as new towns in Japan have been undertaken primarily to create dormitory towns. Nagamine examines the strengths and weaknesses of new town development in Japan. He traces the genesis of public intervention in urban housing in Japan back to the 1920s, compares British and Japanese approaches, and describes the institutional techniques for acquiring land for new towns. Case studies are given of Kozoji New Town (Nagoya) and Senri New Town (Osaka).

NEUSTEAD, A., 'Future Information Cities: Japan's Vision', *Futures*, **21**, June 1989, pp. 263–76. Reviews recent Japanese concepts about the role of information and communication technologies in urban development.

OHOKA, S., 'Urban Development and Regional Development in Japan Taking a New Turn: New Trends Towards the 21st Century', *Business Japan*, **36**, July 1991, pp. 40–43. A brief article summarising social and technological trends influencing Japanese regional development, including the changing importance of information, the growth of the service and software sectors and the increasing demand for recreational facilities. These trends are resulting in the development of specialised cities in Japan, such as technology cities, convention cities, and amusement/market/resort cities. See also other short articles by Ohoka, including 'Metropolitan Bay Development: A Renaissance of Urban Life', *Business Japan*, **36**, August 1991, pp. 38–41; and 'The Importance of Regional Research Core Centers: Research and Development-Type Town Planning', *Business Japan*, **36**, September 1991, pp. 42–43.

OHTA, K., 'The Development of Japanese Transportation Policies in the Context of Regional Development', *Transportation Research: A*, **23** (1) 1989, pp. 91–101. Probes transportation policies in relation to the series of post-war comprehensive national development plans in Japan. Transportation investment has generally supported the general theme of these plans to promote balanced regional development and improved living environments.

RIMMER, P. J., 'Japan's World Cities: Tokyo, Osaka, Nagoya or Tokaido Megalopolis', *Development and Change*, **17**, 1986, pp. 121–58. The author argues that of Japan's three largest cities, only Tokyo could claim to be a world city. Nagoya excels only in national production, and Osaka has lost its interconnections to the global economy to Tokyo. Since the 1970s, Tokyo has experienced physical, economic and social restructuring associated with its world city status. While Tokyo has been free of political conflicts to date, planners have to recognise that the city is now tied into an international chain of production and commerce.

RIMMER, P. J., 'Urban Change and the International Economy: Japanese Construction Contractors and Developers under Three Administrations' in *Pacific Rim Cities in the World Economy* (Comparative Urban and Community Research, Vol. 2),

New Brunswick, NJ, Transaction Publishers, 1989, pp. 156–99. Explores the roles of construction contractors and developers in the remodelling and internationalisation of Japanese cities during the Tanaka, Fukuda and Nakasone administrations.

SAKATA, T., 'New Developments in Urban Management: Present Status and Future Tasks', *Local Government Review (Japan)*, **11**, 1983, pp. 39–55. Examines the relatively new concept in Japan of 'urban management'. Three aspects are discussed: improving the living, working, and recreational environment of cities; relating the city to both local residents and the national government; and maintaining a tax-payer orientation. The article draws on a 1979 report prepared by the Research Committee on Urban Administration and Finance of the Japan City Centre for Local Government Research.

SARGENT, J., 'Industrial Location in Japan with Special Reference to the Semi-conductor Industry', *Geographical Journal*, **153**, 1987, pp. 72–85. Semiconductor manufacturing is one of the most successful of the high-technology industries of Japan. While the location of industry in Japan was characterised by the geographical concentration of manufacturing in the Pacific Belt, Japanese semiconductor manufacturers have opted for locations in the outer region of the country. Kyushu, in particular, has emerged as a major regional concentration of memory chip assembly due to advantageous air transport and other communications, land availability, local government policy and labour supply. However, research and development in this industry remains firmly centred in the capital region. Moreover, the competitive advantage of Kyushu is being eroded by the trend for Japanese semiconductor firms to operate factories overseas to take advantage of cheaper supplies and labour.

SARGENT, J. and WILTSHIRE, R., 'Kamaishi: A Japanese Steel Town in Crisis', *Geography*, **19**, 1988, pp. 354–57. Reviews the development, over 130 years, of iron and steel in the north-eastern coastal city of Kamaishi and the industry's downsizing and restructuring in the 1970s and 1980s. The city's isolation and inadequate infrastructure makes it difficult to attract replacement high-technology industries. See also Wiltshire, R., 'Inter-Regional Personnel Transfers and Structural Changes: The Case of the Kamaishi Steelworks', *Transactions of the Institute of British Geographers*, **NS 17**, 1992, pp. 65–79.

STOHR, W. B. and PONIGHAUS, R., 'Toward a Data-based Evaluation of the Japanese Technopolis Policy: The Effect of New Technological and Organisational Infrastructure on Urban and Regional Development', *Regional Studies*, **26**, 1992, pp. 605–18. Evaluates the local and regional effects of Japan's technopolis policy on the basis of disaggregated time-series data of local and regional economic performance. The data refer to new plant formation per technopolis for the years 1981–89 for eight high-tech industrial sectors, and data per technopolis on production and employment. The study concludes that establishment of technopolises has increased the high-tech share of new manufacturing plants in the peripheral areas of Japan, although the employment-generating effect tends to decline with increasing distance from Tokyo.

WATANABE, S. J., 'Garden City, Japanese Style: The Case of Den-en Toshi Company Ltd, 1918–1928' in Cherry, G. E. (ed.), *Shaping an Urban World*, London, Mansell,

1980, pp. 129–43. Den-en Chofu is a prestigious suburban residential area about 12 kilometres south-west of downtown Tokyo. This study shows how the 'garden city' ideas of Ebeneezer Howard were transferred into Japan during the inter-war years, and used by a large private developer to create the country's first comprehensively planned residential district.

WATANABE, S. J., 'Metropolitanism as a Way of Life: The Case of Tokyo, 1868–1930' in Sutcliffe, A. (ed.), *Metropolis 1890–1940*, London, Mansell, 1984, pp. 403–30. A general history of Tokyo's metropolitan development is presented as a case study for international comparison. The individual character of the Japanese planning system is described through the following subdivisions of its history: pre-modern (until 1868); Meiji (1868–1912); Taisho-early Showa (1912–1930); wartime (1930–1945); and post-war.

YASUDA, Y., 'Tokyo On and Under the Bay', *Japan Quarterly*, 35, April–June 1988, pp. 118–26. A proposal to build a trans-bay highway spanning Tokyo Bay and linking Kanagawa and Chiba prefectures has generated much discussion on related development projects, including building artificial islands and a trans-bay optical-fibre communications loop. But Yasuda doubts that these proposals effectively address Tokyo's pressing congestion problems and raises concerns about the ecological effects. He argues for a new, more environmentally-conscious approach to development.

YAZAWA, S., 'The Technopolis Program in Japan', *Hitotsubashi Journal of Social Studies*, 22, 1990, pp. 7–18. The author suggests that there has been a confusing and inadequate debate about Japan's Technopolis programme. The goals of Technopolis include both aiding Japan's global technological position and improving conditions in less developed regions. The author seeks to clarify the context and realities of the Technopolis initiative.

YOSHINOBU, A., 'Chaos and Order in the Japanese City', *Japan Echo*, **XIV**, 1987, pp. 64–68. Tokyo is characterised as an 'amoeba city', a city continuously in flux and undergoing constant renewal. Buildings are not seen as permanent and urban planning has been relatively shortsighted. Rapid post-war modernisation, population growth, and industrialisation has contributed significantly to the city's chaos. Yet, unlike some Western cities, Tokyo's centre has not died or decayed. Instead, it has remained vital, a result of constant urban renewal. Yoshinobu argues that Tokyo's ability constantly to adapt is a great strength.